RECLAIMING BANISHED VOICES

Stories on the
Road to Compassion

Lawrence J. Lincoln, MD

BALBOA
PRESS
A DIVISION OF HAY HOUSE

Copyright © 2017 Lawrence J. Lincoln, MD.

All rights reserved. No part of this book may be used or reproduced by any means, graphic, electronic, or mechanical, including photocopying, recording, taping or by any information storage retrieval system without the written permission of the author except in the case of brief quotations embodied in critical articles and reviews.

This book is a work of non-fiction. Unless otherwise noted, the author and the publisher make no explicit guarantees as to the accuracy of the information contained in this book and in some cases, names of people and places have been altered to protect their privacy.

Balboa Press books may be ordered through booksellers or by contacting:

Balboa Press
A Division of Hay House
1663 Liberty Drive
Bloomington, IN 47403
www.balboapress.com
1 (877) 407-4847

Because of the dynamic nature of the Internet, any web addresses or links contained in this book may have changed since publication and may no longer be valid. The views expressed in this work are solely those of the author and do not necessarily reflect the views of the publisher, and the publisher hereby disclaims any responsibility for them.

The author of this book does not dispense medical advice or prescribe the use of any technique as a form of treatment for physical, emotional, or medical problems without the advice of a physician, either directly or indirectly. The intent of the author is only to offer information of a general nature to help you in your quest for emotional and spiritual well-being. In the event you use any of the information in this book for yourself, which is your constitutional right, the author and the publisher assume no responsibility for your actions.

Any people depicted in stock imagery provided by Thinkstock are models, and such images are being used for illustrative purposes only.
Certain stock imagery © Thinkstock.

Print information available on the last page.

ISBN: 978-1-5043-9267-9 (sc)
ISBN: 978-1-5043-9269-3 (hc)
ISBN: 978-1-5043-9268-6 (e)

Library of Congress Control Number: 2017918533

Balboa Press rev. date: 12/19/2017

To Anne, my partner, best friend, and love of my life

To our children and grandchildren. What joy.

In memory of Elisabeth Kübler-Ross, MD

Contents

Preface xi

Chapter 1: The "Verkshop" 1

Chapter 2: My Turn 10

Chapter 3: A Banished Child 19
    Pain Is Pain Is Pain 22
    Relapses 23

Chapter 4: Buried under Shame 25
    The Consequence of Self-Hate 26
    Inner Children 29
    Spiritual Practice 33

Chapter 5: The Challenge of Parenting 35
    Jean's Failed Relationship 38
    Pam's Fear of Feelings 46

Chapter 6: Critical Early Years 51

Chapter 7: Early Decisions 57
    Example of Secure Attachment: Mary 58
    Insecure Attachment, Example of Avoidant
    Relationship: Jimmy 59
    Insecure Attachment, Example of Anxious Relationship: Nan 60
    Insecure, Disorganized Attachment: Jeffrey 61

Chapter 8: Earned Attachment 70

Chapter 9: Elusive Memory 82

Real vs. Reality 82
Jill's Final Hours 83
Callie's Compassion 85
Implicit and Explicit Memory 86
Mixed Messages: Joann and Her Mom 89

Chapter 10: Good Grief 95
Matthew's Birthright 95
Diane's Grief 97
Kyle: Without Grief, We Become What We Hate 99
Grieving: No Right Way 100
Charlie's Brief Moment of Tenderness 101

Chapter 11: Hidden Agendas 104
Our Son, Matt, Does Mat Work 106
My Trial by Fire 108
Don's Hidden Little Boy 121

Chapter 12: The Externalization Process 124
Telling My Son Who He Is to Me 131

Chapter 13: Accountability 135
The Source of Willie's Infidelity 135
Boundaries 147

Chapter 14: Forgiveness And Reconciliation 149

Chapter 15: Letting The Love In 160
Natalie's Dying Lesson 160

Chapter 16: Redemption 168
Jim's Redemption 168

Chapter 17: Cultivating Stillness 174
The Answer Is under a Forsythia Bush 174

Chapter 18: Till Death Do Us … 179
Dying Breath 182

Appendix 1: Natural and Distorted Emotions 189
Grief 190

- Roger's Grieving 193
- Distortions of Grief 196
- Anger 197
- Distortions of Anger 199
- Fear 200
- Distortions of Fear 202
- A Father's Misplaced Anger 204
- Healthy Jealousy 207
- Bob's Powerful Judge 209
- Love 211
- Distortions of Love 213
- Carl, the Tough Marine 215

Appendix 2: No Choices: The Victim Triangle 219
- The Victim 221
- The Rescuer 224
- The Perpetrator 226
- Rachael Wants to Go to the Mall 231

Appendix 3: Getting Out of the Triangle 237
Spotting Troublesome Thoughts and Behaviors 237
- Saying the Opposite of What I'm Feeling 237
- Being Careful in My Interactions with Others ... 238
- Giving Unrequested Advice 238
- Gossiping or Judging Others without Compassion 238
- Being Perfectionistic 238
- Beating Myself Up (Believing My Judge) 239
- Speaking for Others or Allowing Others to Speak for Me 239
- Passive-Aggressive Withholding of My True Feelings, Even from Those Who Are Safe 239
- Being Overly Defensive 239
- Not Being the Same Person in All Settings, at Home or Work, Public or Private 239
- Feeling Shame 240

Doing Things Differently 240
- Make Friends with Your Judge 240
- Take Risks to Speak Your Truth 241

    Take a Time-Out 242
    Remember the Fifteen-Second Rule 243
    Say No When I Mean No, with Kindness 245
    Ask for What I Need 246
    Hilda's Unending Need 248
    The Triangle of Health 253

Resources 255

Acknowledgments 259

Preface

Peace cannot be kept by force; it can only be achieved by understanding.
—Albert Einstein

Upon first reading my manuscript, my editor asked me, "Is this a memoir, a treatise on the value of the externalization of emotions, or a book for those searching for elusive contentment?"

"Yes," I answered. But let me start from the beginning.

By the early 1980s, I had reached "someday." I had graduated from Amherst College and Columbia University's College of Physicians and Surgeons, and completed residency and a fellowship in infectious diseases at the University of Pennsylvania. I had married the girl of my dreams. We had two beautiful children, a son and a daughter. I had a successful infectious disease practice and could work as many hours in the day as I wanted.

Often working fourteen-hour days, I became overwhelmed. I was a caring, dedicated physician, but I had no idea how I could keep up this pace for another thirty years. Although I enjoyed my work, I began to dread and resent my immense and unpredictable workload. But I had cultivated the persona of calm, reliable proficiency for so long that I actually believed this was who I was.

In 1983, six years after moving to Tucson, I saw a flier that Dr. Elisabeth Kübler-Ross was speaking at a local high school. I had first heard Elisabeth speak in 1969, about a month after her best-selling book *On Death and Dying* was published. I was taking an elective year in anatomic pathology (performing autopsies) between my second and third years of medical school when I heard that a physician was speaking about death and dying. I thought I should learn about my patients' final journey well before they arrived in the autopsy suite. Elisabeth told many touching stories about the courage of her dying patients, prompting me to rush out and purchase her book. I never got around to reading it. It remained on the shelf as I entered the clinical years at Columbia, followed by five years of residency and fellowship.

In the 1970s, Elisabeth created her Life, Death, and Transition Workshop, a five-day residential program to help the dying live fully until their last breath. Realizing that many of the caregivers who supported the dying needed more help than their wards, Elisabeth opened her workshops to those with current grief, those who suffered from childhood trauma and neglect, and to professionals who were eager to learn about caring for the dying. Vietnam War veterans with PTSD and those on a spiritual journey of self-exploration also began to attend.

During Elisabeth's Tucson lecture in August 1983, she spoke about how accepting one's life was the best preparation for accepting death. I realized I was far from this goal. That night I signed up for her workshop. After initially canceling, because I was too busy to leave my practice, I finally made it to the San Luis Rey Mission in February 1984.

To my surprise, it wasn't the burned-out Dr. Lincoln who predominately participated in this intense workshop but rather a five-year-old boy whose inner voice unexpectedly appeared. In front of ninety-one strangers, he described how a bunch of older kids had piled on and nearly smothered the only other five-year-old boy in my neighborhood.

Once I heard, and more importantly felt, what my inner five-year-old had experienced as he witnessed this cruelty, I reclaimed the little boy who had disappeared from my awareness years ago. At the time, I didn't know I had banished him to protect myself from vulnerability, pain, and humiliation. Nor did I know how life changing this moment of deep compassion for myself would become.

I began to recognize how what seemed to be an unrelated and barely remembered childhood event was impacting my life as a physician, partner, and father. Surprisingly, communicating with and caring for this exiled, internal little boy helped me make the changes that eventually brought acceptance of my life.

After my 1984 workshop, I trained with Elisabeth and her staff. By 1986, I was leading many of her workshops in the US, Canada, Australia, and New Zealand. In January of that year, she joined me in presenting a workshop for medical caregivers, sponsored by Tucson Medical Center, which would evolve into the Growth and Transition Workshop program, now in its thirty-first year. My wife, Anne, and I co-led this program. Over these three decades, it has been a privilege to witness the stories and facilitate the release of emotions of nearly five thousand participants in over three hundred workshops. Many have also reclaimed the banished voices of their childhood.

Life was fulfilling. Besides the residential workshops, I continued my infectious disease practice, and in 1990 I helped create Tucson Medical Center Hospice and became its medical director. But world events would upset my inner equilibrium.

The outward triggers for my writing this book were the multiple attacks of 9/11, our predictable response of meeting violence with violence, and our expectation that the use of force would lead to a peaceful outcome. In a frenzy, I wrote to President Bush, urging patience to allow the enormous outpouring of support from other nations to coalesce into a communal conversation for peace. I met with my congressman and begged him to vote against executive war powers for the invasion of Iraq. I was wasting my time. My powerlessness led to outrage, and anger invaded many hours of my day. I wanted to act, to make somebody pay.

At the peak of my outrage, a dream woke me in the middle of the night. I apparently had requested an audience with long-dead Richard Nixon. I was frisked, and then celestial secret service agents escorted me to within six feet of his throne. Just as I was about to grill (more like lecture) him about our current foreign policy, Mr. Nixon spoke to me in a reverberating, jowl-shaking voice, "Everybody these days is so self-righteous, including you. It is very unbecoming, so stop it."

Shocked and speechless, I accepted his scolding with bent head. (How else was I supposed to respond after being rebuked by a dead ex-president?) Satisfied that I had heard him, Mr. Nixon said he would grant me one question. He was clearly impatient, so I had no time to think. I blurted out, "Are we going to be at war for the next fifty years?"

Mr. Nixon looked right in my eyes and, with some sadness, replied, "Of course." The two secret service men escorted me away. Chastised,

I awoke with the thought that perhaps I had more in common with President Bush than I cared to admit.

It took a while to finally grasp that my internal reaction was way out of proportion to current events. My volatility spoke much more about my internal wounds than about my president. But I was making it about him and, at the same time, bemoaning the polarity in our politics. It had become more important for me to advocate my position than to be part of a solution. Slowly, my reaction to 9/11 brought me back to the five-year-old boy who had witnessed the smothering and to his deeper question about why humans continue to hurt each other. It also solidified my adult query into the origin of revenge.

This is a very personal book. At times, I have felt almost too vulnerable to put it out to the world. Further, I don't wish to tarnish the memory of my family in any way. My reality, to be sure, has impacted the decisions I have made, both consciously and unconsciously. But as we all know, my personal reality no more defines the truth of things than my point of view on how we heal individually and collectively. There isn't a single, universal path to wholeness.

I'm convinced that the cultivation of compassion and self-forgiveness helps us to understand the brokenness of those who have hurt us. Even our enemies are deserving of empathy and respect, without which we continue to project our fears and self-hate onto others and perpetuate revenge as a solution to disagreements.

There are three main topics woven throughout my book which hopefully build on each other to offer a path to compassion. The first relates to my story, which includes some memoir and many internal conversations with the reclaimed voices of my past. The memoir speaks for itself. The numerous internal conversations are my attempt to show that what we say and, more importantly, how we listen to ourselves do matter.

We talk to ourselves silently all day long. For some of us, the speaker is our judge, the internal voice who berates us with subliminal criticism nearly twenty-four hours a day; or perhaps it's the taskmaster, whose mantra is, "Yes, but what have you done lately?" Often the two voices are in cahoots, one demanding performance and the other perfection. At other times, an internal voice puffs us up with our own self-importance, infusing its monologue with judgment of others and our own entitlement, arrogance, and self-righteousness. These speakers tie up the transmission lines of our unconsciousness with the message that we are either unworthy or all important so we almost never hear the whisperings of our hearts. Instead, we succumb to the internalized subliminal voices of others.

Many, like me, don't realize we have the opportunity to rediscover the passionate voices from our past that can teach us who we really are. The process requires not only willingness but also imagination. Inviting the voices I tried to silence back into my life has provided fresh intimacy, humor, tenderness, and strength, and it has become my spiritual practice. Referring to those voices as "inner children" is simply one of many useful metaphors for self-awareness.

The second topic woven throughout the book is parenting. Why so much writing about that topic? One internal little voice chimes in, "You weren't so great a parent to us or to Matt and Rachael (our biologic children) until you started to pay attention to what I was feeling and what I had to tell you." Each of us has the opportunity to create a new internal parent. As I listen to the discarded voices of my youth, they teach me which part of my childhood wiring they want me to retain and emulate, and which they want me to discard. The art of listening to myself has benefitted not only me but also all my loved ones. Becoming a good parent to myself is an ongoing acquired skill as I continue to accept and appreciate my own uniqueness—that is, who I actually am rather than who I pretended to be. The development of a healthy internal parent matches my capacity to live a compassionate life.

The third subject woven throughout the book encompasses the psychological teachings from the workshops, exemplified in the many stories of workshop participants as well as my medical and hospice patients. In medical school, I spent nearly three years learning all the basic science before I was allowed, or even felt comfortable, to sit at a patient's bedside. I had only rudimentary lectures in the field of mental health. In my work with Elisabeth, I have had the pleasure of empirical learning, made possible by the thousands of participants who entrusted themselves and their childhood voices to my presence. Although this book contains a few actual stories, with names changed and permission given, almost all are composite examples that demonstrate how very much alike we humans are, even though we carry our own unique histories. Our workshop participants and my medical patients have been, and continue to be, my professors of the human spirit. Their stories populate this book, with my gratitude.

I have included teachings from our workshops, which Anne and I have personally found invaluable and which have helped to integrate the emotional work for many participants. I have placed them at the end of my story, as appendices, and have suggested where in the narrative it would be useful to read them. For those who would prefer to plow through the personal stories in the book, the teachings can be a resource later.

Some have commented on how emotional some of the stories are. I invite my readers to notice whether they become uncomfortable with the pain or even the tenderness in these stories, and to use this information to inquire who inside is having those feelings.

Over the years, some of the staff of the Elisabeth Kübler-Ross Center, including Anne Taylor Lincoln, have amplified, modified, and supplemented the original material Elisabeth presented in her Life, Death, and Transition Workshop. I thank Elisabeth and all those who enriched her teachings. If I have contributed to this body of work, it is the particular way I champion my relationship with the inner voices of my past, which is the main subject of this book.

What I have included in my book says much more about how I think than about the actual workings of the human brain, mind, and soul. I don't believe any of the models of human psychology can possibly capture or explain the exquisite nature of human experience. But I do encourage the reader to try on my pair of shoes. If they fit, at least for now, you are welcome to take them home with you. If they are giving you blisters, by all means find a different cobbler.

Reclaiming Banished Voices is neither a political polemic nor a sales pitch for our workshops. It is about the cultivation of self-awareness and the deepening of an internal intimacy, which can spread outward to our families and our larger communities, help to reverse the consequences of subliminal self-hate, and sanctify our yearning for forgiveness and connection. This book is also about being accountable and learning to take responsibility for our own feelings and behaviors while holding others accountable with the same compassion, honesty, and humility inherent in the knowledge that none of us is perfect.

It has taken me a long time and multiple iterations to write this book. After much encouragement, I added my personal narrative as a thread that weaves throughout the book. If it is helpful, it is because I'm just a regular guy wanting regular things, living an unheroic life. It is my hope that these stories will be another catalyst for self-reflection. Perhaps, as I have, you will find it equally useful to include a daily inner dialogue in the many components of your spiritual journey.

Chapter 1
THE "VERKSHOP"

> We shall not cease from exploration, and the end of all our exploring will be to arrive where we started and know the place for the first time.
> —T. S. Eliot

It was in 1969 that I first heard Elisabeth speak, just after she had written *On Death and Dying*. I was a second-year med student at Columbia University in New York City. Figuring I might see a dying patient someday, I attended her Saturday morning presentation. Although the largest auditorium was reserved for her talk, only about fifty attended. We were treated to a series of moving stories about the courage and suffering of the dying and their beloved caregivers. I rushed out to buy her book but left it sitting on my shelf, unread, as I continued my rigorous medical education.

One of the stories Elisabeth told was her visit to meet a nine-year-old boy who was dying of leukemia. Consumed by nearly six years of chemotherapy regimens, with only brief periods of remission, Jimmy never had a chance to learn to ride his brand-new two-wheeler bike, which sat in his room with the training wheels still on. Just a few weeks from his death, Jimmy told Elisabeth that his only unfinished business was to ride his bike around the block all by himself. Elisabeth said she would help.

She convinced Jimmy's mom to let her pale and very weak little boy take what would be his final journey. They carried the bike to the sidewalk and assisted Jimmy to climb on. Embarrassed that, at nine years old, he had to ride with training wheels, Jimmy nonetheless pedaled slowly away from his mom and Elisabeth. The two women held onto each other and sent up silent prayers as he made his first turn and disappeared around the corner. It seemed an eternity before Jimmy and his triumphant smile came into view as he made the final turn at the other end of their block. It would be just a few weeks later, on the day prior to his death, that Jimmy presented his bike to his younger brother on the condition that he take the damn training wheels off. I have only recently realized that another part of me was listening to Jimmy's story besides the competent medical student who had been performing autopsies at Columbia Presbyterian Medical Center.

Fourteen years later, in 1983, while I was making my predawn rounds at Tucson Medical Center, I saw a circular announcing that Elisabeth Kübler-Ross would be lecturing at a local high school. I began my hospital rounds at four o'clock in the morning to avoid competition with other physicians, who also wanted to review and write in the medical charts, and to see all my hospitalized infectious disease patients before my internal medicine office hours began. Otherwise, I wouldn't get home in time to have dinner with my family; help bathe my young children, Matt and Rachael; and read them a bedtime story.

Another reason for "rounding" so early was to get in and out of the hospital before the other docs arrived. Many of my consults came when other docs spotted me in the halls. "Larry, I just remembered that I wanted you to see Mrs. So-and-So. She's been in the ICU for six weeks and is still running fevers." Picturing four volumes of charts, which would take me an hour to wade through before I could even see the patient, I put on a smile, thanked my colleague for his or her consult, and seethed my way to the ICU. Little did I know it was a five-year-old boy inside me who was the ticking bomb.

As soon as I saw the flyer announcing Elisabeth's lecture, I impulsively dialed the number, not realizing, until a very sleepy voice answered, that I was calling the seller at six o'clock in the morning. What I now know is that my internal little boy dialed the number because he was very eager to once again see the woman who had been Jimmy's champion. Recently, he also told me that he harbored the fourteen-year hope that one day Elisabeth would champion him.

I knew all about being awakened from a sound sleep. Although I had been up and working for two hours, I had no excuse. But young children don't think about time of day when they know what they want. Fortunately, the sleepy woman at the other end of the line was as gracious as anyone could be. On this auspicious morning, I bought four tickets, including one for Anne, who had never heard Elisabeth speak, and two for friends who had lost a son to leukemia several years before.

Elisabeth was a triplet, born into an upper middle-class Swiss family in 1926. Having an identical twin, Erika, Elisabeth was never seen as a separate person. Even her parents called them by combined names. In one of her lectures, Elisabeth described how one sister excelled in school while the other disappointed, yet both were given Cs on their report cards. In fact, the only warm-blooded creature who could tell the girls apart was Elisabeth's pet black bunny, which her father insisted she take to the butcher to prepare for a wartime meal.

Another colorful story was about Elisabeth standing in for her sister on a date. At home sick, Erika didn't want her boyfriend to ask her competitor to the dance. Agreeing to this absurd plan, Elisabeth asked Erika how far she'd gone with the guy and dressed in her sister's clothes. When she realized the boy didn't suspect anything throughout the entire evening, Elisabeth knew she would have to leave Switzerland to have her own life. Her need for individual recognition was a blessing to the world, and at times it was perhaps a personal burden, driving her to work incessantly and place herself in the center of controversy.

When the war ended, Elisabeth did relief work in Zurich and then visited Majdanek concentration camp in Poland. There she met a Jewish woman, who told her that, under the right circumstances, all of us are capable of doing what the Germans had done. Seeing railroad cars filled with children's shoes, Elisabeth pondered how the guards could have exterminated small boys and girls during the day and worry about their own children with chicken pox when they got home at night.

When Elisabeth graduated from medical school in Zurich, she married an American classmate. After losing her slot in a pediatric residency when she became pregnant, she opted for training in psychiatry. Upset by how health care professionals avoided talking about death, Elisabeth asked her surgical oncology colleagues whether she could interview their dying patients. When they responded by saying they had no dying patients, she asked whether she could speak to those with cancer. Finally, one colleague consented if Elisabeth promised she wouldn't tell his patients they had cancer.

After introducing herself as a physician who was available to talk about whatever they wanted, Elisabeth quickly discovered that almost all these patients knew they had cancer and were dying. Soon others began requesting to speak to Dr. Kübler-Ross. Later, she created a seminar at the University of Chicago Hospital, where she interviewed dying patients in front of a multidisciplinary audience. These conversations led to her book writing, which, along with her storytelling gift, made her an instant worldwide authority. It's ironic that, more than four decades later, so much energy continues to focus on the limitations of her grief model, when Elisabeth stopped talking about the "five stages" immediately after she wrote *On Death and Dying*. In twelve years of working with her, I never once heard Elisabeth mention them.

Elisabeth was as spellbinding in 1983 as she had been fourteen years earlier. At one point, when she was talking about accepting one's own death, she awakened a deep sadness in me. My eyes filled with tears as I heard an internal voice whisper, *Cancer wouldn't be so bad. I could stop all the bullshit and just be Larry again.* It would be an honorable way to get off the treadmill. I now know that accepting one's own death requires accepting one's own life, but prior to that moment, much of my life remained hidden.

We were walking through the parking lot to our cars when I uncharacteristically stopped Anne and our friends. I had to go back and speak to Dr. Kübler-Ross, who was surrounded by well-wishers waiting to get autographed copies of her books. Typically, I would have patiently waited my turn or just given up, but this time I pushed my way through thirty or forty people. Before Elisabeth even saw me, I bent over and whispered my thanks in her ear. This tiny, gifted woman, surrounded by her publications and admirers, turned and stared up at me for maybe fifteen seconds. Shoving a brochure in my hand, in her Swiss-German accent, she said, "You come to my next verkshop."

When we arrived home after the lecture, I placed the brochure on my pile of future possibilities, but this time the small, determined voice said, *Oh, no, you don't.* At ten o'clock in the evening, I filled out the application, wrote the deposit check, licked the stamp, and drove to the nearest mailbox. Something wasn't going to let me bury this application in my pile of unfulfilled dreams.

Had I not mailed it that night, the brochure would have gone on the ever-growing pile of brochures for seminars, exotic foreign travel, and medical meetings that eventually would be discarded to make room for the next round of circulars.

Three months passed, but as the workshop date drew near, I was too busy to attend it. That earnest first step of driving the application to the mailbox, along with the urgency I had felt on the night of the lecture, was forgotten. Work came first. I phoned the Kübler-Ross Center to cancel, assuming I would lose my deposit, and that would be that. Instead, the coordinator said she would transfer my deposit to the February 1984 program near San Diego. The universe wasn't going to let me off the hook.

I was on call the weekend before the workshop, so I signed over the care of my patients to my partners Monday morning from a pay phone at the airport. As I hopped a shuttle to the San Luis Rey Mission—a place where priests are made—in Escondido, California, I was still reviewing my hospital cases to be sure I had left no loose ends. It was only when the van pulled up to the mission gate that I felt a drop of sweat trickle down my back. This wasn't going to be a scientific conference.

I grabbed my suitcase and climbed the steps to the mission. Two cheerful, bright-eyed women were greeting and assigning rooms to a waiting group of participants. They asked me to fill out a name tag, first name only. I printed "Larry."

When my turn came for a room assignment, one of the facilitators greeted me with a huge smile. "Hi, Larr!" Giving her my brightest, biggest smile back, I thought, *Oh man, I've got to be bubbly for five days.* I rolled my suitcase down the hall past a communal bathroom. *I'm not even going to be able to take a crap in private this week.*

When I arrived in my room, I realized I had a roommate and that he had taken all the hangers in the closet. I shoved my suitcase under the bed, rested my head on the pillow, and tried to disappear into sleep. I was burned out with worrying and caring for others. I needed time to myself, and I wasn't going to get it.

Elisabeth had begun leading workshops for the dying in the mid-1970s, giving them a safe place to express their fears, make sense of unsettled issues in their past, grieve the future they wouldn't live to see, and find meaning in their final days. Due to their physical limitations, the dying often would need caregivers to assist them. Elisabeth soon discovered that the healthy caregivers were burdened with similar issues and often needed the workshops more than the dying did. Over time, a wide range of people attended her Life, Death, and Transition Workshop, which dealt with not only life and death issues but also childhood neglect or abuse, what became known as PTSD (post-traumatic stress disorder) in returning Vietnam veterans, and caregiver burnout. Also, many professionals came to watch Elisabeth work her magic, since she had an uncanny gift for seeing what people needed, even before they knew what they needed.

We met in a large, empty rectangular room with a worn carpet that somehow fit with the novice-priest aesthetic. Small, elevated windows allowed only indirect sunlight, adding to the gloominess and matching my mood. Elisabeth, along with her two greeters, sat in front next to a faded blackboard with years of white chalk embedded in the slate. On the floor in front of Elisabeth was a twin-size mattress and surprisingly a tall stack of thick phone books. In my wildest imaginings, I couldn't guess how they would be used. In the acceptance letter the center had sent to me, which I'd finally read in the van, I was told to bring a phone book as well as a pair of work gloves. I figured there were plenty of phone books, but I wondered where I'd find a pair of gloves.

The ninety-two participants sat on folding chairs arranged in five rows of semicircles. I chose an end seat in the fourth row. I knew better than to seem so eager as to sit in the front row or so obviously skeptical by lurking in the back. I had advanced degrees in invisibility, and I wanted a clear shot at the exit.

The next thing I knew, helpers were passing out songbooks, and we began singing old church songs spiced up with a few New Age melodies. *What a waste of time. I paid good money and am using up a precious week of medical coverage to sing "Kumbaya." What was I thinking?*

After our sing-along, we spent most of the afternoon introducing ourselves. We were instructed to briefly say why we were here. When it was my turn, I followed her instructions and finished in thirty seconds. Others needed ten minutes to say what could have been said in one-tenth the time. *If I wanted to listen to people talk, I could have stayed in my office.*

I was definitely in judgment mode. But it didn't take long for others to break through my crust of fear and skepticism with stories of horrendous grief. Some could barely get any sounds out beyond choking sobs. By the end of the introductions, I was exhausted and humbled.

The following morning, we received some basic teaching and then rapidly moved to the core of the five-day workshop, which Elisabeth called "externalization" or "mat work." Without introduction or explanation of what was to come, a young woman seemed to know just what to do. She walked to the front and sat on the mattress in front of Elisabeth. In great detail, she described a horrifying story of medical arrogance and mishap because a doctor had refused to listen to her. As her anger bubbled to the surface, Elisabeth handed her a pair of gloves followed by a thick rubber hose, and she threw one of the phone books onto the mat. Pointing to the book, Elisabeth said, "He's right here. Tell him."

Imagining the doctor inhabited its pages, the young woman smashed the hose on the phone book with all her might, all the while screaming her rage at him for his arrogant mutilation of her beloved. Drenched in sweat, she was finally able to release pent-up rage that had been eating her alive.

Now that her anger toward the doctor no longer encumbered her, tears of pure grief followed. Elisabeth handed her a pillow, which she cradled in her arms as she told her man how much she missed him and how grateful she was for the brief, rich time they'd had together and finally for his loving and accepting her as no one else ever had.

Most of the group shed tears along with her. As she finished crying, a great stillness came over her. She looked up at Elisabeth, then turned to the rest of us and nodded, as if to say, *Yes, this is who I am. This is how powerfully I love.*

I couldn't believe that a seemingly ordinary young woman could carry so much murderous anger and pain behind her very competent, intelligent, and perfectly rational exterior. When she was finished, Elisabeth looked at the rest of us and said, "Although you think that you're crying for her, you are really crying for yourself."

I was more than a little skeptical: I knew whom I was crying for, and it wasn't for me. Besides, it seemed a bit crazy to rip through a bunch of phone books with a rubber hose while talking to someone who wasn't even there. Then I reflected on watching this young woman apparently suspend her skepticism and empty out months of pent-up anger without hurting anyone, or anything, except some yellow pages. After I had witnessed and shed tears for a few more participants, I began to believe this process might really be useful for *them*. But there was no way I was going to pour *my* guts out or whine about my little problems in front of ninety strangers.

For the rest of the first day of externalization, I hid in the middle of the pack. I shed silent tears, all the while minimizing my pain as a way of separating myself from what I was seeing. For years I had successfully avoided exposing who I really was, even to myself. I certainly wasn't going to do so in public. Besides, what did I have to complain about except a little burnout? It dawned on me that I had learned as a young boy to keep my feelings—as opposed to my thoughts—to myself because no one was really interested in how I felt. Well-meaning parents and teachers emphasized rationality, talking me out of illogical feelings. Although exhausted by my stirred-up feelings, I couldn't help but listen to every story until we finally ended the first day of externalization well past midnight.

By the second morning of externalization, I'd had enough. After a meager few hours of sleep, my skeptical mind reconstituted. Although I was willing to concede that the mat work seemed to help those who shared, I knew I wouldn't go up to the mat. I told myself my burnout at work was too insignificant to waste people's time. Of course, that was the unspoken message I had learned about my feelings. *Not only are they not important, but they get in the way of performance.* I wasn't about to admit to myself that I was too scared to go to the mat. I wasn't going to lose control. Besides, I might not do it right. Making a fool of myself ranked way up there with death. If nothing else, I was competent.

I was kicking myself for using precious time off to subject myself to more human pain and misery. I could have been on a beach in Hawaii. All I really needed was some quiet time to rest and recoup. But for now, I needed to figure out how I was going to get through one more sixteen-hour day of mat work.

It is said that there are no coincidences. Sometimes I doubt this statement until I'm reminded again and again to keep my eyes and heart open. That morning I collected my breakfast tray and walked to the farthest corner of the huge dining room, nearly thirty yards from anyone else in our group. I sat facing the wall, assuming my body language would make it clear to everyone to let me eat my breakfast in peace. Just as I was taking my first spoonful of oatmeal, a young, wide-eyed schoolteacher sat down directly across from me. If my look could kill ...

Undaunted, she proceeded to chat away about where she came from and the kids she taught, and she finally asked me who I was and what I did in the real world. Gradually, I gave in to her good humor, and we had a very relaxed, sane conversation, completely avoiding any reference to the workshop. *Okay, I can hang out with her and get through one more day of this torture.* We walked into the meeting room together, and I settled in with my survival strategy. The universe had other plans.

Chapter 2

MY TURN

There are two ways to live: you can live as if nothing is a miracle; you can live as if everything is a miracle.
—Albert Einstein

My new friend guided me to a middle seat in the second row. A bit close, but I had a solid plan. I even let myself sing a few songs. I was settling in for a long day of listening to others. During the moment of silence after the singing, I took a few deep, reassuring breaths and then opened my eyes to look around a bit. I felt centered.

Then my new friend opened her eyes and turned to me. "I'm such a perfectionist. If I don't get up there now, I never will." And damn if she didn't walk right up and sit down on the mat.

My instant reaction was, *I've been set up!* Who was this person who had followed me to the far corner of the dining room, proceeded to ratchet down my anxiety, and then betrayed me by doing the one thing I was hoping to avoid? Was she employed by the Kübler-Ross Center? I looked around to see whether anyone else was suspicious, but everyone, including Elisabeth, was waiting for my new friend to begin her story. To even consider this young woman had been sent to manipulate me, out of all the participants, is an indication of how scared I was to be vulnerable in public, not to mention my feelings of self-importance. Some things die hard.

Suffice it to say, I had no clue about the profound grief this good-humored young woman was carrying around. It amazed me that I had seen no evidence of her pain during our breakfast conversation. She was just another regular person—as opposed to me, who was so unique. As I shed tears for her, I still resisted the idea that I would ever take the long walk from my chair to the mat. Even if I had been set up, it wasn't going to work. Two young voices who hadn't communicated with each other for more than thirty years were about to overrule me, and yet for their own reasons, they were about to become allies against a skeptical, entrenched Dr. Lincoln.

Looking back, the first voice that appeared was from what felt like a six-year-old, the competitive perfectionist who had been my most trusted supporter in not wanting to make a fool out of myself. But he had taken the bait. *If she can do it, so can I.* I reined him in just as he was about to jump out of the chair and join the other participant on the mat. But the genie was out of the bottle.

Next I heard the timid, quiet voice of a five-year-old boy I had buried long ago. In retrospect, he had been the one who made me fill out the application and take it to the mailbox. He trusted this tiny Swiss woman, who told stories about children dying of cancer and wasn't afraid to champion their cause. No sooner had I prevented the six-year-old from bolting to the mat when his younger counterpart whispered, *If it's true that when I cry I'm crying for myself, then I'm damn well going to cry for myself.*

Years ago, he had decided that crying was taboo. So he shut down, filled with shame, humiliation, and impotent rage; but the moment he gave himself permission to let the feelings come, he supplied me with a symbolic image. He stood alone on the porch, watching all the laughing and yelling older boys run off to play without him. To my five-year-old self, they were laughing at him. I *hated* those kids for being cruel and for leaving me to spend so much time by myself.

While my new friend was sharing her grief, my little boy stood up to be sure Elisabeth saw he was going on the mat next. When he caught her eye, he pointed to his chest and then to the mat. Silenced for thirty-three years, this little guy was finally going to tell someone what had happened. He had watched Elisabeth very carefully with all the other participants the day before and had decided he would be safe. So he was going to the mat with or without me. Kids can be impatient. It seemed like a very long time until my breakfast companion finished her story. Finally, the mat was free, and Elisabeth nodded to me.

By the time I walked to the mat, my feelings had evaporated. My five-year-old was gone, and the macho, competitive six-year-old who was destined to replace him bailed out as well. So here I was, Dr. Larry Lincoln, sitting on a mattress in front of ninety-plus strangers.

I looked to Elisabeth for some guidance. She remained silent. I began to talk about my burnout. Although I felt the tears of the five-year-old boy who had brought me to the mat, I was unclear about what he wanted to say to Elisabeth. His history remained suppressed, behind a veil. I felt awkward and exposed, not really knowing what to do, not sure even what had brought me to the mat. So I talked about my current life.

Over years of leading workshops, I've seen that many participants demonstrated exactly this disconnect, either acting like composed adults who kept a lid on the past or being completely out of control, flooded with feelings and only a vague sense of their origin. One woman put it so well when she said, "I had to be a grown-up as a little girl, and now I'm a bawling kid as an adult."

I described my current work schedule to Elisabeth, going on and on about thirty infectious disease patients in the hospital, on top of a full internal medicine office practice. With more feeling, I told her that one of my hospitalized patients had terminal leukemia. She had failed to go into remission after three rounds of chemotherapy. Her prognosis was grim. Any further treatment was futile, yet she and her family insisted on more treatment, even against the advice of her oncologist. After much negotiation, the oncologist administered a last-ditch salvage regimen that made her extremely sick. Due to her lack of infection-fighting white blood cells, she developed a fungal infection in both lungs. The only available treatment was amphotericin B, an intravenous drug that caused her to have, despite all the tricks I knew, bone-shaking rigors followed by high fevers with each infusion. Each morning her family required about forty-five minutes of time I didn't have for me to explain again why the drug was making her sick, that (in 1984) there were no alternatives, and that it wouldn't do anything to fight the leukemia, just the infection.

Every day the family berated me for making Mom sick and yet insisted that I continue the treatment. Every day was the same lengthy discussion. At this point in my story, I looked at the group and said most people believe doctors keep people alive unnecessarily, but the truth was that I was being forced to put someone through hell for no good reason.

I grabbed the red rubber radiator hose and began smashing a phone book, telling the family of my patient that their mother was dying, that she was being tortured, and that I was being tortured, too. As I smashed apart the first book and picked up the next one, I screamed, "I'm done explaining the same thing the same way day after day to you. Your mother isn't the only sick person in the world! I'm working fifteen hours a day to keep up with all my other patients, and I'm not going to waste another hour while you make me responsible for your screwed-up decision."

I threw down the hose. I looked at Elisabeth and said, *"I'm tired."* With that came a flood of tears, followed by an unstoppable confession.

Feelings aren't linear. The grief from my professional exhaustion tapped into the reservoir of tears from when I was five. My little guy proceeded to tell Elisabeth his story.

I had grown up in a lower middle-class neighborhood of post-World War II row houses in Wilmington, Delaware. They were two-story brick homes of about nine hundred square feet, built to accommodate the explosion of children who would become the baby-boom generation. The houses were duplexes with two families sharing a common porch. The neighborhood was packed with kids, most of us squeezing into the second bedroom and sharing a single bathroom with our parents. Privacy was a rare commodity. We all knew each other's business. In the early 1950s, it was a segregated, all-white, equal-opportunity neighborhood; kids called each other "kikes," "wops," "krauts," and "Polacks."

The next paragraphs are a more complete version of what my inner little boy told Elisabeth that morning. He wants you, the reader, to hear the story in his words:

> I'm five. I live in a neighborhood with row houses. We share our porch with the family next door. She screams at her husband and kids. I don't talk to them. The milkman brings them bottles with the cream on the top. Ours is "homogenized." I want to open their milk and drink the top.

One family has twelve kids. They're Catholic. I'm Jewish. They have three bedrooms, so I think six kids in each room. We have two bedrooms. Three boys in one room, Mom and Dad in the other. They put water on their cereal, one of the boys told me. I like milk. I feel bad for them. Maybe that's why the older kids are mean.

Mr. Frederick has a white fence. He'll kill us if we try to get our ball out of his yard. (It was a baseball black hole.) There are a lot of older boys on the block, but I don't play with the older kids. I'm too little. I don't want to get hurt. I don't want them to see me cry.

My older brother, Steve—he's six and really good at baseball. He can throw the ball fast. He plays with them. I stay at home, or I watch.

There is a soda plant across the street from the end of our block. The empty lot next to it is where the kids play tackle football and baseball. One day I went with the boy whose dad owns the soda plant. It was filled with bags of sugar all the way to the ceiling. He climbed up the pile and jumped off. He broke a bag and the sugar spilled out all over. I was sure his father would be mad and hit us. We opened bottles of soda and shook them up, with our hand covering the hole. Cream soda shoots the farthest.

One day, an older boy, maybe fourteen, brought a bow and arrow to the lot. The arrow had a very sharp end with three barbs. He said it was a hunting arrow. He shot it almost straight up in the air. We ran the other way as fast as we could. It went so high we couldn't see it. It took a long time to come out of the sky. I was scared it would hit me.

He shot it again. This time, "crazy Louie"—he's twelve or fourteen too—started running where the arrow was shot. The other kids screamed and laughed. Louie ran as fast as he could. The arrow disappeared in the sky. I wanted to turn around and not look, but I had to look. I was so scared the arrow would come down right through the back of Louie's neck. He kept running. I saw the arrow coming down, heading right toward Louie. I started to cry. But the arrow landed right in front of him, and he jumped over it with his next step. He pulled the arrow out of the ground and held it over his head and screamed. Everyone laughed and cheered. I went home.

We collect empty soda bottles in our wagon and take them to the store next to the lot. I get two cents for each bottle and buy wax lips and pink-and-white candy dots stuck to a long piece of white paper. Sometimes I put a penny in a slot to get two round pieces of bubblegum. One time I put ten pieces in my mouth at the same time. My mouth was so full, I had to spit.

When I get older, I'm going to take my wagon across the highway and carry bags of groceries for the ladies. I can get a nickel or a dime if I carry them to their houses. I just hope the big kids don't push me out of the way when the ladies come out of the store and look for me. I know the big kids will laugh at me.

I trick-or-treated on Halloween. I got gobs of candy, but one of the older kids tried to take my bag and made me lose some of it but not all. After that, I went home after every block and dumped what I had on the bed. Then I went back out again with an empty bag.

One day, the lot was really muddy from the rain, and there was nothing to do. The older kids hung out down the street from my house. I went over to see what they were doing. Kids were pushing and shoving each other, swearing and laughing. The biggest kids had cigarettes. Then, one kid, who was eight years old, yelled out, "Nigger pile" and threw Teddy on the ground. I don't know that word. I'll have to ask my mom.

Teddy is the only other five-year-old. He lives down the street and up another block, closer to the highway. Anyway, the boy jumped on Teddy, and then all the other kids piled on. Teddy screamed, but the pile got so big I couldn't hear him anymore. The pile was so high that kids slid off. They would move back and get a running start so they could jump back on the pile. They were having fun. I was scared Teddy couldn't breathe.

When the kids in the middle of the pile got tired of being jumped on by the kids who fell off, they pushed off the top kids. Then all the kids got off Teddy. He didn't move. All the other kids ran away but me. I wanted to help Teddy, but I just stood there. I thought he was dead.

Finally, Teddy got up slowly and walked away. We didn't say anything to each other. I felt real bad. I went home to see my mom. I didn't tell her or anybody what happened. I'm not going to ask her about that word.

I never saw Teddy again.

Sitting on the mat, my five-year-old told Elisabeth that Teddy had almost died and that he'd done nothing to stop it. He'd covered his face, ashamed of what he didn't do. Adult Dr. Lincoln, thirty-three years later, was worn out with keeping other people alive. Was I trying to make up for not helping Teddy? Buried under all the layers of adult competence and self-composure, the fear never dissipated. In fact, it had magnified from the effort to hide it.

From that day on, I believed those neighborhood boys had learned everything there was to know about me, that I was weak and scared and *other*, just like Teddy and whomever they were abhorrently calling "niggers." I was Other. They could justify whatever they wanted to do to us, to me, just as long as they didn't get caught, didn't get into trouble for their behavior, because we weren't of them. They felt nothing but disdain for our weakness and cowardice. From that day on, I segregated myself from them, just like Teddy did. I falsely believed I knew all about them as well. They became Other to me, and I fostered an equal disdain for them. My fear and rage made it impossible to see they were as terrified as I was.

Tentatively, my five-year-old reached for the hose, tears streaming down his face. Taking the risk to do now what he had been unable to do so long ago, he confronted the mob. As it turned out, many of my five-year-old tears weren't of sadness but of rage, swallowed by a scared little boy who didn't feel safe enough to show any anger. He was still afraid of what the mob could do to him.

All he could do was ask the neighborhood boys a question. "Why?" When no answer came, he asked again. "Why?" His request became a demand. "Why?" And he split the phone book into pieces with the hose. Then he didn't care about the why; he gave them a taste of their own medicine.

I had no idea I was so angry with the neighborhood kids for scaring and humiliating Teddy and me. It was amazing to voice the feelings I didn't even realize existed and, at the same time, observe myself doing so.

At one point, as he was demolishing his fourth or fifth phone book—there was a cord of phone books behind Elisabeth to refill the diminishing pile next to the mat—making those kids feel what it was like to be smothered, my observing mind asked with incredulity, *Am I really doing this?* But no sooner had my observer asked the silent question when the five-year-old inside responded to my interrupting observer.

Shut up and pay attention. You picked on the littlest boy! You're bullies. Cowards. Cowards. Cowards! You smothered him. He couldn't breathe. I couldn't breathe. You could have killed him. Now I'm going to kill you! He ripped through two more phone books.

No, I'm not going to kill you. I'm going to smother you.

Using both arms, he piled together a mass of strewn yellow pages. Then he grabbed the pillow and mashed it over the pile, suffocating the mob of older boys. He pushed down with all his might so they couldn't move, couldn't breathe. Finally, just before they ran out of air, he lifted the pillow.

If you ever scare another little kid like that again, I'll kill you.

I could feel his fear of those bigger boys and of his own anger melt away with each destroyed book. Toward the end of his rampage, I sensed the exhilaration in his own unchecked power—and his freedom from years of humiliation.

Then I heard the little guy make a sworn oath to those neighborhood kids. *I'll show you all one day. You can run away from me today, but one day I'll be faster and stronger ... and kinder and better.* The penny dropped. Thirty-three years later, the competitive boy who had been born out of the ashes of that day was still trying to prove to a bunch of kids that he was better than they were.

When I was finished telling my story and releasing the years of anger and grief, the room was completely quiet. I looked up to see the group nodding. Their eyes said, *We hear you. So that is who this Dr. Larry Lincoln is. Take care of that little boy.*

My adult burnout was the catalyst that had brought me back to an earlier grief. Loss triggers loss. I was no longer superman. I had rejoined the human race.

Chapter 3

A BANISHED CHILD

> There is no light without shadow and no psychic wholeness without imperfection. To round itself out, life calls not for perfection but for completeness; and for this the "thorn in the flesh" is needed, the suffering of defects without which there is no progress and no ascent.
> —C. G. Jung

My catharsis from the workshop was an immediate gift. Unloading years of rage, which I didn't even know I carried inside, left me with a new lightness of spirit. Although I had very little sleep at the workshop and returned to an intense on-call weekend, my office patients the following week commented that I looked refreshed from my week-long vacation. Several said I looked years younger. Inside, my little one giggled, tempted to say, "Of course I look younger. I'm five!"

The change in my sleep pattern surprised me. Prior to the workshop, I averaged five or six total hours of rest per night. After the workshop, I enjoyed a few minutes of quiet wakefulness before entering a restful sleep that lasted eight full hours, which I hadn't done since high school.

The benefit of catharsis alone would have gradually succumbed to the burden of my busy schedule and daily responsibilities. However, insights kept coming, reinforcing the connection between my adult self and my inner children.

I refer to the child within for two reasons. First, when I can genuinely picture myself at age five, I am better able to appreciate *his* reality, including his terror. I look at my five-year-old granddaughter and say to myself, "I was that little!" Second, during my time on the mat, I recognized the change in my voice when I told the story from his perspective.

No, I don't have multiple personalities. Like most of us, I possess a complex human psyche that encompasses the multiple voices of my life experiences and memories. Many are already incorporated into my psychic autobiography. I tried to bury one particular voice because I was ashamed of his weakness, clumsiness, and frailty.

Before I experienced and expressed the feelings specific to a five-year-old event, I would have been put off by child-within language. This was 1984, long before the construct of the inner child had reached mainstream pop psychology and *Saturday Night Live*. It was simply what I was experiencing, and it was powerful.

Throughout the first day of externalization, I also began to experience the power of the group process. Those who had the courage to tell their powerful stories and release the pent-up sounds of rage and the sobs of grief touched others, propelling them to come to the mat. In return, for those brave enough to tell their story, the silent witnessing of the group would be sufficient to tip the scales and steer them toward self-compassion. It was mutually beneficial.

Ancient cultures have known the power of community to heal the wounded and to bring those who are lost back into the fold. Anne once taught me a story of a tribe that created a personal song for every newborn. The song would be sung to the child during all the special milestones of his or her life. It was the duty and commitment of the tribe to remember this song so that each child knew he or she was not only part of a larger whole but also a unique, important, and separate being. If someone strayed from his or her core values, the tribe would bring the person into the center of the village and sing his or her song, reminding each lost soul of how uniquely precious he or she was to the tribe.

In our witnessing during that first day of the workshop, the group was, in a sense, silently singing to each person his or her unique song. It was profound—to be heard and seen by so many. We began to understand that although we had different, individual histories, physical appearances, talents, and gifts, we all belonged to the same tribe.

Dr. Dan Siegel says, "It isn't what happens to us that determines our future. Rather, it is how we make sense of it." I would add that it is how we find a resting place for it. I would never have made sense of my past without experiencing the raw emotions of those days. Even if I had been able to pull up the memory, I wouldn't have appreciated its effect on me without my little one showing me his pain. I am eternally grateful that I had a safe place for those inner voices to appear. It was the re-experiencing of those events, amid the safety, that created a palpable biography. My linear brain absorbed and integrated my story, and I found compassion for a part of myself that I had abandoned to survive and move ahead in life. I now understood the cost of that abandonment.

Now that I knew about that banished little boy, not just in my head but in my gut, it would no longer be useful to blame anyone for my past. It would now be *my responsibility* to care for myself the way my little guy always wanted to be treated.

I was surprised to discover that, after being so vulnerable, I felt stronger, more centered, and, if anything, more competent than I had been when I was working so hard to appear that way. I hadn't realized how much energy I was expending to contain feelings I didn't even know I had.

Something had shifted inside me. Having released scary feelings in a safe way, I would no longer need to be so careful with my thoughts and behavior. If I got mad, I wasn't going to kill someone. If I shed a tear in public, it didn't signify I was weak and incompetent. If I admitted I was scared or anxious, it didn't mean I was a coward and couldn't be trusted in difficult situations.

Instead of managing my feelings, I began to own them. When I stepped off the mat, I didn't immediately make these intellectual correlations. Rather, I reveled in the freedom that came from safely releasing so much anger and openly shedding so many tears.

It may sound overly dramatic to fear that if I got angry I might kill someone, but it isn't. Four- and five-year-olds have magical thinking, believing their thoughts alone are capable of coming true. When a parent dies, young children often believe they have killed them with their angry thoughts. Certainly, as a logical adult physician, I would never kill anyone, but killing isn't logical. I have heard over and over from others who have safely released the pent-up murderous anger of their youth that they were afraid they could kill someone if they ever lost control. Unfortunately, we often read or hear about an unsuspecting person committing murder in a fit of rage, taking it out on someone who symbolizes a childhood abuser. I ponder the number of prison cells filled with people who haven't had a safe place to grieve and reclaim their true selves.

Pain Is Pain Is Pain

Over the years, I have shared my story with workshop participants about bullying. Sometimes they laugh nervously and tell me they grew up with "pile ons" too, even if labeled differently. Rarely have they asked whether I knew what became of Teddy. Never have I been probed to say more about how the event affected me. After all, I was just an observer.

More than thirty years passed before I had an inkling of how this event had affected me: my terror and humiliation, my shame about doing nothing to prevent or stop the assault, and my rage at the older boys' cruelty and misuse of power.

Why did this incident touch me in such a powerful way? My older brother, Steve, had thrived in our neighborhood. Although I don't remember his being there that day, I'm not sure he would have seen it with my eyes. Was I being too sensitive? Too timid? Why was I the kid who made mountains out of molehills? I had to remind myself that my pain is neither more nor less valid than anyone else's. Pain is a sign of neither a character defect nor a competition.

At our workshops, participants often compare their pain with those who tell other stories. Sometimes a participant might question whether someone is overdramatizing his or her story. He or she may have learned that no one listens to him or her unless he or she sounds and appears in a crisis. Some tell their story with an angry edge, expecting listeners to minimize their reality as others have done in the past. Often the angry storytellers see how they have projected their own doubts and self-rejection on others.

Others won't take the risk of having others confirm what they already believe about themselves, that they are using their past as an excuse for failing to be happy. Others believe their story is trivial. Self-judgment prevents them from taking ownership of their experience.

I'm sure my parents queried each other many times about how they could have produced such different sons. Many people understand the concept that each sibling is born into a different family. Steve was born in Hawaii, just as World War II was coming to an end. My parents described that time as "living in paradise," with lots of good friends who shared the camaraderie of wartime experiences. When Mom and Dad returned stateside, they moved in with my paternal grandparents and Dad's embittered sister, who was trapped in a wheelchair by muscular dystrophy. My dad was gone all day, hustling for a buck and leaving Mom to negotiate her new household. I can only speculate on how being born in this household affected me.

I have learned that the *why* doesn't matter as much as owning and accepting my interpretation of the events of that day. This insight may seem self-evident, even easy, at least intellectually, but owning my experience on a deeply emotional and spiritual level has been, and continues to be, the journey. Learning to honor my reality humbly, honestly, and soberly has taken time and requires a safe place to allow my five-year-old to show me how he actually felt that day. Pain is pain. This is my story—and I'm sticking to it.

Relapses

After returning home from the workshop, I was different. In fact, just today, Anne admonished me to be sure I tell readers how I was changed. I became a different partner, father, friend, and physician. I was able to listen in a deeper way, offering advice only when asked, trusting that others were capable of finding their own truth and not having to fix everything. I was cured—or so I thought. I plunged back into life with a new focus. I enjoyed my interactions at work. Often I came home with touching stories rather than sighs of exhaustion. I was more effective, and I got even busier.

Once again I began to ignore my little boy, who just wanted to play and have some of my attention. Old habits, along with long-held coping and surviving strategies, aren't easy to discard. My subconscious has a strong pull, and I must relearn the same lessons over and over again. He tugged at my sleeve to pay attention to him, but I was too busy with my transformed life. He escalated his request, and I started to get irritable again. Still I pushed on until people began telling me I looked tired again. The little guy was shutting down.

I continue to learn that emotional and spiritual care is a lifelong commitment—not a one-time leap off the cliff into Bliss, a three-day fix at a workshop, or a single meditation retreat. It's more like daily shaving with a blade: sometimes it's a sharp, clean removal; other times it's a slow, dull scraping of accumulated regrown stubble.

Chapter 4

BURIED UNDER SHAME

> Your vision will become clear only when you can look into your own heart. Who looks outside, dreams; who looks inside, awakes.
> —C. G. Jung

Although my story can be read as a dramatic single event, most traumas are a series of daily betrayals that gnaw at a child's soul. Sometimes the injury is as dramatic as sexual exploitation or life-threatening beatings. More often betrayals are an accumulation of ridicule, criticism, neglect, overindulgence, or simply the denial of a child's inner reality.

Rather than feel helpless and powerless, children take responsibility for events they are powerless to control. I blamed and condemned the innocent, sweet, gentle, trusting part of me as weak and cowardly for doing nothing to stop Teddy's trauma. Along with my feelings, I interred a scared, small boy under his own pile of self-contempt. I replaced him with a calculating, determined, and quietly competitive kid who was determined never to be vulnerable again. He would *show them all one day. Get even.* I became a quiet version of what I hated.

By the time I could seek revenge in the neighborhood, we had moved away, and I had written them off anyway. Instead, I projected the identity of those neighborhood kids onto my teammates and opponents on the football field and wrestling mat. I remember being overly aggressive with opposing football players when I tackled them. Just recently, I realized I never lost a "wrestle off" with teammates in high school or college, because they were, for me, the kids in my neighborhood. Much to the frustration of my college wrestling coach, I performed much better in the wrestle offs than I did in the actual matches against other teams. Beating an opponent outside the neighborhood didn't matter as much to me. Only in competitive sports, where there were rules of conduct, could I release my aggression. After all, I wasn't like "them"; I didn't hurt people. I was a nice guy.

Whenever I try to rationalize Teddy's smothering as kids just being kids, my little one hears he is overly sensitive. He loses twice: first, he lived through the event; second, I've basically said to him that his response was wrong. He was the problem.

I've also rationalized that it made him/me tougher, and it was the driver for higher achievement. Both responses minimize my inner experience of that day. They tell a scared little boy that he should just forget about it and move on, which is exactly what I tried to do. "Move on and keep going" became my mantra; the price I paid for burying the memory of Teddy was my burnout. I tried to prove to myself that I was better than those neighborhood kids in every way: stronger, tougher, kinder, and smarter … not like them.

I had to be perfect. I didn't understand that the engine for such focus was a driven five-year-old boy/man who came out of the ashes of Teddy's abuse. He would run and continue to run scared for his entire life. He wore me out.

The Consequence of Self-Hate

No event, and no response to it, occurs in a vacuum. In many ways, the "smothering" was a powerful symbol in my young life. Several other responses to that act of cruelty and violence might have been possible, but my history—including hay fever and asthma—and the culture in my family produced my response.

I developed severe allergic rhinitis and was a mouth breather. Sometimes at night I'd wake up with so much mucus in the back of my throat that it temporarily obstructed my breath. I would suffer a brief moment of near panic until I could cough and clear my airway. By the time I was five, I knew the fear of not being able to breathe. I didn't know I had asthma until my late teens, but I probably had exercise-induced bronchospasm several years before it was diagnosed. I noticed, especially during wrestling, that my effort and rate of breathing always seemed greater than those of my teammates and opponents. I couldn't understand why I had to expend so much energy just to get air when I trained harder than almost everybody else.

I attended a wonderful girls' private school that was co-ed from kindergarten through second grade. Fortunately for me, the board of trustees decided to make the entire school co-ed one year at a time, beginning with my class. At the start of fourth grade, they hired a male phys ed teacher, who later became our varsity football coach. He also became a second father to me.

In the fall of my fourth-grade year, he had us race about a mile-long course through the woods behind the school. Besides being very competitive, I wanted to impress my new teacher. Between not knowing the route and being very short of breath, I got behind the head of the pack very early in the race. It was torture to push myself to stay within sight of the leader, especially since I didn't know how far I would have to run. Finally, I came out of the woods, about twenty yards behind the winner. The next thing I knew I was in the arms of my new teacher, being carried to the nurse's office. I had fainted from an undiagnosed asthma attack. Unfortunately, I wasn't treated for the condition until after my high school wrestling career many years later.

During my freshman year in a New England college, I experienced my first full-blown asthma attack while running wind sprints up Memorial Hill. I eventually got myself to the college infirmary, where I spent the night receiving what is now very primitive treatment for asthma. By morning, I was back in class and exercising indoors. I didn't connect the panic I had felt that night in the infirmary with childhood hay fever, let alone the smothering of a little boy.

I still wonder today what happened to Teddy. There were many possible aftermaths. If Teddy had a stronger, older brother, there might have been retribution, an upholding of family honor, a small clan war on our block. Perhaps his mother or father could have called the police. The fathers might have beaten their kids when the police showed up at their homes. The scenario that actually happened, I believe, is the most common response to violence and abuse. Nothing.

Nothing happened because victims keep quiet. I cannot be certain what happened when Teddy got home, but I strongly suspect that he, like my five-year-old, didn't tell his mom or dad. His shame and humiliation would have been too great. And even if he had told, say, his mom, she likely would have minimized the event or responded with irritation for scaring her.

I said nothing to my mom because I already knew upsetting her wasn't a good idea. When Mom was scared, she could lash out, and I didn't want another scene on top of the one I had just experienced. Teddy's father and my dad would likely have told us not to come crying to them but to go back out there and fight, even if we got another beating. Dad told me many stories of his bravery and tenacity against bigger kids. He wanted me to be tough enough to survive such adversity. He wanted me not to turn away from bullies. I wanted that, too. I guess it worked.

My best guess is that Teddy did what I did; he kept quiet and kept his distance. My silence lasted so long that, in preparing him for this book, I only recently told my older brother, Steve, about the smothering. Although the perpetrators probably didn't give it another second's thought, at least one victim was forever changed.

I don't believe it was a coincidence that I never saw Teddy again. I'm sure he made excuses to avoid coming down the block and around the corner to where the neighborhood kids played. When I doubt my reality, I even wonder whether he remembers the event and could corroborate my story.

When children don't have a safe place to process their grief, they make up their own stories. *There is something wrong with who I am for Mom to ignore me, for Dad to beat my siblings. If I were just a better kid—prettier, smarter, braver, happier, stronger—none of this would be happening.* In taking the blame, children simultaneously feel unworthy and unlovable yet all-powerful and responsible for all the suffering in their world.

Yet the self-hate of early childhood is often unconscious. It tints the lenses of our lives so early that we accept the hue as normal. I have heard so many participants say how amazed they were at their level of self-hate, and how freeing it was to remove the glasses and see themselves clearly for the first time.

Some of us remain victims, feeling hopeless, unable to change, always at the mercy of the world. Others identify with the bully. *No one will help me get what I need. It's me against the world, so I'm just going to take what I want. Someone has to be scared, and it's not going to be me.* Still others act out lifelong atonement. These three roles—victim, perpetrator, rescuer—live inside each of us (see appendix 2). I still wonder who Teddy became.

I regret to this day that I never went to see him. Of course, I know better now, but I don't think it even crossed my mind to walk the two blocks and knock on his door. I suppose I didn't want to be reminded of my own shame and humiliation and my guilt for silence and passivity. I kept our secret, even from Teddy.

I hope Teddy's parents showed empathy, if he told them. I hope they expressed their outrage, giving voice to Teddy's own anger. And I hope Teddy saw in his parents' eyes that what happened that day wasn't his fault; it wasn't due to his weakness or cowardice. I hope they taught him that cruelty and insensitivity come from those who have also been bullied. Repair is possible with this kind of loving support.

What I know today is that I didn't trust myself or anyone else with my shame and fear. This wasn't a conscious decision. It was survival. My psyche not only buried the little boy but also erased the memory of that day from my consciousness. It allowed me to go about my life, looking like most other five-year-olds—going to kindergarten, learning to read, and playing on the playground. Our brains are ingenious and protect us from what we're incapable of processing in the moment. There were consequences, but I survived and later would come to terms with the future ripples.

Inner Children

I often have the feeling that my earlier years belonged to someone else, that I have incarnated multiple times in one lifetime: infant; toddler; timid, sometimes sickly little boy; hard-driving boy-man; socially clueless person, stubborn adolescent/college kid; medical student; doctor; husband; partner; father; infectious disease specialist; workshop leader; and hospice physician.

I visit my old neighborhood and marvel at how it looks through aging eyes, allowing old feelings to bubble up. I go to Washington Heights and sit in the original amphitheaters at Columbia University's College of Physicians and Surgeons, wondering whether I was actually that kid taking notes in a pharmacology lecture. No feelings come in the amphitheater, as if that part of my brain shut down to make room for all the data I was required to absorb. I ask myself how long my current ego incarnation has been. Maybe ten to fifteen years. But in ten more years, fully retired and slowing down, will even this incarnation fade behind the veil?

Before my first workshop, I assumed what I saw was who I was. Certainly, I had no clue that inner voices, filled with their own bodily and emotional memories, lay dormant within me, waiting for the right time to present themselves for my approval, care, and affection. My inner ones waited because I wasn't ready. I was too busy. I was too frightened to hear what they had to tell me. I wasn't prepared to face my shame, feel my sadness, or acknowledge that I too had a smotherer living inside me. I had no time for that kind of inquiry or vulnerability. I needed to protect the persona I had cultivated. I needed control.

But memories also have a life of their own. They may remain dormant, allowing us to don a mask of normalcy. But, in adulthood, stressful situations (an unexpected major loss or a chronic, exhaustive burden) weaken our fortress and allow unwanted memories to make forays into our consciousness. By 1983, I could no longer shore up my peripheral defenses by working longer and harder. I was very fortunate to find a safe and respectful place when these memories overran the gates of my carefully guarded kingdom.

Our logical minds organize memories chronologically. Our emotional minds store them as feelings and images. Chicken soup warming on the stove brings me back to Grandmom's house. The death of an acquaintance or watching a poignant movie plunges me into intense sadness because each connects to a loss from years ago. Feelings leapfrog over the years and have the capacity to educate us if we don't re-entomb them.

Initially, I believed I used my imagination to create the voices of my inner children to bring life to my memories, putting ages and faces to significant periods in my life. I named them "infant," "toddler," "scared five-year-old," "driven six-year-old boy-man," and "adolescent." There was a certain arrogance that it was I who gave my inner children their life and that I would treat them with beneficence. I saw this relationship as a one-way street: I would show them compassion, and they, in turn, would show their gratitude by being happy, compliant little children … and leave me to get on with my life.

I now know that the silenced voices of my past demanded life, just as an oppressed people demand their freedom. Sometimes the timing isn't ideal for the adult to hear the whisperings of these banished voices, any more than it is for the slave owner or dictator. Maybe it never is. Freedom can be messy, chaotic, and scary, making us feel crazy and out of control. Hopefully, we have support and a bit of luck during our transformation.

Sometimes a rebellion is quelled, at least temporarily. Some attempts at freedom do end in failure; but the potential benefit to an individual, important personal relationships, and society is too powerful to stanch the urge for growth. It may take many generations in one family before the memories of violence, neglect, criticism, or sexual abuse demand life to end a cycle of addiction and ignorance. It may take centuries for an enslaved people to compel their oppressors to look in the mirror so they see how they project their own terror and self-hate onto their victims. I would have to own my fear, rage, and vulnerability before I could walk in the shoes of those neighborhood boys, understand we weren't so different from each other, and claim my right to fully belong in the world.

The process of awakening takes patience, endurance, commitment, courage, and compassion. My time came in 1984. Fortunately for me, I crested a hill during my first workshop. Even though I couldn't see a final destination, just knowing there was a path (rather than an endless or pointless climb) gave me hope, even if I didn't completely understand the point or know the final outcome. That hope was sufficient to keep me from putting the genie—my little ones—back in the bottle. I had no idea how much they would teach me and how they would change my life.

Over the last several decades, the concept of the inner child has moved from a psychological construct, beyond pop psychology, and into mainstream media. In fact, the inner child is doing his postdoc in comedy. In several recent movies, he acts out all our worst nightmares, humiliating the adult he lives in. He is rebellious, impulsive, out of control, funny, pathetic, or vicious whenever the feeling comes over him. He has no filter, and he says what's on his mind, no matter what the consequences will be for the adult he inhabits. He highjacks our lives. He is our worst nightmare.

When we use our inner child as the excuse for our behavior, we get looks of disbelief and disdain that we cannot control our impulses and take responsibility for our behavior. In Hollywood, inner children are used to amuse us, and we leave them in the theater along with our empty popcorn container.

Real men don't have inner children. They keep the past where it belongs. I knew about all that. But inner children, just like real alive kids, tend to act out when they are ignored. What is funny on the silver screen is terrifying or humiliating in real life: having road rage, bullying a waiter, dragging our child off his or her feet because he or she doesn't move fast enough for us, having uncontrollable crying spells that come seemingly out of nowhere, experiencing paralyzing fear, showing trash-talking bravado, and possessing insatiable neediness. We judge and punish ourselves and each other for such behavior. It's no laughing matter outside the movie plex. Unclaimed and unprotected inner children, left alone in their envy, fear, and vengeance, have thrown many nations into war.

I have discovered many inner voices besides the five-year-old. As I move into retirement and another decade, I have recently felt the voice of an infant much too young to speak. He asks whether I am getting close to death. He has been with me for the last twenty-five years of my hospice work, witnessing thousands of deaths and wondering what it will be like for him (us). He cuts through all the medical issues, doesn't ask me whether one of my coronary arteries is about to occlude or whether a silent cancer is spreading through my body. He simply wants to know whether he will be left alone in his crib without anyone to hear his cry.

Hearing the infant's question, my timid five-year-old child asked whether he will struggle for air or panic with suffocation during his (our) last hours of life? He also wants a thoughtful answer from me. These childlike questions often elicit the wisest, gentlest, and most honest part of me.

Spiritual Practice

For many years after my first workshop, the squeaky wheel got the grease. Only when I recognized I was significantly out of sorts did I consider asking myself what was being triggered from my past. I would ponder what age was the source of my grief or my brooding irritability. I barely even recognized my anxiety and fear. When I made the effort to engage a voice from my past, I was rewarded with precious information, much of which led to a deeper appreciation of the unsettled feelings I carried as a child as well as new insights about how the past impacted my current relationships and behavior.

I often got an earful from a younger part of myself for ignoring him until a crisis occurred in my present life. He let me know that if I continued to ignore him, he could up the ante again until he shut me down. Allowing him to express his resentments and sadness about how my current adult life was triggering his pain, I always sensed his appreciation that I took the time to listen and get to know him better. Often just telling me how he felt gave me the clarity to take better care of him and therefore myself. Relationships also improved. As many workshop participants have confessed, I sometimes made promises that I would talk to him on a regular basis, even when life was good. And I broke my promises regularly.

After years of intermittent contact, mainly to put out emotional brushfires, I committed to daily check-ins with whatever inner voice wanted time. I learned to listen without pep talks and lectures. I discovered that the frequency of loving contact with the voices of my past was inversely related to self-preoccupation, neediness, and irritability in my adult life. The gratitude of my little ones for the quality time we spent together spilled over into interactions in my daily life. I also noticed that my natural desire to be similarly available to my patients, colleagues, and family increased.

If spirituality is about a deep connection with something larger than oneself, as well as the development of a meaningful life, then I had inadvertently found a tool that opened me to spirit. Checking in with my little ones twice a day has become my spiritual practice. I suppose it's a directed form of a loving-kindness meditation.

Each evening before sleep and every morning before I leap out of bed, I gather them up and ask for questions and comments about our day. I wait to see which child, which incarnation, will speak first. Sometimes they all let me know they are tired and just want to go to sleep. Other nights at least one voice will want to talk about something that upset him or made him happy that day. I am often surprised by what I hear. You would think I would know ahead of time everything my childhood voices would say to me. If that were the case, I would have quit listening, and they would have quit talking years ago.

I listen, smile, squeeze an imaginary hand, and nod to acknowledge their feelings. I thank them for their insights and ask whether they have any questions for me. It is at least a two-way conversation between my younger voices and me; sometimes it's a roundtable. Rarely does it take more than a few minutes since we have become quite proficient in saying what is on our collective minds. Sometimes when I hear about how part of me is scared, I notice I'm not breathing. He and I take deep, relaxing breaths. Other times I massage my face to soften the muscles carrying childhood anger. We laugh at what a bulldog we can be, holding on to resentment. Finally, we end our good-nights by thanking God for all his blessings.

It takes imagination to see and feel the children who live inside me. They provoke tenderness from me that simple memories cannot. But when I gather them together each night, I am not simply singing them a lullaby. They amaze me with how each experienced my day differently, how they bring texture and clarity to my interactions, how they spot the fear, rage, guilt, or grief in those I encounter every day at work, in the grocery store, and even in my family. My inner children are my best emotional consultants. Best of all, they make me laugh with their humor as well as their astonishing insight. Our check-ins are, at times, poignant or playful, and at other times they are a quick "Good morning" or "Sleep tight." For me, engaging in this particular form of self-awareness adds intricately textured insights to my adult consciousness.

Chapter 5

THE CHALLENGE OF PARENTING

> The only possible recourse a baby has when his screams
> are ignored is to repress his distress, which is tantamount
> to mutilating his soul, for the result is an interference with
> his ability to feel, to be aware, and to remember.
> —Alice Miller

> As Johann Wolfgang von Goethe wrote, "Treat people
> as if they were what they ought to be and you help
> them become what they are capable of being."
> —Daniel J. Siegel, *Brainstorm: The Power
> and Purpose of the Teenage Brain*

In an ideal world, parents adore their child from the moment he or she is born. They commit to their child's physical needs for nourishment and hygiene, and attune to this new soul, who has arrived with only a birthday suit and a scream. The newborn needs parents who will put him or her above their own needs and have the endurance to be with him or her even when the child seems inconsolable. This work is hugely significant, made possible only by the miracle of indescribable maternal, instinctual love.

I had the pleasure of witnessing how our daughter, Rachael, greets her young son each time he awakens or when she returns from teaching or even from a brief outing for coffee. Henry's little brain sees the face of pure joy. On the most primitive level, Henry knows he is loved and, equally important, that his existence brings happiness. Many children never learn that who they are is a gift to the world. No words explain the power of such love for an infant.

It's not easy to raise children, and even great parents aren't perfect. As they continue to learn their child's unique language, their baby begins to trust. I remember visiting our son, Matt, and daughter-in-law, Lindsay, after the birth of their first child, Scout. Lindsay expressed how hard new motherhood was for her; Scout was slow to gain weight because her intestines were immature. We were all a bit worried, but the buck stopped with the nursing mom. Lindsay doubted herself at times. Was she nursing properly? Was her milk nutritious enough? Was Scout bonding with her?

We had seen Scout for a few days right after her birth. When she was hungry, she screamed until her mouth was on the breast. On our second visit, about three or four weeks later, Scout already demonstrated that she could trust her mom. One morning I was rocking her when she began to scream. It had been about an hour and a half since her last meal, so the timing was right. I brought my screaming granddaughter into the kitchen and turned her over to Lindsay. This time the wailing stopped as soon as she heard Lindsay say, "I'm right here, Scouty."

Once she heard Lindsay's voice, Scout's scream became an imploring whimper, as if to say, "Hurray, Mommy. You know what I want!" At one month old, Scout already trusted that her mom would recognize and respond to her needs in a timely manner. Scout had also developed a primitive language, rewarding Lindsay for her attentiveness.

Even infants have feelings, which need to be acknowledged and supported. Behind the feelings is almost always a request: feed me, play with me, sing to me, hold me, change me, let me rest for a while. Both Matt and Lindsay have permitted Scout and sister Zoe to have a full range of feelings, acknowledging when they are hurting or angry. They haven't shamed the girls for being afraid or given them something to cry about when they expressed two-year-old frustration or rebellion. Allowed to interpret events in their world the way they experience them, which isn't necessarily the way their parents feel, the girls have learned to trust their internal gyroscopes and remain lively and spontaneous. They don't have to watch Mom or Dad to see how they are supposed to feel. At the same time,

Matt and Lindsay have established consistent routines around mealtimes and nap times and an inviolate bedtime ritual, which confirms to their girls that all is stable and right in their world as they enter dreamtime.

After the development of language, children can be taught to name their feelings, which is the beginning of self-reflection and self-awareness. They learn what makes them happy, mad, sad, or scared; they learn that their feelings can hurt others and that their feelings aren't the universal truth. Others may feel differently.

Healthy adults have learned when and where to have their temper tantrums so they don't sabotage relationships. When we are unsure or confused, we know how to ask for a reality check from those we trust to help us sort out whether our current feelings are proportional to the stimulus or whether we are reacting to events from our past. The development of introspection is one prerequisite for accountability and personal responsibility.

Of course, kids watch their parents and learn best from what they see rather than from what they are told. I think that is what is meant by the sins (unhealthy behaviors) of the fathers and mothers being passed on from generation to generation.

When parents make mistakes, a healthy child will protest. Healthy parents will acknowledge their child's feelings, hear his or her request, and even apologize when they have overreacted. They teach their kids that everyone makes mistakes and that no one has to be perfect. Mistakes aren't failures, just simply mistakes. The empathy children receive from their parents also teaches them to respond to others with concern and kindness, to walk in other people's shoes.

If parents are unable to tolerate these normal, healthy responses, they respond in ways that defeat the child. Harsh responses, the misuse of force, ridicule, punishment, or exile erodes a child's trust in his or her own spontaneous interpretation of events. Parents who demand specific feelings and responses may get obedience, but it may be at the cost of the loss of spontaneity and self-trust. It takes a lot of psychic energy to contain feelings, energy that should be used for play and exploration. Unfortunately, children who are taught not to feel become the next generation of parents who must control their offspring so they don't feel out of control themselves. And the cycle keeps repeating.

Overt criticism or abuse can be confusing because it provides at least some acknowledgment from the parent that his or her child exists. Many adults who have been the object of terrible abuse have described how a part of them craved the attention. Some love was better than no love at all. The desire to be loved, in itself, becomes a source of shame in the setting of such abuse. It takes a lot of repair to separate the basic human need to be loved from feelings of being defective, bad, needy, or dirty.

Unlike with overt abuse, emotionally neglected kids are unseen and unheard. This lack of acknowledgment can be even more damaging than intrusive parental behavior. Kids may quit trying altogether or prostitute themselves for a morsel of attention. As adults, they may become resentful and entitled, demanding the attention they didn't receive as children, or remain unworthy beggars. Many relationships struggle under the weight of childhood neglect.

Jean's Failed Relationship

Jean came to a workshop because her eight-year relationship was on the rocks. Her life partner, Darlene, told her she "couldn't do it anymore." In return, Jean complained that Darlene was never there for her and didn't know how to be in a relationship.

Jean was one of six children. Her father worked long hours and was too tired to interact with his children at the end of the day. Her mom worked part time and was responsible for the material aspects of the home, but otherwise she just wanted to curl up with a book. Jean was an athlete, but neither parent made the effort to see her play. She was pretty much on her own. In school, she was seen as a loner; and she sent out vibes that she didn't need anyone, which confirmed her world view. At the same time, Jean resented her classmates because she felt excluded and disliked.

Jean found a partner who was emotionally distant and self-absorbed. It felt familiar. Of course, the unconscious hope that this time it would be different didn't materialize. Even before they committed to each other, all the warning signs pointed to her lonely, resentful little girl not getting what she needed. But hope is powerful—sometimes lifesaving, other times self-defeating.

Jean doted on Darlene, giving her partner all the attention and care Jean had always wanted. When Darlene didn't reciprocate, Jean felt hurt and unworthy once again. The more Darlene took her for granted, the needier Jean felt, and the more manipulative she became. Jean tried harder, hoping to obtain a crumb of acknowledgment and gratitude. She hated herself for giving herself away, as she had as a little girl; and she hated her partner for making her feel this way all over again. But Jean couldn't help herself. She tried to withdraw and be less demanding, but her internal little girl grew lonely, even more desperate for affection and approval. Then Jean's neediness made Darlene more withholding and distant. Jean was angry all the time.

At work, Jean met another woman who treated her differently, showered her with compliments, and made her feel attractive and desirable. One thing led to another. Although the affair was brief, Jean felt guilty for ignoring her values and even more angry with Darlene for making her look for love outside their relationship.

Darlene refused to go to counseling. She saw it as one more needy request Jean was making. Besides, in Darlene's family, they didn't talk to strangers about private business. Eventually, Jean and Darlene separated, each pointing fingers at the other for the failure of their marriage.

In counseling Jean began the process of grieving what she never had as a child. It was painful to feel the emptiness of her childhood—and embarrassing to admit that she had spent her entire courtship and marriage prostituting herself to get her partner to fill the empty hole of her childhood neglect.

Although it was too late for this relationship, Jean began to take responsibility for her part. Gradually, she began to understand that she had been expecting Darlene, who lacked the skills and desire, to repair her childhood injury. She also realized her own shame had kept her from even telling her partner about the part of her life she wanted her to repair. Yet she expected Darlene to show more compassion for the part of her she had spent a lifetime condemning. Jean hadn't realized how much she hated the needy little girl inside, who seemed so unworthy of her parents' love and attention.

At our workshop, Jean was stuck. Despite her anger at her ex-partner and parents, she couldn't pick up the hose. Instead, she repeatedly returned to how needy she was and how she should just get on with her life.

I tossed a phone book on the mat. "That's the little girl you call needy, the one you want to shut up so you can move on." Jean grabbed the hose and tore into her little girl, splitting the phone book and shredding the pages with her self-hate. Words of self-judgment spilled out, culminating with, "You're pathetic. No matter what people give you, it's never enough. No one will ever want to be with you."

I asked Jean who else gave her little girl that message. "They never actually said it, but that was the message from my mom and dad. They did it with a look."

I cleared the mat of a pile of yellow pages and placed a fresh book in front of her. "It's time that you allow your little girl to respond to her critics." Finally, Jean gave herself permission to tell her mom and dad they had never been there for her, tearing through two more phone books before her anger was spent. Then the tears came for what she never had.

Jean found compassion for her needy little girl. It dawned on her how uncaring she had been to stay with someone who, because of her own wounding, couldn't see or cherish Jean's neglected inner child. Using a soft pillow, Jean cradled her little one, telling her how sorry she was for treating her the same way her parents and ex-partner had.

Months later I received a note from Jean. Although she was lonely, not being in a relationship, she was hopeful that someday she would meet the right woman. In the meantime, she took responsibility for giving to her little one the attention, love, and care she'd never received. In return, her little one could warn Jean when she dated someone who didn't appreciate her. The communication between the adult and the child prevented Jean from once again looking for love in all the wrong places. She would no longer settle for companionship if it meant neglecting herself was the price.

Another form of neglect is to never be trained in the tasks of daily life. I have seen many people work hard in therapy to heal childhood neglect and abuse yet fail to make progress because they cannot make changes in their adult lives. They lack the skills they could have learned in childhood as well as the discipline and energy to get up in the morning, plant their feet on the ground, and do what needs to be done. Even though the little ones have grieved what they never had, they remain adrift because they lack an inner grown-up who knows how to function in the world. Unable to clean their home, buy groceries, prepare healthy food, live in their bodies, and find meaningful work, they continue to neglect their little ones around the basics of life.

Because of their own upbringing, my parents were unable to give me what I needed emotionally. Mom had been orphaned and sent to live with an "aunt and uncle" who used, and likely abused, her. It was a Cinderella life, minus the slipper. Mom learned how to survive. She worked hard and kept an immaculate house. But when I brought her my fears or grief, she minimized their importance because I scared her, and she felt responsible. She didn't know that all I needed was a sympathetic ear. She couldn't give me what she'd never had.

My vulnerability also frightened her because she believed I had to be tough to survive in a harsh world. She would tell me I had nothing to complain about and then give me something productive to do. In fact, "Do something productive" was her mantra, and I took it to heart. If I complained that I was bored, Mom responded with the old Yiddish expression, "*Shlug dein kopf im vand*," which translates as "Hit your head against the wall."

Mom hated the treatment she'd received as a child. She was a smart, sweet, kind, encouraging woman who wanted only the best for her three boys. Despite herself, she reverted to her aunt's words. I learned very early in life to keep my inner reality to myself. It is no wonder that I didn't tell her about Teddy's ordeal.

Mom was timid, believing that she didn't belong in most social settings. She was afraid to drive but pushed herself to do so out of necessity. Later in life, she stopped well before she needed to, trapping herself at home when Dad was out and about. Yet she took risks for her three sons.

When Steve was four years old, Mom heard about a caring, exceptional teacher who had started a girls' finishing school, which was co-ed from kindergarten through second grade. Determined to give her sons the opportunity she never had, and without telling my dad, Mom rode two city buses to the school and asked to see the new headmistress. "I have three sons who need a good education, and I have no money," she told Mrs. Meyers. Fortunately for me, Mrs. Myers took a liking to this brave, young mother.

Mom made sure her sons would have the opportunities she never did and that we could take care of ourselves. She taught us and expected us to make our beds, clean up our shared bedroom, and help with the dishes. When we were a little older, we vacuumed and scrubbed the bathroom and kitchen floors on our knees with a bucket and rags. Only then could we play. I learned that I was to get all my work done before I rewarded myself. This lesson has been a blessing and a curse.

Dad was a scrapper and a hustler, and he was a great salesman. He knew intuitively that people wanted a good deal and just how to present it to them. Before World War II, he worked for a five-and-dime. During the war, he used his skills for naval procurement in Hawaii. He opened a pool hall, booked horses, and ran numbers immediately after the war. He also gambled at the track until Mom gave him an ultimatum.

When I was nine, Dad began a new career, selling shrubbery door to door to new homeowners. Within a year, he was the top salesman in the country. He then opened his own garden mart, renting space outside a local department store. He sold shrubbery, seed, and fertilizer during the spring and fall as well as Christmas trees in December. At ages twelve and eleven, Steve and I worked every Saturday and Sunday at the garden mart, loading fifty-pound bags of lime and fertilizer into people's trunks. When school closed for Christmas break at noon on Friday and our friends began their celebrations, Steve and I could be found bundled up, selling, tying, and loading Christmas trees by early that afternoon. No one appreciated Christmas day more than we did.

I remember one afternoon when I was about thirteen when Dad embarrassed me in front of a customer. I went back to Mom, who worked the cash register, and told her that if he ever did that again, I would quit. "Don't tell me. Tell your father" was her reply. So I did.

Dad's response was, "Do things right, and I won't embarrass you again."

A black-and-white thinker, Dad could nonetheless distill a complicated set of variables into a very clear and simple solution. I spent hours listening to him and his entrepreneur friends banter, tell stories, and analyze their world. I have been grateful for this analytical training all my life—in school and later as a clinician in infectious diseases.

Dad taught us to add and subtract when we were four and five years old. We played a game of who could add up the numbers on a license plate on the car ahead of us the fastest. We learned about money, paid our bills on time, got discounts for cash from subcontractors, and bargained for a better price.

A natural storyteller, Dad loved describing his childhood and business exploits in great detail. He could go on and on about how he merchandized his products or how he made deals with suppliers, buying in volume and paying in cash for big discounts. His eyes lit up with a fresh audience to mesmerize, but he never noticed when he was exhausting his listeners. Mom would kick him under the table and say, "*Genug*" (Yiddish for "enough"), but Dad would continue unraveling the same story our guests had heard many times before. I became a very good listener, always careful not to talk so much that I would bore my audience … or get a bruised shin.

Dad also taught me about generosity. He loved helping others, taking more pride in the success of people he helped than in his own achievements. On the flip side, he would often be miffed if they didn't take his advice or show enough gratitude. I learned to pay close attention to any deeper motives I might have, asking myself, "Who am I really doing this for?" Years later, Elisabeth clarified this issue for me with one of her universal laws. "All true benefits are mutual."

Each in his or her own way, Mom and Dad prepared us for the larger world. If I had to choose, I would take good coaching over emotional attunement, even though clearly both are desirable for a balanced life. Fortunately, I would find a safe place to reclaim my inner world. In retrospect, I now thank Mom and Dad not only for the many things they were able to give me but also for what they couldn't. Their deficiencies led me to Elisabeth and the blessed gift of helping others reclaim their lives.

If abuse and neglect litter one shoulder of the road of emotional health, the opposite shoulder is cluttered with overindulgence. Encouraging our children to have their feelings is important. Just as important, however, is teaching them that others may have equally valid and different feelings and that each of us is responsible for what we do with them.

Parents who have difficulty sitting with their own painful emotions may also have difficulty dealing with the hurt, fear, and anger their children express. My mom dealt with my feelings by minimizing them, as she did with her own. She didn't want to hear about my doubts and fears because they stirred up her own. My dad dealt with negative feelings by offering mini lectures of advice. But when it came to our sibling disagreements, Dad had no tolerance.

My brother and I had explored Grandmom's house for years, including the subterranean nooks and crannies. In one basement corner was a roughly six-foot-square coal bin, which stoked the original furnace, providing hot water for baths and the clanging winter radiators. A coal chute ran up to the only small basement window, facilitating a speedy delivery of the black lumps of fuel directly into the bin. I remember blackening my hands with the residual coal fragments that remained three or four inches deep, documenting the history of a long-ago replaced furnace. I also remembered the four barber straps hanging neatly on their nails along the wooden stairs leading into the basement.

The straps were like the ones in the barbershop, where dad took us for our haircuts. An image of the old barber lathering up the face of a bearded customer with white foamy soap reminded me of Mom scooping mounds of whipped cream onto homemade strawberry shortcake. Opening his straight razor, the barber ceremoniously stroked it back and forth along the three-inch-wide brown leather strap, making the blade ready to whiten the shadowed face of his trusting customer. I didn't realize until a few years later that my grandfather had another use for his collection of leather.

I was eight years old when my dad took me down to Grandmom's basement to tell me about the second purpose of my grandfather's straps. Dad recounted how his father used them to beat my uncles and him when they broke my grandfather's rules. Usually grandfather marched his boys to the basement to carry out his sentencing. But one time he waited until they were asleep.

My dad vividly recounted one summer night when his younger brother, Moish, snuck back in the house way past curfew. Dad and he shared the same bed, since there were too few bedrooms for six kids. It was sweltering weather, so they wore only underpants. Waiting for his sons to be fast asleep, Granddad stormed into the room, pulled off the sheet, flipped on the overhead light, and began beating both with a strap.

When Dad was fourteen, my grandfather ordered him to the basement to punish him for yet another minor disobedience. With his own stoic rage, my dad announced to his father that he could beat him until he killed him, but he would never make him cry again. Dad made no sound while his father whipped him until he was too tired to swing the heavy strap over his head. "It was the last time my father ever touched me," Dad proclaimed.

I knew Dad was trying to tell me (without actually saying it) that he wasn't his father. I believe Dad took me down to the basement to stop himself from breaking his oath. Although Dad had broken his silent oath a few times, he never hurt me again after our tour in the basement. Moish also never laid a violent hand on his children.

At Grandmom's house, when Steve and I were four and three, we began fighting over who would play with our new record player. I'm sure we dragged the needle over the record several times, increasing the frustration of both our parents and Grandmom. I'm also sure Mom counseled us to take turns several times, without effect. Steve and I continued to grab each other's hands off the player. Without warning, Dad jumped up, ran over to us, and smashed our new toy with his foot. I can still picture the wooden box splintering and the sound of the metal being crushed. If we couldn't share our new toy, then neither of us would use it ... ever again.

The few times Dad also used his belt on us were always when we fought. When our bickering exceeded his tolerance, he shut us up with the belt. We'd scream before the first swipe. Usually one or two whacks, and it would be over. He never lost control. All it took was one beating to create the fear of future harm.

Much parental abuse is the result of being inadvertently triggered and overwhelmed by the innocent behavior of children. The few times Dad came after us with his belt were sudden and explosive. Although I don't know why, I suspect a young voice inside him needed to shut us up.

Our inability to deal with our own feelings may cause us to minimize or even abort our children's expressions of pain and discomfort. It can also go the other way. Magnifying their child's feelings, parents may try to fix what doesn't need fixing. This type of overindulgence has unintended consequences. Fixing a child's feelings may result in dependence and less resilience. She may learn she is incapable of surviving strong emotions or life's inevitable hardships. Creating an expectation that they will intervene any time she is upset, parents may inadvertently reinforce a payoff for drama and manipulation with whatever feeling gets their parents' attention. On the one hand, we teach our children they are too fragile to survive without us; on the other hand, we teach them they are too powerful, able to control the behavior of their parents with dramatic feelings.

Lawrence J. Lincoln, MD

Pam's Fear of Feelings

Pam was in her late thirties when she came to a workshop, presumably to deal with a painful breakup with her fiancé. The sounds of the hose on the phone books initially overwhelmed Pam as well as the overwhelming grief of other participants. But she hung in there. Gradually, she began to see that other participants became quieter and centered after they allowed themselves to release stored-up emotions. Pam decided to take a risk.

I was in the room when Pam came to the mat, trembling with fear. Her mouth was too dry to speak. Anne, who was facilitating the work, gave her a sip of water. Pam faced the group and told her story of lifelong anxiety and of how she spent most of her energy protecting herself from being afraid. Then, as if a lightbulb went on in her head, she declared, "I'm afraid of being afraid. I can't believe it. I'm afraid of being afraid!"

Pam was clearly a brilliant and talented young woman. She excelled at school, demonstrating superior intellectual and problem-solving abilities. School was easy for her because it was predictable and consistent. However, in other areas of life, Pam was tentative and anxious. She called her mom many times a day to talk about social interactions, a difficulty with a teacher, or a change of plans. Pam's calls also reinforced her mom's anxiety. Mom's coworkers were used to the frequent calls from her daughter interrupting them; these took precedence over all other activity.

When Pam was upset, Mom gave prescriptive advice. In doing so, her mom inadvertently taught Pam that her feelings might overwhelm her. Perhaps she also didn't believe her daughter was strong enough to make her own decisions. When mom's anxiety peaked, she would sometimes yell at Pam and break off the conversation. Both mom and daughter felt overwhelmed.

As Pam entered high school, social pressures increased along with her anxiety. Her parents took her to counseling and to a psychiatrist, who began antianxiety medications, which would blunt her fear. Initial improvement gave way to the habitual pattern of parental consultations and further dependence. In the meantime, Pam could get whatever she wanted when she was scared, sad, or depressed. Although her parents wondered whether Pam was sometimes manipulating them, they couldn't take the risk of setting limits. Besides, Pam wasn't consciously aware of the payoff.

Besides medication, Pam tried meditation, but anxiety kept interrupting her practice. Her mom arranged for massages and took her shopping for her new clothes to take Pam's mind off her worries. Pam's parents were so frightened by her strong feelings that they focused on making them go away.

Sometimes it's helpful to get a reality check from others. Anne asked the group whether they would raise their hands if they had a similar fear of their strong feelings. Many hands went up. Others spoke about how paralyzing that fear of fear could be. Pam saw she wasn't alone.

Anne asked her whether she would like to experiment with getting some of her feelings out, and Pam agreed. She could pick up the hose and release a bit of anger at her ex-boyfriend. That was enough. She was exhausted. Before she left the mat, Anne asked Pam to look around the room and describe what she saw in the eyes of the group. Pam took her time. When she was finished, she turned to Anne and said, "They think I'm brave."

After the workshop, Pam sent us a letter. She told us that the biggest thing she got out of the workshop was that there was another way to deal with her feelings. She had spent all her life trying to contain them, without much success. Now she was in counseling with a therapist who encouraged her to express her fears, anger, and grief. Her new psychiatrist had assisted her in weaning off medication that had caused her to numb herself. She was making real progress. Pam also wrote that she was weaning herself from relying on her Mom, which was difficult for both of them. But both were enjoying playing together rather than gnashing their teeth together.

Anne and I have had to relearn multiple times, even with our grown-up children, to keep our advice to ourselves. We discovered that giving constant advice was about our own fears and perfectionism, and about transmitting to our kids that they might have perfectly packaged lives. We are all much more complex and interesting than that. Anne and I take turns reminding each other to listen and make appropriate sympathetic murmurings without offering our brilliant prescriptions. We have discovered by keeping our mouths shut that our kids are amazingly wise and capable of ingenious analysis and decisions. We are learning to trust, mostly. But like all parents, *we want our kids to be happy*, so we lapse.

Perhaps the person Dad wanted to help the most, and who categorically refused his advice, was my younger brother, Artie. They tormented each other with Dad's unending and unrequested (though often very good) advice. Artie ignored, argued, refuted, and showed disdained for this advice. He misinterpreted Dad's suggestions as evidence that he was never good enough and would never be equal to his older brothers. Artie could match our dad word for word, resulting in many painful battles between these two kindhearted, pigheaded warriors.

Another form of overindulgence, false praise, can also be confusing, since it doesn't match a child's own inner knowing. If children believe they deserve praise for everything they do, they will resent and resist others who give them constructive feedback. Or they will lose trust in their parents for lying to them. Encouragement, rather than false praise, fuels a child's pursuits and allows a child to discover, on his or her own, his or her passion, talents, and shortcomings.

Finding the balance between supporting our children's feelings and normalizing them isn't easy. I found myself weaving all over the road, making frequent midcourse corrections. Constantly forced to analyze when my advice or demands were grounded in my fears or guilt, I gradually became clear when my advice was self-serving. Sometimes my kids declined my advice and told me to work on my issues. The more I owned my motives, the more I found that our kids were more open to my suggestions. Because they didn't feel criticized or incompetent, they were able to accept or reject help with poise.

Another indulgence is to give our children all the material things they want. When we spoil our children, we deprive them of important, real-world lessons about human desires, self-discipline, and the satisfaction of hard work.

Desire for something is a feeling. As with other feelings, we just have them. Trouble finds us when we try *not* to feel or when we give in to acting on all our feelings and desires. Parents can acknowledge their children's desires while not necessarily fulfilling them and teach their kids to work for something they really want. Perhaps most importantly parents can model restraint, teaching that desires come and go whether we fulfill them or not. What seems so important at age seven (or thirty-seven) may become passé by age eight (or thirty-eight), whether we have obtained our desires or not. Having all our wants fulfilled may make it more difficult to recognize and prioritize the one or two passions that may have lasting importance throughout our lives. Like all parenting, teaching this life lesson is easier said than done.

At times, it felt like Matt and Rachael, like all kids, were never satisfied. We would give, give, give, and then they would ask for more. I grew up relatively poor, raised by parents who struggled for every nickel and dime. My mom and dad let me know that "money doesn't grow on trees." Although they gave me the most important things, such as a good education, they took me to outlet stores for my clothes while classmates wore brand names. I did without.

When Matt and Rachael seemingly wanted everything, competing voices from my past bombarded me. One voice came from a little boy who told me to give them whatever they wanted to make up for what he'd never had. Another voice would get angry that Matt and Rachael were so spoiled and grabby (my reality, not theirs). After all, my inner child wasn't allowed to want things, so why should they? If I wasn't mindful, I could indulge their every wish, or I could judge and resent them for having the same desires I had or for being so ungrateful for all I had given them. Neither response was particularly helpful.

Prior to my work with Elisabeth (Matt was ten, Rachael eight), I was less aware of my competing inner voices. I just knew I was inconsistent as a parent. If I was confused about my behavior, you can imagine how confused Matt and Rachael must have been. It took many years to be able to acknowledge their desires, make a conscious decision on whether to give them a gift, make them work for it, or just tell them how great it would be if they had a magic lamp with a genie inside. Over time I learned to tell them about my desires: ones I chose to work for, ones that dissipated before I made the money to fulfill them, and ones I still wanted but would likely never have because the cost—in money or to my loved ones—was too great.

Among many other things, I have learned from my children that having desires is human and that I (including my internal children) am not bad or hedonistic for having them. Somehow I give myself a gift when I tell my little guy how wonderful it would be if we could get what we want, even when I know I won't act on the desire.

When we spoil our children with material things, we create little, and later, big tyrants who believe they are the center of the universe and that all others are there to serve them, agree with them, and give them everything they want. Narcissism and entitlement strip us of empathy and concern for others and create an obstacle to intimacy.

Both emotional abuse/neglect and overindulgence lead to conditional relationships, whereby we use others to fulfill our unmet needs. Relationship becomes a means to an end rather than an end in itself. By giving our children everything they want, we inadvertently teach them that fulfilling their personal desires equals love. This can be a hard belief to unlearn.

Raising kids is difficult. Fortunately, we don't have to be perfect; and neither should our children have to be. Given the safety to protest when they aren't being heard or when they are being intruded on, children will learn to listen and trust their own inner authority and develop resilience. With further guidance, they also learn accountability for their thoughts, feelings, and actions.

Chapter 6

CRITICAL EARLY YEARS

> The greatest tragedy of the family is the unlived lives of the parents.
> —C. G. Jung

We humans are complex creatures. From moment to moment, we are loving and violent, cooperative and greedy, searching for oneness with all things and then bragging about our own higher consciousness, yearning for approval and acceptance while criticizing and judging others, turning ourselves over to God while micromanaging our lives and those of our loved ones. We search for higher meaning for our existence while we unravel our genetic code in attempts to explain our behavior. We attribute events to fate while we die fighting for freedom of choice. We wonder how it's possible that Hitler could order the death of six million men, women, and children just because of their Jewish heritage or how ISIL can terrorize their Muslim brothers and sisters to take control of a patch of territory that is being abandoned by inhabitants and decimated by bombs. At the same time, we in the West can justify, even glorify, our own acts of violence that others perceive as equally brutal.

Most of us go about our days living decent lives, too busy most of the time to fret over anything except what is right in front of us. While we fall under the spell of life maintenance, preoccupied by providing and acquiring for our families and ourselves, we might be comforted—if only unconsciously—in seeing the evil in others as qualitatively distinct from ourselves. While we aspire to do life happily, we often succumb to resentment for all the time wasted on mundane activity and take our frustrations out on those we love most.

But our behavior has no relationship to mass murder. Or does it? Does evil inhabit a select group of monsters that heroes must defeat, or does the capacity for evil and good reside in each of us on some kind of continuum?

It can seem overwhelming to make sense of all this, but my humanity requires that I try. With all the tools at our disposal, we are studying and disseminating information about the human brain at an enormous rate. But will understanding the function of the human brain lead to happiness, peace on earth, or a cleaner planet? What must happen to change human behavior? For over sixty years, my little one has continued to reframe the same question. Where and how do my earliest memories fit into this puzzle? We are told that long-term memory begins at age three to four, which is about the time of my earliest recollections.

Born in my paternal grandparents' home months after my mom, dad, and brother Steve returned from Hawaii after the war, I looked strikingly similar to Grandmom's oldest son, Joseph, who had died in his late teens. I must have been in her arms much of the time because I cannot recall ever being in my mother's.

Mom confided in my wife, Anne, a practicing psychotherapist and trusted friend, that she had been sexually abused in the home of her aunt and uncle. I wonder whether Mom was unable to touch her young boys because she didn't want to risk hurting us the way she had been. I speculate that the situation was too confusing for her, so she kept us at a distance. Or maybe it was the stress of returning to reality from their Hawaiian paradise and living with in-laws.

Dad opened a pool hall, which was a front for bookmaking horse races and the numbers game, a prelude to a pick-three lottery that paid 500:1 with odds of 1,000:1. Dad also tried to make a living by betting on horses. Like all gamblers, he would tell us he either won or broke even. It must have been a rough lifestyle for an orphaned girl who craved safety and security.

Mom relished hugs from her college-age boys. I believe her injured little one thrived on the safe touch from her grown sons and later her daughters-in-law. Fortunately for Matt and Rachael, we get a second chance as grandparents. My mom showered her grandchildren with physical affection.

We moved to our postwar row house when I was two or three. On Friday mornings, my father would load me in the car, drive to the kosher butcher on Front Street for a freshly killed hen, and deposit our two warm bodies (the chicken and me) at Grandmom's house. I would spend the day entranced, watching Grandmom pluck the feathers, clean the chicken, make the soup, and prepare the bird for Sabbath dinner. I was often rewarded with the hen's tiny yellow undescended egg yolks in my soup.

I remember no conversation on those Fridays. Grandmom knew Russian, Yiddish, German, and some English, but she mostly spoke very little. What I still remember, however, is resting my head in her lap when she took a break from cooking. I still feel those magical hands on my scalp.

A couple of years ago, a study was published about genetically identical newborn rats, which were given to foster mothers with distinctly different parenting behaviors. The rat pups given to mothers who licked them frequently and consistently grew into calm adults. Not easily startled, these adult rats didn't suffer surges of stress hormones after minor irritating stimuli. Pups given to mothers who didn't lick them after birth became easily irritable and chronically anxious. They manifested bursts of stress hormones with minor stressors. What was surprising was that the brains of these genetically identical rats revealed *anatomic* differences in the hippocampus due to the nurturing they did or didn't receive.

Elisabeth Kübler-Ross used to say we could survive and thrive if we had just one person who loved us unconditionally. I was blessed to have Grandmom give me, in those earliest years, what I don't remember receiving from Mom. Yet I have *no* doubt that my mom and dad loved us fiercely. Both always wanted the best for me, cheered my efforts, and celebrated my accomplishments. This certainty lives not so much in my body as in my intellect. What my infant/toddler body remembers are only the soft, strong hands of his grandmother.

Recently, in the midst of a conversation about whether we are capable of change and completely letting go of the past, I asked an old friend whether she had a body memory of being held, nurtured, and safe in the arms of her mom or dad.

Her answer was an immediate no. As we continued our conversation, ancient tears filled her eyes, further supporting her response. I also carry an ancient sadness that comes on me at times. I look inside, asking myself who is shedding those tears or awakening me at night with wordless grief.

Save the Children estimated that eight million children were living in orphanages around the world, and perhaps as many as one hundred million (UNICEF estimate) children were orphaned or abandoned. The magnitude of lifelong psychic injury and neglect doesn't bode well for a reduction in chaos and violence in the world, nor for the health of the next generations parented by these children, who have no internal concept of what a baby might need.

It took many years before I knew I could ask such a question and hear an answer from the youngest part of me, "It's me," he says. "But I can't tell you why I am sad. I don't have the memory or the words."

In such moments, all I can do is bring him close and honor his grief, even though I don't fully understand its source. I imagine holding him so he can feel my heart beating against his chest and my arms cradling him in his sadness. After many years of being held by my adult, the infant-toddler inside has obtained a peace from knowing I will be there when I recognize his call. But he and I know his grief will remain. He no longer cares so much about the why of his grief, although we have certainly looked for answers in this life and in past lives, karma, food, work, exercise, prayer, and in the distant past, even drugs. Right now, I know the surest path to his contentment is for me to acknowledge his grief and remind him of his grandmother as well as Anne, Matt, and Rachael, who know who he is and love him unconditionally.

Mom and Dad carried generational pain into their new family. I forgive them for not knowing as my grown children are forgiving my ignorance. I also thank them for doing the best they could.

As I write about my earliest memory, I am struck with the reality that a three-year-old boy could sit quietly all day while his grandmother cooked. My grandchildren show no inclination toward such passive behavior. Was this my inherent temperament, or did precognitive events shape my nature?

Neuroscientists have demonstrated that the brain isn't a fully formed organ at birth (much like in the study with newborn rats) and that the quality of early relationships has profound effects on not only the functioning but also the anatomy of this developing organ.

An ongoing study of Romanian orphans reported the results of removing children from the notorious deprivation of understaffed, undertrained institutional care at an average age of twenty-four months and placing them in foster care. In this study, after eighteen months in foster care, about half of the children were securely attached to their caregiver, but most of the benefit occurred for the girls. Also, a preponderance of behavioral disorders was found in the boys. (It makes me wonder what will happen when these boys grow to military age.) Whether this has to do with inherent resilience in females or cultural differences in treatment of the sexes in foster homes isn't known.

Another important difference described in these neglected, deprived children was the lack of discernment about going with a stranger. A majority of the institutionalized children at age four and a half were perfectly willing to go with a complete stranger, whereas almost none of the control group would. This lack of caution could put these kids at great risk of abuse and manipulation. My mind flashes to all the orphans in the failed states in Africa and their risk of becoming child soldiers, prostitutes, or slaves.

The brain scans of these deprived children showed reduction in size in the areas necessary for emotional maturity and higher reasoning. This result isn't surprising because we've known for years that children who have strabismus (crossed eyes) lose the ability to see out of the eye they don't use unless the dominant eye is patched. Although the nondominant eye remains anatomically normal, the visual processing center in the back of the brain (occipital cortex) atrophies due to disuse, rendering the eye functionally blind. Patching the dominant eye forces the use of the nondominant eye as well as its corresponding visual center in the brain.

Similarly, the lack of connection with another human results in both anatomical and functional loss—in this instance, functional loss of the parts of the brain that are necessary for healthy relationships. Repair is possible. The brain is remarkably plastic. But even with consistent love and care, repair takes a long time. The orphan study supports early intervention. It was very encouraging to me to read that many of the orphans placed in foster care had a chance for a normal life.

Much like the infant rats, the information and experiences our brains receive during the preverbal years are crucial in determining which circuits are activated, reinforced, and habituated (hardwired). These circuits set our threshold for stress and influence how we handle psychic injuries and behave with others during both moments of tenderness and distress. In essence, these circuits help us to self-regulate and increase our resilience.

Do I get angry and defensive with criticism, even if it's thoughtful and well intended? Do I have trouble with authority? Do I seek help when I'm confused? Do I berate myself or lash out at others? Am I able to apologize, or must I be right all the time? Do I expend much of my energy worrying about and involving myself in the moods of others? Do I avoid close relationships altogether? Do I take innocent comments by others personally? Do I enjoy being with people because, by and large, I feel their love and support, or do I mistrust what others say and do? Am I chronically anxious, basically calm, or calm until I blow a fuse? The best current theory of development has moved the pendulum back toward the importance of the patterns of relationships during the earliest months and years of life, more specifically the relationship between infant and mother (or primary caregiver).

Recognizing the importance of the mother-infant relationship often brings up difficult feelings. Some older moms (and dads) become defensive or feel guilty about mistakes with their kids, and some new moms become perfectionistic. These feelings confirm the love they have for their children. I continue to make amends to my grown children as past mistakes reveal themselves, but first I needed to understand and have compassion for a young, inexperienced father who was doing the best he could with the knowledge he had. It is both humbling and freeing. Parents who are unwilling to acknowledge their imperfections place the blame on their screwed-up kids, who are unable to meet unrealistic expectations.

Today I suppose it was a combination of nature and nurture that a three-year-old boy would be so content to sit and watch his near-silent grandmother prepare her Sabbath meal. I wonder what primal decision, lingering in the mist of my precognitive memory, I made about the world during my first few years in Grandmom's house.

Chapter 7

EARLY DECISIONS

> Early experience shapes the structure and function of
> the brain. This reveals the fundamental way in which
> gene expression is determined by experience.
> —Daniel J. Siegel

Infancy isn't a passive process. A child is absorbing his or her experiences and making lifelong decisions about how he or she will interact with this new world well before he or she acquires language and biographical memory. What is amazing is that these precognitive decisions have lifelong implications.

Our son, Matt, had severe food allergies, with anaphylaxis to dairy and eggs as well as asthma, requiring hospitalization and injections of epinephrine during his first year. Despite lots of love and attention, he became a very cautious little boy, knowing without language that his body (his universe) put him at risk. Matt engaged in new activities very reluctantly, needing much reassurance and encouragement. When he was a young adult, we told him about how he nearly went into anaphylactic shock when a pediatric allergist skin tested him for eggs and milk, despite our description of his severe reactions to these foods. We postulated to Matt that his early life-threatening allergies may have intensified his reluctance to engage in new activities, be it playing a sport, changing schools, or moving to a new home. Once Matt had these unknown pieces to his life puzzle, he was better able to understand his initial gut reaction to change without succumbing to it.

Mary Ainsworth, a psychologist who was one of the early researchers in the field of attachment, designed an experiment in the 1970s to see whether a child as young as a one-year old had already made decisions about his or her relationships. The Infant Strange Situation remains a linchpin of attachment research and was used to score the Romanian orphan study. Basically, a mother brings her child into a room with an array of interesting toys. As the child begins to explore, a stranger comes in and interacts with the mother and then the child while the mother sneaks out of the room. After a few minutes, Mom returns, comforts her child, and leaves again—this time with the stranger. Minutes later, first the stranger returns and then the mother. The observers record the amount of exploration and play the child engages in as well as the child's reaction to his or her separation from, and reunion with, his or her mother. (See resources for details of the experiment.) Ainsworth's groundbreaking experiment confirmed that a one-year-old child makes logical decisions about the nature of his or her relationships well before he or she has language.

Example of Secure Attachment: Mary

Mary is a happy and playful little girl. Initially, she displays both a healthy curiosity and a wariness of strangers. So long as Mom is in the room, Mary eventually begins to interact with the stranger. When Mom leaves, Mary is tearful but begins to play with some toys. When Mary hears the door open and sees her mom, she lights up with delight, runs to Mom as if she is her best friend in the whole world, and reaches up for a warm reunion. After a brief period of love and reassurance, Mary squirms out of Mom's embrace to explore her environment again.

Secure attachment creates the foundation for our ability to trust that close relationships are possible and desirable. Intimacy is based on interdependence and mutual trust, not one-up, one-down, someone-wins-and-someone-loses relationships. At one year, Mary feels the mutually beneficial partnership that has developed with her mom, which will likely carry over into adulthood.

Insecure Attachment, Example of Avoidant Relationship: Jimmy

Jimmy is an independent, little one-year-old. He has experienced detached parenting. His mom, preoccupied with her life, didn't recognize his earliest needs for touch and nurturing. Jimmy's basic material needs were met but only when he cried long enough. It took a disproportionate amount of time for his mom to read his infant attempts at communication. Employing trial-and-error efforts to quiet his crying, she might feed Jimmy when his diaper was soaked or assume he needed a nap when he wanted nurturing touch and stimulation.

During the experiment, Jimmy begins to explore and play with the toys well before Mom leaves the room. When she returns, Jimmy briefly glances at his mother but continues to play with his toys. By one year, he already has learned that this woman won't meet his needs and will likely reject him if he reaches for her.

Jimmy's reaction to his mother is no different than to a stranger. He assumes neither will meet his needs. Without intervention, he will grow up to be a self-sufficient, "independent little man," not daring to risk being in need. He is likely to carry a primordial grief for what he never had, for what we all crave.

Jimmy will keep others at a distance out of arrogance (they aren't good enough) or fear of rejection. For survival in an unresponsive world, Jimmy will submerge the preverbal feelings of longing, unaware of the grieving infant inside him. This style of relating has been labeled "Insecure-Avoidant Attachment." This decision serves as a powerful psychological defense for a child who has learned Mother won't be there for him.

Unfortunately, early defenses can become liabilities for a full, rich adult life. Although children who grow up with an avoidant attachment style with their mom don't suffer intellectually, they have push-pull adult relationships, at once wanting companionship and pushing it away. The assumption that they will be rejected can be so strong that they never allow themselves the vulnerability to ask for help or love. If those around them don't somehow psychically offer the attention and affection they crave, the avoidant becomes resentful. Yet if love and affection come too directly, they push it away. Being dependent, vulnerable, or even in need feels life threatening.

Insecure Attachment, Example of Anxious Relationship: Nan

Nan is an adorable little girl, who frequently checks on Mom's whereabouts. Because of anxiety and depression, Nan's mom has been unpredictable during Nan's infancy. At times, Mom is appropriately attentive and affectionate; at other times she is sad, scared, frustrated, or overbearing. Mom's lack of consistency confuses her daughter.

Nan is very distraught when Mom leaves the room. She cries a long time, frequently looking at the door where her mom exited. When Mom does return, Nan runs to her for reassurance and remains clinging to her. Seeing Nan's distress, Mom is overly protective, reluctantly releasing Nan when she eventually wants to play. There is intense energy between the child and mother.

Nan has already learned that she must defer her own needs and focus on Mom. Mom must be okay for her to be okay. Her energy will be outwardly focused, putting aside internal needs to be sure her world is safe, to be sure others are pleased with her, that she is worthy of love. Later in childhood, Nan's anxiety may impact attention and performance in school.

Nan will need a lot of reassurance that she is good enough. It's likely she'll try to overcompensate in relationships, assuming too much responsibility for the behavior of her partner. It's exhausting to be so hypervigilant, so concerned with the moods and preferences of others. At times Nan may explode in frustration or shut down under the weight of it all.

Nan has learned from her mother that wide, sometimes dramatic, mood swings will get her the attention she wants. She, in turn, requires a similar amount of vigilance by her partner and children.

Childhood logic and hope inform Nan that if she tries hard enough, she will fix Mom and make her happy. If she pays close attention to the moods and whims of others, she may find a way to be lovable or at least safe from the unpredictable behaviors of others. This strategy incurs a heavy burden later in life.

Many who display this attachment style remain in relationships that are unfulfilling. They settle for one-sided relationships, feeling as if they are doing all the giving and getting little in return. Even when external life is good, they don't know what to do, because they have never listened to the whisperings of their own hearts. Eventually they must ask, "Who am I outside of partner, mother, sister?"

Insecure, Disorganized Attachment: Jeffrey

Several years after Ainsworth's original experiment, a fourth attachment style was added to her model. Researchers noted a different behavior among children known to be abused, terrified, or overly intruded upon by the very people who were supposed to love and care for them.

Jeffrey's mother is unable to see that crying is merely his attempt to get what he needs. She takes it all personally, as if his screams are accusing her of being a horrible mother. Infuriated, she shakes or pinches him to stop him from making noise. She drowns out his crying by turning up the TV until Jeffrey gives up. Jeffrey endures hunger and a wet diaper until his mother is good and ready to deal with him. Jeffrey spends hours in his crib, his only company being a bottle propped on a pillow.

During his experiment, Jeffrey interacts with the stranger without the normal concern, even when his mother is away for more than a few minutes. When Jeffrey is alone, he plays with the toys without enthusiasm. When his mother returns, he displays his inner chaos and confusion by taking a step toward her, then turning away, then taking a step toward her, then turning away until he literally spins in circles.

Adults who survive this level of chaos report few childhood memories. They express difficulty concentrating in school and are distracted at work. Often emotions flood them without their knowing why this is happening to them. They feel and act out of control in response to what most of us would consider a minor irritation, a small snub, or a playful jab. Ironically, when children who suffer abuse become too much for their parents to handle, they are identified as the problem, as if their nature is to be bad kids. Later, when they lose control as adults, they receive the same condemning looks from peers and loved ones, confirming their own feelings of inadequacy.

Some children survive childhood maltreatment and neglect by mimicking the scripts of their parents. In social situations, they parrot adult behaviors, looking like very well-behaved and perfect little grown-ups. Fear of disapproval produces the outward appearance of normalcy. Inside, they live with the loss of their true voice and sometimes with the self-disgust of their capitulation. Later, their inner child may rebel in dangerous and outrageous ways to break the yoke of well-meaning parenting.

Many workshop participants have begun their story with, "We were the perfect family on the outside. We held hands walking to church. We were polite, happy children. We fooled everybody in town. It didn't matter what went on behind closed doors or how we felt on the inside. What mattered was how we looked to the world. If I looked happy, I was happy. And God help me if I didn't look happy."

The CDC/Kaiser Permanente Adverse Childhood Experiences Study from 1995–1997 reviewed the childhood experiences of seventeen thousand members and analyzed the effects of childhood abuse and household dysfunction on the mental and physical heath of this population. The study confirmed that prolonged childhood maltreatment and/or neglect have been shown to increase the risk of mental and emotional disorders as well as the likelihood of alcohol and drug abuse. Other consequences include arrests for violent crimes and chronic medical conditions such as obesity, type 2 diabetes with all its associated cardiovascular and kidney complications, chronic lung disease, cirrhosis of the liver, and lifestyle-linked cancers. Childhood neglect and abuse may be the biggest risk factor for early mortality from all causes, including disease, stress, street violence, and war.

After writing about Ainsworth's experiment, I turned off the lights and arranged the pillow for my first position of the night. I drifted off to sleep, thinking about my attachment style with my mother. After reading about attachment and doing a lot of my own growth work, I was still unclear if I could diagnose myself.

Three hours later, I awakened with the urge to jump out of bed. Assuming my bladder was the source of the feeling, I went to the bathroom and returned to bed. I could not get comfortable. The urge to bolt out of bed returned. I sat up in the dark and reviewed my last thoughts before sleep. Attachment. Maybe if I started with Mom, I'd figure out how to make some headway.

Mom kept to herself. She was not, as she described herself, a social butterfly. She mistrusted most people, regularly questioning their motives. Once her parents died (to this day, I don't know what actually happened to them), she and her sister were separated from their brothers and fostered in an unsafe home.

I grew up listening to her kitchen-table psychoanalysis of friends and neighbors, taking their inventory with a skeptical, sometimes cynical, slant. She disdained those who groveled for attention or appeared materialistic. Mom never treated herself by shopping except when she bounced from her baseline—"I don't need anything or want anything"—to angry entitlement—"Your father joined the country club and plays golf three times a week. I'm going to get that dress." (Dad was always thrilled when Mom treated herself.) It was only much later in life that Mom occasionally bought something for herself with joy and tenderness.

My dad, on the other hand, unabashedly wanted recognition for his talents. Pop was a great storyteller, recounting his merchandising achievements, the deals he made, and the great advice he gave to random strangers. Actually, he didn't have to exaggerate. He was a brilliant businessman and helped a lot of people. But Mom must have heard the same stories a thousand times.

Tonight, waiting for sleep to take me, I have a new insight. Whereas I used to think Mom was mad that Pop held people hostage, I now wonder whether she was furious with the little boy inside Dad who would risk humiliating himself for recognition and attention while being equally angry with her own needy little girl for wanting the same thing.

Unable to bear the pain of feeling unworthy, Mom used quiet disdain and mistrust as her shield. Warm and endearing with those she trusted, she put on a good face in social situations but avoided them when she could. Her lonely little girl could worm her way into anyone's heart. People loved my mom, but she didn't truly believe she was adorable until her dying breath.

When Dad was frail and dying of heart disease and mom had progressive dementia, I knew it was nearing time for around-the-clock support. Then I received a page at four o'clock in the morning from my answering service that Dad had fallen and been unable to get off the floor since midnight. In her confusion, Mom hadn't been able to find our home number. After several hours, she dialed my office number and spoke to the answering service. That day I arranged for them to move to a care home, where Dad died about three weeks later at the age of ninety-four. Mom settled in amazingly well despite the loss of her mate of sixty-three years and her comfortable and familiar home.

The most touching moment of her yearlong stay at the care home came about a month after Dad died. On that day, she pulled me into her room, closed the door behind us, and whispered conspiratorially, "They love me here." There was genuine pride and happiness in her voice, but there was also surprise and relief that she was, in fact, lovable.

Mom's dementia worsened, as did her congestive heart failure. One morning she awakened with severe shortness of breath and told the staff at the care home she wanted "to go to Larry's hospital." Although I had been a hospice medical director for more than fifteen years, when it came time to choose between traditional cardiac care in the hospital or admission to our hospice unit, I needed to call my brother Steve to get his permission for end-of-life care. My head knew Mom wanted all this to be over with, but I still had this nagging feeling I was killing my mom. Fortunately, Steve reassured me that hospice was the right choice. He and his wife, Crystal, arrived the next day.

Mom declined over the next several days. We pulled out old photos, told stories, and laughed a lot. On her last morning, Steve, Crystal, Anne, and I were all there, taking turns holding Mom's hand. I had just sat down to gently massage Mom's feet when Anne turned our discussion to how Mom's lack of self-esteem had prevented her from achieving amazing things with her life. We all commented on the wasted potential of a brilliant woman. Then, as if prompted by a divine choral master, all four of us simultaneously yelled, "Mom, we love you ... Everybody loved you!" I believe that a sad, lonely, abandoned little girl inhaled the singsong words uttered by the people she loved most, then washed herself clean with them, releasing all self-doubt as she let out her last sighing breath.

That's where my mind takes me at two o'clock in the morning, sitting in my dark bedroom. I am thinking that Mom taught me not to rely on other people (including her), partly because she couldn't give me the deep, relaxed affection she'd so sternly denied herself. I suppose that, on the whole, I have an avoidant style of attachment with both Mom and Dad. Yet here I sit, upright in the dark, so anxious that I want to jump out of bed and run around the house. (For the record, this doesn't happen often.) Somehow my anxiety doesn't fit with the cool, self-contained avoidance I present to the world.

And that's when it dawns on me. Maybe I was anxiously attached to Mom as well. I always had my eye on her moods, trying to calm her when she was scared and feeling relief when she was happy. Dad's lifestyle scared her plenty. He'd secretly go to the savings and loan and borrow money to play the horses. I would ask to go with him to the track and sit next to him all day while he handicapped the horses. I silently prayed that his picks would win so Mom would be happy when we got home.

I remember the day when Dad hit five races in a row. He brought home more than $1,200 and spread it all out on the table. I was sure Mom would be happy. Instead, she grabbed the money and said, "We're driving to California to see my sister before you give the money back to Delaware Park."

Another day I remember Dad betting $200 to show on Hasty Scenes, the overall favorite, who would pay $230 if he came in third or better. That was an unusually large bet for our poor family in the early 1950s, when $30 could have filled a Radio Flyer with groceries that would have fed the five of us for a week. The bet didn't make sense to my childhood mind, to risk $200 for a $30 payoff, but Dad was a brilliant handicapper, so I kept my mouth shut. From my analysis of the Telegraph, the racing form that contained the detailed histories of prior races, Hasty Scenes was a "closer," usually hanging back in the middle of the pack until he rounded the last turn. On that day, Hasty Scenes was running his race, hanging back between fifth or sixth on the backstretch, but when he came through the last turn, nothing happened. The jockey put the whip to him, but he didn't respond.

I felt like the world had come to an end. I started to cry in front of all the people who surrounded us. I'm sure Dad was angry with himself for the bet, ashamed of causing me such distress, or disappointed that I was crying. But instead of consoling me, he squeezed my arm and whispered, "If you don't stop crying, we'll leave right now, and I will never take you to the track again."

That was my last day at the track.

Instead of doing what four- to eight-year-old boys usually did, I frequently accompanied Dad to the track, enjoying the camaraderie and the stories of the other happy gamblers. By the time I was seven, Dad had me handicapping my own races. I liked the intellectual challenge, even though I was too young to bet. Besides, even the smallest wager of two dollars was way out of my league. But underneath the excitement and spectacle of the track, I was the secret guardian of our family, protecting a very scared, insecure little girl (my mom) from her fear of being homeless again. I also protected the rest of our family when her fear turned to anger.

Tonight in the darkness, a grown man of sixty-eight, I decided it's possible to possess different attachment styles to different parts of my mother. I had an anxious attachment to my mother's scared little girl and an avoidant attachment to her practical, self-denying, hardworking adult.

It's complicated. It's the middle of the night, and I'm trying to diagnose myself. What do I know? Besides, my little one doesn't really care about theories, even if they are useful to psychologists.

Now that I have this brilliant insight, I should be relieved and relaxed. I want to go back to sleep, but I'm still restless. The more I try to sleep, the more frustrated I become. I am about to learn with deeper clarity that the feelings beneath my thoughts are the source of my insomnia. After what seems like several hours of insomnia, I finally remember to ask myself, "Who in there is having all this anxiety?"

Within seconds, a very young inner child says, "I am. Don't you remember I used to get so uptight that Mom would have to give me those purple pills?" Mom didn't know how to soothe my anxiety any more than she knew how to calm herself, except by keeping a very organized and spotlessly clean home. Having consulted our family doctor, Mom occasionally gave me the tiny purple pill, pretty much the only tranquilizer available at the time. I wonder which of us benefitted more from those pills.

Over the years, I have learned to be patient and not rush to give advice or a pep talk to my younger self. I silently acknowledge this memory I have forgotten. "I remember now, feeling so tense at times when I was little like you." I wait, trying to picture a troubled little boy who was unaware of what was wrong or how to stop the sensations that were overwhelming him. I feel my eyes fill and hear a very small voice say, with a mixture of desperation and shame, "I can't fix all of this."

All I can answer is, "No, you couldn't fix it then, and I am so sorry that you thought you had to." I can feel his little body take in a breath of relief. I continue to imagine holding him in my arms while he finishes crying. Then, to my surprise, he blurts out with some urgency, "I can't go to sleep yet."

Like many children whose parents didn't know how to hear their inner thoughts, my little guy still is unable to trust—even me after almost thirty years of communicating with him this way. Just a few moments earlier, he had watched me ignore (or not realize) that it was he who was struggling with the urge to move. Instead of being gentle with him, I was telling myself to just calm down and go back to sleep.

By saying he wasn't ready to go back to sleep, he was telling me he was suspicious of my motives for comforting him, that I was doing it to shut him up so I could go back to sleep. He didn't want to hear me say, "Okay, we've talked long enough, so it's time for you to feel calm and happy now."

Kids can smell the hidden agendas of adults. I think all parents have them. Some are conscious choices, but many are driven by all the conflicting needs of adults managing their busy lives as well as the unconscious emotional needs of their own little voices inside. It makes me sad this night to hear the fear of my little one that I will abandon him in his distress.

"Little guy, I will stay awake and hold you all night, if that is what we need to do. You are more important to me than a few more hours of sleep."

I feel his muscles relax and enjoy the easy movement of his chest as he takes cleansing breaths. I sense that he trusts that he doesn't have to fix anything and that he will be cared for. After a few minutes, I lie back down on the bed, finding a new position for the pillows, ready to be with my little guy in silence. Five or ten minutes later, I think I hear him mumble something about "little purple pills" as we drift into a deep, replenishing sleep.

Many good references about attachment theory explain in more detail the importance of these critical infant relationships. I describe Ainsworth's experiment to emphasize how early our brains make unconscious decisions that affect our lifelong relationships. Fortunately, early intervention, or having a long-term loving relationship can do much to repair these early patterns (see next chapter).

Of course, we may have different attachment styles to different people, which can provide some ballast in rough seas. I was securely attached to my grandmother, despite our mostly nonverbal communication. I was lucky, having been born in her home and reminding her of her oldest son.

I had an avoidant attachment to my dad. He was an extrovert and not only outward focused but also completely submerged under the weight of providing for his family and compensating for his own childhood poverty. I was quiet, somewhat sickly with allergies, and an introvert who needed an emotional connection. In no way could Dad meet my internal needs because they weren't in his repertoire. I didn't turn to him for advice (although he regularly gave it) or consolation. I learned that if I were to have any relationship with Dad, I would have to meet him on his terms. So, we talked about horse racing, business, sports, finances, ice cream flavors … whatever he wanted to talk to me about. I learned valuable analytical skills, such as how to function with honesty and integrity in the marketplace of life and, above all, how to listen. Although my head knew and understood I had to meet Dad on his terms, my little boy never completely freed himself from disappointment, sadness, and resentment that his father never once asked him how he was, who he was, or why he was choosing the path he was on.

Stepping back, I see that this disconnect with Dad may have actually intensified my need for, and appreciation of, a rich internal life. Now, eight years after Dad's death, I can say that I am equally grateful for what he wasn't able to provide as for what he did. I wouldn't have been drawn to the work of Elisabeth Kübler-Ross. Although I deeply appreciate my father now, when Anne and I were in the thick of looking after my parents during the last eight years of their lives, I needed to give my little one plenty of time and space to grieve or swear in frustration. Anne allowed—even encouraged—me to express my frustration so I could come back to being a kind, dutiful, helpful, and loving son.

During those years of caregiving, my little one really didn't want to hear that Dad wasn't doing it intentionally, which of course was true. He already knew Dad loved and respected me. He just needed the space to blow off steam.

I was able to find compassion for a man who worked hard to give his sons much more than he ever had and for my father's "little boy," whom an ignorant and physically punitive father had raised. Dad did his best to break the generational cycle of physical abuse. That he couldn't completely shed his childhood skin and passed on some unwanted traits to his sons isn't surprising and sometimes still surfaces as a source of grief. I, in turn, haven't completely shed my childhood skin and so am a source of grief for, and a reason for compassion from, my kids.

Revisiting painful moments in our past is scary. We don't want to feel vulnerable or admit those we love may have been the source of our pain. We don't wish to rehash buried anger and fear because we don't want to admit we aren't so different from those who hurt us and so are capable of injuring the next generation. But if we wish to develop deep compassion, we must have the courage to own what Elisabeth Kübler-Ross called the Mother Teresa and Hitler inside each of us.

Chapter 8

EARNED ATTACHMENT

> Our sorrows and wounds are healed only when
> we touch them with compassion.
> —Buddha

All isn't lost if we are insecurely attached to our primary caregivers. Studies have shown that a healthy, long-term relationship or several years with a good therapist can modify insecure attachment. I was blessed to meet the love of my life more than fifty years ago. Over those years and with a lot of personal work, we have been fortunate to raise each other again and help our "little ones" attach securely to ourselves and each other. Ours would be an example of "earned attachment."

As a teenager, I was painfully shy. I had no idea how to make small talk. Having no sisters, I knew little about being with girls. I was too inhibited to dance, so I concentrated on sports and studies. I appeased my parents by listening to their suggestions, not arguing with what they told me, then doing what I wanted. Silent rebellion.

My inner adolescent still wants to avoid large gatherings (more than four to six people) and displays a quiet, stubborn streak. The individual sport of wrestling definitely suited his personality. I have recently realized that he could also be quite impulsive, for which I am mostly very grateful.

When I was fifteen, I went to a dance held at a local country club. Mostly at such parties, I wandered around, talking to friends individually, so I could avoid feeling so out of place and invisible in a larger group. After about two hours, I was bored and ready to leave. I'm not sure what was going on in my mind when I decided to go to this particular dance. Maybe I had the romantic notion that I would meet the girl of my dreams, but it sure wasn't happening. I remember climbing the stairs to the second floor, looking for a ride home. I passed by a sitting room occupied by kids from a rival school. I stopped at the door and peered in, just in case I recognized someone. Sitting on the sofa, with guys on either side, was the most beautiful human being I had ever seen. I am sure I stared with my mouth open until another kid bumped me out of the way. I ran downstairs, found a friend who might know who she was, and dragged him to the second floor. I warned him to be cool and subtle as we passed by the room. He looked inside and was about to point at her when I yanked him away.

"Do you know her name?" I asked. He did. I did further research, learning where she lived, whether she had a boyfriend, and what grade she was in. Anne was two and a half years younger and two grades behind. I was definitely too old to be asking out a twelve- to thirteen-year-old. Besides, I didn't have the chutzpah.

Later that year, a good friend of mine, who was in Anne's grade, dated her for a few months. When he told me, I acted nonchalant. Fortunately, their relationship was short lived. During my last years in high school, I dated a few girls, but it never seemed right. My path didn't really cross Anne's again after that first glimpse. Time passed. I graduated and left for Amherst College in Massachusetts.

Freshman year at Amherst was notoriously difficult academically. All of us were mandated to take the core curriculum, which included math, physics, history, classics, a foreign language, and a writing course. I was good in the sciences, but the English and fine arts majors struggled to survive calculus and physics. In turn, the daily two hundred to three hundred pages of assigned reading for history and classics brutalized me, and the infamous English 1 writing course just about broke me.

My writing instructor, William Coles, notorious for challenging (intimidating) his students, returned my first assignment, pockmarked with comments like "Bulletproof" and "Who do you think you are, Norman Vincent Peale?" A bit horrified I was accused of being a preacher, I nevertheless prayed that my papers would never make the daily selection for class discussion, knowing that mine wouldn't be chosen as an example of great writing. Coles was brutal, charismatic, and demanding. I loved the guy. I wish he were alive to take out his red pencil today.

The Amherst core curriculum was boot camp. I studied in the library until it closed, then in my room until one o'clock in the morning. I set my alarm for five o'clock and started all over again. My driven little man was pushed to his limit, but he wasn't going to quit. Before breakfast, I would walk over to Memorial Hill, gaze at the panorama of technicolor leaves, lick my wounds, and wonder whether I could keep this pace up for four years. I was homesick. I wanted the comfort of Tatnall School, where I knew exactly what was required of me. I also wanted my mom's home-cooked meals and the security and privacy of my own bedroom.

About six weeks into the first semester, the football coach, who had been the quarterback at the University of Delaware and was a good friend of my high school coach, called to see whether I wanted to fly home for the weekend. They were going to scout the U. of D. football team. There was a free seat in the four-seater airplane, and it was mine if I wanted it. I threw my books in a suitcase and jumped aboard.

After studying all day Saturday, I decided to go out. I called my friend, who had dated Anne two years before. He told me that there was a dance at Tower Hill (her school) that night. Though it was closed to other schools, I told him I wanted to crash it. While my friend was always game, I knew that, for me, this adventure would take the kind of social courage I lacked. I procured a bottle of vodka.

My brown paper bag and I climbed into my friend's car, and we made a quick stop for lemonade. After two quick cups of courage, we walked right in the Tower Hill gym. While my buddy stopped to say hello to a football friend, I split off in search of Anne Taylor. She was dancing with a junior classmate. I cut in.

Here I was, just where I wanted to be, and I had no plan. We danced a bit, and she asked me who I was. "What?" I screamed over the loudspeakers.

"Your name?" Anne yelled in my ear. I stopped dancing, right in the middle of the gymnasium. College freshman mathematics: the inverse relationship of blood alcohol to multitasking. It was either talk or dance. At about eighty decibels, I told her my name, then blurted out the truth. "I crashed Tower Hill so I could dance with you one time. I'm leaving now, but I was wondering if I could write to you from Amherst."

I put it all on the line. "Hillers" dancing around us began to stare. I waited for Anne's answer or the hand of a teacher-bouncer on my shoulder. I would be either a total romantic or an arrogant Tatnall jerk. I suppose she decided she didn't have much to lose, my being more than three hundred miles away. I would like to believe, even now, that some primitive, past-life recognition was happening near midcourt.

Anne pulled me outside one of the gym doors. "Do you want my address?"

"I know where you live," I told her. "I'll write you next week. Thanks for our dance." I walked away to tell my friend I was ready to go.

"We just got here!" he said. I insisted.

I have done a lot of wonderfully impulsive things in my life, and mostly they came from a deep intuitive, knowing place, but none (including the way I met Elisabeth) have compared to that October night in 1964. Anne and I corresponded regularly. She told me years later that she was wooed by my writing. She should have been my English I instructor.

We married six years later. It wasn't easy. I was Jewish and came from the wrong side of the tracks. Anne came from a southern Episcopal family, her mother's pedigree dating back to the American Revolution. Our parents had only one thing in common: the belief that this relationship was a bad idea. We proved them wrong.

Besides her physical beauty, Anne has been a passionate, loyal, intelligent, and fiercely loving partner, mom, and now grandmother. She is also an extremely gifted psychotherapist and workshop leader. She has always wanted the best for me, even as she at times struggled to find her own place in life.

In 1970, Anne joined me and the New York tenement cockroaches in our seventy-five-dollars-per-month rent-controlled Washington Heights apartment. For my last two years of medical school at Columbia University, Anne scrambled to find a job as an elementary school teacher. Her first job took her to Harlem as a substitute teacher. She had guts to be traveling there during the time of riots, drugs, and Black Power. A sixth-grade boy took it upon himself to be her protector, walking her to and from her car each day. The following year, Anne was offered a last-minute second-grade position in the school directly across the street from Presbyterian Hospital. The principal made the terrible mistake of having the other six second-grade teachers choose children to transfer into Anne's class. As you might expect, they didn't send the brightest, cheeriest, and best-behaved kids to this rookie teacher. Half the children in Anne's class were patients at Psychiatric Institute, suffering from childhood trauma and neglect. Anne was more herder than teacher that year. But she never missed a day of school.

When I arrived home from the hospital, Anne would greet me with, "Sit down, eat your dinner—and no talking." I instantly changed from white coat medical student to second-grader.

Anne had a great class of kids the following year but had to say good-bye to them in late November, when we decided to have a last adventure before residency and children. Using our savings and Anne's small inheritance from a great uncle, we arranged a series of medical school electives so we could spend a month each in Perth and Sydney, Australia, followed by two months in Hualien, Taiwan.

We invited Anne's sister to join us in Taiwan. She was a junior in high school and struggling to find her own place in the world. In retrospect, we had no business trying to rescue a teenager when we barely knew ourselves. The two sisters had some rough times, and I was often the mediator, a role I was used to playing as the middle child in my family. Those months were hard and wonderful, binding us together in what has grown to be a precious sibling relationship.

In Taiwan, we provided portable medical clinics for the aboriginal tribal people of the island, who had been relegated to the mountainous regions first by invading Chinese centuries ago and then by the defeated armies of Chiang Kai-shek after World War II. They grew bananas and ginger on the hillsides, making about sixty cents a day. Anne and her sister set up the tabletop pharmacy, while Dr. Brown, the missionary surgeon, and I tended to a line of patients, one after the other. We had no exam tables and no privacy. The next person in line waited in easy earshot, three feet away, while I ministered to her neighbor. A young tribal woman, who worked at the hospital, acted as my translator. She spoke Japanese, the unifying language among the eight aboriginal tribes on the island, since the Japanese occupation prior to World War II.

On the first morning of clinic, I saw about ten patients, most complaining of dyspepsia. I assumed that the stress of living marginal lives, without adequate protein or heat during the cold, damp winters, without running water or electricity, and with the use of communal outhouses was the cause of their indigestion. I prescribed antacids, which our pharmacists dispensed from our limited supply of medications. Surprised by the repetitive nature of these complaints, I nonetheless continued the brief examinations of my fully clothed patients, ordering the same treatment.

When my interpreter explained the plan to my tenth patient, she frowned and spoke several clearly questioning words. My translator shook her head and tried to send her on her way. This time I interrupted and asked what was happening. Initially, my helper shook her head and wouldn't tell me. I insisted.

With her head down, she demurely told me the woman complained that a nine-inch worm had crawled out of her nose that morning. She said Maalox wouldn't help her. I looked at my translator in disbelief and asked whether all the previous people I had seen also suffered from roundworm infestation. More importantly, why had she not told me?

With tears in her eyes, my young nurse translator said she didn't want me to lose face in front of the tribe. After a short break to find some respectful, common ground between our two cultures, I apologized for making her lose face as well. She had cried in front of our patients. With mutual humility, we both agreed that serving our patients would supersede protecting me from my ignorance. Although I was the doctor, I could still be her student. My interest in infectious diseases blossomed during our time in Taiwan.

In June 1972, I began my internal medicine internship at the hospital of the University of Pennsylvania. Anne and I decided this would be a good time for pregnancy and children, since I would be on call every second or third night for the next two or three years. Usually, this required staying up all night, admitting new patients, and putting out fires. In those days, when I was on the ICU rotations, it meant I was awake thirty-six out of every forty-eight hours. Anne and I learned that sleep trumped everything else, including food or intimacy. On the weekends, Anne would invite friends for dinner to break up the long hours alone. I would come home, attempt to make pleasant conversation while having a bite to eat, and then wander into the bedroom and fall asleep in my clothes without so much as a "Nice seeing you."

Matt and Rachael were born in 1973 and 1975. There are no words to express the joy of seeing my own children come screaming out of my partner's womb and the relief and gratitude that they arrived with ten fingers and toes. Now, at ages forty-one and forty, they continue to be the greatest gifts of our lives.

In 1977, after I completed my infectious disease fellowship, we moved to Tucson. Several months before, Anne and I had driven through the Southwest looking for jobs. We fell in love with the mountains and desert, so I spent an extra couple of days knocking on doors and looking for an infectious disease job. The local infectious disease doctor told me there was barely enough work for one specialist. About to give up, I drove past Holbrook-Hill Clinic, a beautiful new building across from Tucson Medical Center, made a U-turn, parked in the lot, and asked the receptionist whether I could speak to the managing physician. Initially she told me it would be impossible without an appointment. I persisted, explaining that I had flown from Philadelphia to look for work in Tucson. She brought me to Dr. Stephens, who, dressed like an Easterner in the quintessential three-piece suit, was both formal and gracious. He told me that regretfully the clinic had no need for a new doctor since they had just hired Dr. Michael Boxer from St. Louis. I jumped in disbelief, telling him Mike Boxer had been my organic chemistry lab instructor at Amherst. After a brief reunion with Mike, Anne and I prepared to explore other cities in California the next day. In the meantime, my former lab instructor was twisting arms, insisting that the clinic hire me despite the financial risk. Late that afternoon, we were invited to dinner with several of the docs and their wives, and I accepted my first job.

We left Tucson the next morning, shell-shocked by the rapidity of events. In fact, we were so anxious about our quick decision that I flew out again six weeks later, just to be sure about the job and to begin looking for housing. Three days later, just before boarding my plane home, I called Anne to tell her I had bought a house. I was more worried about Anne liking my impulsive house purchase than about the job. It was one thing to crash a school dance but quite another to buy a house Anne had never seen. I was way out on a limb. Four months later, on 7/7/77, we flew to Tucson with our two children. Anne loved the house.

The first two weeks were very slow at work. I saw some emergency visits and a few new patients, who were being distributed among the younger doctors. Late into my second week, I got a somewhat frantic call from a gastroenterologist to come right over to the ICU to see a seventy-year-old man with high fevers and delirium. He and his wife had just returned from a month-long trip to India. The patient had a negative blood smear for malaria. Looking septic, he was placed on three broad-spectrum antibiotics, which would treat bacterial infections from staph to typhoid. He continued to decline, exhibiting high fevers and increasing confusion. His Valley Fever (a fungus infection endemic to the desert Southwest) tests were also negative.

Despite a negative blood smear, the referring physician was sure he had malaria or some other esoteric parasitic infection, which was rapidly draining the life from him. I rushed over to see my first infectious disease patient, worried that I wouldn't find the cause of his critical illness. I poured over his chart, reviewed his x-rays, which revealed a small patch of pneumonia, and examined my patient, who was too delirious to give me his history. Except for scattered crackling sounds in the lower lobe of one lung, at the site of the infiltrate on his chest x-ray, I had no hint of a cause for his illness. He had no skin lesions, and his exam didn't point toward meningitis. With his loss of mental function, he would need a spinal tap.

Next, I walked to the lab and reviewed his malaria smear. I saw no parasites. By then, his wife had arrived in the waiting room. I took an extensive medical history before asking her to give me a day-by-day description of their trip to India. Nothing she told me was helpful. I then reviewed my findings and explained that her husband needed a bronchoscopy to obtain samples from the lung and that I would order additional laboratory tests. I'm sure she could read the concern all over my face.

I had turned to go back to the ICU but stopped myself. Just to be as thorough as possible, I asked whether by any chance they had parrots at home. "Why, yes," she said. "In fact, one of the birds is really sick right now." I nearly screamed. Limiting myself to a big hug, I rushed back to the ICU, discontinued all antibiotics, and began intravenous tetracycline for psittacosis, a disease common to birds and which can cause a serious pneumonia in humans.

The ICU staff was quite concerned that this new, very young specialist had stopped all the strong antibiotics. I called the referring physician, told him his patient had psittacosis, that the India trip was a red herring, and reviewed my plan of action. He responded with, "Is this supposed to be funny?"

Within twenty-four hours, the fever broke, and the patient was lucid and hungry. He was discharged five days later, just before the psittacosis titer came back extremely positive. The ICU staff became an immediate, and often insistent, source of referrals for their sickest patients, and my days of leisurely medicine were over.

I had reached the magic "someday" when I had everything I had hoped for: a great wife, two wonderful children, a steady source of income, and now sudden esteem from the medical community. Within eighteen months, the clinic that hired me broke apart, so I joined another pair of internists. My practice continued to grow. After two years of long, unpredictable, and stressful days at work, I began to wonder whether I could keep up this pace for another thirty years. A voice inside me, the origin about which I knew nothing, resented the time away from my family, the stress of being responsible for so many people, and the very long days. I began to dream of a way out.

In the summer of 1979, my brother Steve shipped out samples of Haagen-Dazs ice cream. Anne's sister had already introduced us to their carob and honey vanilla flavors in Boston several years before, but the strawberry and chocolate chocolate-chip made us converts. The company was nearly unknown in Tucson and had just begun franchising stores. We shared the ice cream with another couple, our first friends in Tucson. Within two days, I called New Jersey to set up a visit at company headquarters, while our friends secured a location for a store. This would be the twenty-fourth dip store to open in the nation. Maybe ice cream would be my ticket to a quieter life.

Anne and Nancy did the heavy lifting at the store, since Joe and I still had our full-time careers. Anne was excited to have an opportunity to manage and develop a business, and to contribute in a significant way to the prosperity of our family.

As it turned out, each of the four of us had very different needs and goals around the business, often leading to hard feelings. Over the next four years, we opened two more stores, adding to our stress. Unable to meet each other's needs, Anne and I disagreed and argued almost daily, each defending and advocating a different point of view. We were busier than ever—and now our marriage was at risk.

It didn't cross our minds to seek professional help. We had no idea that unmet childhood needs were being triggered and that we were unconsciously hurting and betraying "little ones."

It all came to a head in the summer of 1982, when Anne told me she needed to leave. It felt much longer than a week before she called to say she would be returning home. Somehow the separation, with its very real risk of breaking up our precious family, caused both of us to disarm. We stopped fighting. Even though we shared an unspoken, primitive sense that we were both doing the best we could, just trying to survive, and not trying to hurt each other, we had no language to talk about what had happened. The truce held, and we continued to lick our wounds.

Two or three times that year, we stole an overnight together in Phoenix. Each time we fought all the way on the drive north on I-10. But once there, we enjoyed our time together, remembering why we'd fallen in love with each other. By the third trip, as we once again began to fight, we began laughing at the absurdity of this predictable event. We both were learning that our love would survive these disagreements. As trust deepened between us, we worked with our business partners to return our stores to the parent company.

By fall 1983, Anne and I returned to solid footing, but our lives remained overly busy. I started earlier and pushed through my day until my desk and pager were clear. I was successful by any external criteria, enjoyed seeing nearly all my patients, and appreciated touching moments of interaction daily. Yet on an existential level I knew something was missing. Despite many internal pep talks, I couldn't let go of that feeling. Maybe the problem was medicine.

At this point I seriously considered leaving my profession and teaching at a private school much like the one I had attended, with the dream of someday becoming a headmaster. Out of desperation, I impulsively flew to Anaheim, where the National Independent School Association meetings were being held. I queried a variety of teachers to find a school on the West Coast that would somehow match my dream. Once I heard about Polytechnic School in Pasadena, I ran around the conference halls and pushed past crowds of teachers until I found Alexander Babcock, its headmaster. After talking for nearly an hour, he invited Anne and me to visit. Although it must have been scary, Anne enthusiastically joined me, showing a willingness to follow my impulsive search for meaning.

Polytechnic was a beautiful school, with engaged students, dedicated teachers, and supportive parents. It was perfect, except I had bills to pay and two kids to educate. My head out-voted my heart. We returned to Tucson, and I pushed down all the voices of resistance. I told myself to put away childish dreams. With tough resignation, I planted my feet on the floor each morning and shifted into high gear. This was the life I chose. It was time that I accepted it.

Within a few weeks of my decision, I was making my predawn rounds on the oncology floor when I saw a flyer announcing that Elisabeth Kübler-Ross would be giving a public lecture at a local high school. I bought four tickets, wanting Anne to hear this brilliant, inspiring woman, whom I had first heard fourteen years ago, and believing I could help two dear friends who had lost a son to leukemia. Little did I know that Elisabeth's talk would initiate a guided tour into my past, where I would soon meet the younger self I was determined to keep submerged.

Over the next several years, Anne and I began to put the pieces of our life puzzles together. We found a common language to share our stories and introduced our little ones to each other. We began to recognize our wounds and honor the needs and strengths of our younger selves. We not only began to nurture ourselves but also to cherish, protect, and nurture one another. We were very fortunate to trust each other enough to risk deep self-disclosure.

In 1985, we moved our family from Tucson back to our roots in Delaware. I left my medical practice to work with Elisabeth full-time, while Anne completed a master's degree in counseling at the University of Delaware and continued to staff workshops. During those two years, I traveled about 50 percent of the time; that was too much for Anne and our two preadolescent children. In 1987, we decided to return to Tucson. While continuing to lead workshops, I resumed my infectious disease consultations, and Anne began her counseling practice. Life was busy and very rich.

Secure attachment occurs when our primary caregiver meets our emotional and physical needs in a timely manner. As Anne and I learned to attune to our own inner voices, we simultaneously did that for each other. Although we continued to be triggered at times, we never used the information we had learned about our early childhood to purposely attack or hurt the other. The more stories we have shared, the deeper the feelings of trust and safety have evolved. My little ones know Anne has seen them, with all their fears, rage, grief, and shame—and yet she still loves them. They know she will protect them with her life. I believe she knows I accept and protect her, too.

Through our ongoing personal exploration, Anne and I have given our little ones the gift of earned, secure attachment.

Chapter 9
ELUSIVE MEMORY

> The past beats inside me like a second heart.
> —John Banville, *The Sea*

Real vs. Reality

Memory is tricky, fluid, and susceptible to change with ongoing experiences. Eyewitnesses of the same event often provide widely differing accounts, not just differing interpretation, of what they actually saw. Researchers have also documented that the level of certainty of an observer doesn't correlate with the accuracy of his or her observation. Since we recreate, and therefore may modify, a memory each time we remember it, we are constantly rewriting our autobiographies.

Suppose I could now magically view Teddy's ordeal on YouTube, and it looked nothing like what I remembered. Much like a child who wakes up screaming in the night because there is a monster in his room, I needed someone first and foremost to acknowledge and show concern for my feelings and then check under the bed and in the closet with me. Unfortunately, I didn't trust my parents with the information, so they didn't have the opportunity to comfort me and then walk with me to Teddy's home to see how he was doing. That way I would have been able in real time to merge my reality with what really happened.

Jill's Final Hours

About fifteen years ago, while leading one of Elisabeth's Life, Death, and Transition Workshops, I met Jill, a woman with advanced cancer who arrived from a neighboring state the night before the workshop began. I had spoken to her earlier to be sure she was well enough to attend. She told me she had stopped radiation and chemotherapy. Although quite weak, she could get around with help. I arranged a scholarship for a friend, who couldn't afford the workshop fee, to act as an assistant for Jill.

That evening, several other women arrived and were assigned to Jill's bunkhouse. At about midnight, one of the participants broke into our staff meeting in a panic. Jill was gasping for air and in great distress. As I ran to the bunkhouse, another participant called 911.

When I saw Jill, I knew she was taking her last breaths. Within a minute of my assessment, the paramedics arrived, moving in with oxygen, ready to start an IV and place a tube into Jill's trachea.

Fortunately, Jill and I had discussed this eventuality during our phone call, even though she strongly doubted there would be a problem. Jill had made it very clear to me that she didn't want resuscitation or hospitalization. Even though I didn't have her living will in my hand, I held off the very determined medics and stayed by Jill's side while she took her last breath. Six other women witnessed the entire scene.

Jill's death was difficult, sudden, and unexpected. As a physician, I hate these kinds of surprises.

After the medics took Jill's body, I remained with the other women in the bunkhouse to debrief. Although our left brains had all witnessed the same sequence of events and were capable of reconstructing the scene in very similar language, our right brains had widely varying experiences.

One woman was furious. "Why didn't you do something? She was fine a half hour ago! She wasn't ready to die. You gave up, just like the doctors who let my mother die of asthma."

Another woman, a medical caregiver, was indignant that she had been placed, without her consent, in a bunkhouse with a sick patient. It turned out that she had come to the workshop to get away from the hospital, to consider whether she wanted to continue carrying the burden of her profession.

I was still shaky myself from the need to make such an immediate and unexpected life-or-death decision in such a public manner and then to have to call Jill's mother and tell her that her daughter had died.

Then, to my utter surprise, another woman shared that this was the most beautiful death she could ever imagine. Each of us had created our own unique, personal, holistic experience of Jill's unexpected death.

On the fourth day of the workshop, we held a memorial service for Jill, sending up our prayers for her next journey. For those of us who witnessed her death, Jill became a catalyst for growth, an amazing gift. We were able to process how being a part of such a poignant moment touched deeper issues in our lives. Each of us integrated what seemed like unrelated personal issues with our reactions to Jill's death. I learned in a very palpable way that memory is more than facts. It is also how we feel and respond to them. It is the sum total of our memories that makes us who we are.

How do we trust memories given that they are so susceptible to reinterpretation? Many workshop participants have said they suspected they were molested, although they couldn't remember exactly what happened. They wanted the facts, as if knowing would either justify or melt away their feelings. Others have been absolutely certain of very specific events of early childhood that were equally unverifiable.

My experience has been that giving ourselves permission to tell our story is powerful medicine. Ironically, for many, the more they trusted their inner reality, the less urgent was their need to know for certain what actually happened. In essence, grieving has the power to transmute our past through compassion and self-forgiveness.

Compassion often diminishes the urge to confront a suspected abuser or seek revenge. Those who have prematurely confronted their suspected abuser have often revictimized themselves. Rather than receiving an apology, they suffer the condemnation of being called "unstable, troublemaking, or attention seeking"—all of which they may have been accused of in the past. Once again, they are labeled "the problem."

Callie's Compassion

Callie was in her early forties when I met her. She had recently celebrated her daughter's ninth birthday and had proudly lost one hundred pounds with exercise and a careful eating plan. But nightmares and sleeplessness began to wreak havoc in her life. She began to miss work due to fatigue and had outbursts of anger at her very loving and supportive husband.

Although she had a vague sense that this upheaval had to do with molestation by her brother, she tried to drive it out of her mind. She abandoned her one-year disciplined exercise and food program, ate compulsively for several months, and gained back nearly fifty pounds. This loss of control compounded her self-loathing now that she once again looked like the fat teenager she had been.

Over several months, Callie realized that her abuse had started when she turned nine and that her daughter's ninth birthday had unleashed all the pent-up emotions she thought she had dealt with. With a lot of work, she reclaimed the fat little girl she had despised and tried to banish. Callie restarted her walking program, using the time to have internal conversations with the wounded part of herself. Together they discussed her fear of becoming thin and more attractive to men. This time around, Callie's weight came off with much less resistance and effort, since it now was a joint decision of the adult and the newly supported prepubescent little girl.

Gradually, Callie realized the dysfunction in her family had affected her older brother just as much. With a heart full of compassion, she met with her brother to let him know she understood how the family pain and ignorance had led to his intruding on her sexual space. They both lacked the love and support they desperately needed.

Callie made no accusation, no demand for compensation, and expressed no condemnation. She simply spoke her truth. Callie and her brother cried together for two lonely, desperate children. Not only did her brother apologize, but he told Callie that none of it was her fault and that he hoped she would let go of any shame she had carried all these years. Whereas in the past Callie had avoided family gatherings when her brother was present, they now were quiet allies. Later, they honored each other by asking advice about their children and sharing their mutual vulnerability. True reconciliation.

Nelson Mandela sought such healing in South Africa with the Truth and Reconciliation Commission, made possible by his capacity to see the fear, ignorance, and humanity of his captors and his willingness to forgive them. Mandela simply requested an accounting. He didn't seek revenge or humiliation. He knew that under threat of punishment, most perpetrators would confess and apologize, which would only intensify lingering resentment. That he didn't demand remorse often created the space for true regret and reconciliation.

Mandela believed in the power of story, of bringing to light what festers in the darkness. I wonder whether the suppression of ethnic discord in Yugoslavia under the fifty-year dictatorship of Tito led to the ethnic killing soon after his death. I wonder whether the current policy of not uttering the words *Hutu* or *Tutsi* in Rwanda will lead to assimilation or another conflagration. Can we truly banish voices of hatred, or do they need to be heard in the light of day?

I believe both Mandela and Callie experienced an inner transformation before they could bring about external change. Tito imposed peace on the ethnic groups for several generations, during which time Yugoslavia modernized and prospered. It was heartbreaking and very discouraging to see old hatreds destroy the encouraging progress that had been achieved.

For more than thirty years, I buried the memory of Teddy's smothering. My young psyche did what it needed to do to survive. Although I forgot about Teddy until opportunity jostled the memory loose, I nevertheless experienced feelings triggered by the event and overcompensated with driven behaviors. So, did I really forget? Or perhaps the better question is, how and why did I fail to create a readily accessible memory that might have spared me many years of existential unhappiness amid seemingly great outward success?

Implicit and Explicit Memory

Implicit memory stores sensory, emotional and kinesthetic information that is subliminal, unintentional, and unconscious. This process is mostly a function of the right hemisphere of the brain. Explicit memory, on the other hand, is conscious, intentional, factual, and biographical; and it gives us a sense of ourselves over time. This resides in the left hemisphere.

Implicit memory allows us to perform activities that require no conscious thought, such as tying our shoes, using utensils to eat our food, or typing on a keyboard (at least for some of us). In his book *Musicophilia*, neurologist Oliver Sacks tells the story of a gifted choral director, who suffered total amnesia for over twenty years as the consequence of herpes simplex encephalitis. Each moment of his life was like his first awakening. It is believed that his infection destroyed the hippocampus, a structure on the inside of the temporal lobes that is necessary for new chronologic memory and learning. This is explicit memory.

Yet this gentleman, who had lost all biographic memory, not only recognized his wife but retained his love of music and was capable of completing daily tasks of hygiene. In the midst of permanent, complete memory loss, he could sing and even direct his former choir in a hymn yet not remember he did so one minute later. Clearly there are primitive centers in the brain where tasks necessary for survival abide. Sack's patient also displayed a wide range of emotion, from fear and frustration to the pleasure of music and the devotion and love of his wife. Procedural and emotional memory, called implicit memory, is stored elsewhere.

This explains why infants are capable of emotional and procedural learning before the hippocampus comes on line at around eighteen months, about the same time as the development of language. Yet, as Ainsworth's experiment demonstrated, autobiographical memory isn't required for children to make important emotional decisions about their world.

Neuroscience has shown that surges of stress hormones can temporarily shut down the hippocampus. During moments of childhood trauma (rage, physical or sexual violence, condemnation, or neglect), war, or severe accidents, we might capture the event only as implicit memory, storing the emotional content without corresponding intellectual or conscious history. Initially protective, this dissociative process prevents us from being overwhelmed during a time when we are powerless and helpless. Ironically, when we are no longer in the stressful situation, we are unable to use our cognitive left brain to integrate the experience, because we haven't generated the explicit memory.

This helps to explain why adults with disorganized attachment have very few childhood memories and experience emotional flooding triggered by what, for others, would be seemingly innocuous interactions. They also have difficulty understanding their current behavior in relation to childhood experiences. Unable to make sense of their past, these adults have difficulty controlling their outbursts and soothing themselves. Lacking an internal rheostat, they experience emotions either full on or full off, leaving them (and those around them) wondering whether sometimes a demon has taken possession.

Similarly, adults with PTSD can be flooded with emotion due to a noise, an odor, even a tone of voice or facial appearance that triggers an implicit memory. We have heard about soldiers, long returned from battle, being thrown back into a wartime event when a car backfires. Because the original experience wasn't imprinted in the hippocampus, the soldier experiences the event once again in real time. The images they see in their mind's eye are life threatening, causing a release of stress hormones as if they were back in battle.

Ironically, had someone asked me whether I had ever witnessed boys jumping on top of another kid, I would have probably said I had, but I strongly doubt I would have been flooded with the emotions attached to the memory. I might have reported the event as if I were an objective bystander. Disconnected from my emotional experience of the smothering, I wouldn't have understood the impact this event had on my life.

It's my belief that it's necessary to process what's stored in our emotional brains, as well as in our bodies, for forgiveness and compassion to occur. When the Vietnam veterans who attended Elisabeth's workshops had a safe place to reexperience and release the emotions attached to their wartime terrors, they were later able to use the cognitive memory to reassure themselves that they were no longer in the war zone. Also, having a group of civilians validate their experience helped the vets believe they weren't crazy.

Memories don't have to come out as a flood, which can be overwhelming. Our psyche will choose the time, place, and pace of information to be revealed. I don't believe it should be forced. At our workshops, we don't push our participants to go deeper than their defenses allow.

When the brain is functioning well, the two hemispheres communicate with each other to confirm whether the information they are receiving matches or is discordant. Our brains call forth past interactions and experiences to verify whether tone and language match. If so, we feel reassured and can trust what we hear and see.

When there is a mismatch, we go on high alert.

Mixed Messages: Joann and Her Mom

I recently met Joann, a thirty-five-year-old nursing administrator who was in therapy, working through unfinished business with her extremely anxious mother. Trying to protect her daughter from the rejection and ridicule she'd suffered as a child, Mom orchestrated every aspect of Joann's life. She bought her clothes, scheduled every detail of her social life, and frequently compared Joann to her friends. Stung by the inherent criticism of these comparisons, Joann often burst into tears (she never got angry, because on some level she believed her mother was too fragile to take it). Typically, her mother responded to her tears with one of two phrases: "Joann, you're just sensitive" or "Joann, you know I love you."

In either case, Joann registered the tone and emotion behind her mother's words as condescending, even though her left brain might otherwise hear the words as statements of fact. Words that could have been comforting were more painful than if they were never spoken because of the discordant right-left brain perceptions.

The tone of her mother's words was further confirmation for Joann that her mother thought she was weak and fragile and needed the hovering protection that drove Joann crazy. Ironically, Joann's passivity supported this image of fragility, even though she thought she suppressed her anger to protect her mother. Their mutual belief that the other was too weak to take the truth was equally disrespectful.

Her mother's tone of voice also confirmed to Joann that she wasn't seen or heard for who she was. The conflict got to the point that Joann wanted to strangle her mother with each unrequested parcel of advice. Underneath it all, Joann was furious with herself for needing her mother. She couldn't live with her but couldn't live without her. Mutual anxiety fueled this complicated but loving relationship.

If pushed, Joann's mother probably would have denied she was being critical of her daughter. Rather, she would have said Joann needed all the love, attention, and direction her mother could give her because she was so emotional and flustered when things didn't go her way. This would have been Mom's statement of fact, not judgment.

The discordance of tone and language caused Joann to flip-flop from distrusting her own truth, at once feeling hopeless and crazy, and being absolutely infuriated with, and rebelling against, her controlling mother. Joann needed a safe place to release her rage without hurting herself or her mom. She needed to grieve the wasted years of being overprotected, of not being allowed to learn from her own mistakes. So long as Mom orchestrated her every move, Joann couldn't celebrate any of her successes.

Joann discovered her voice in the setting of our weekend workshop. Sitting on the mat, she looked at me for a long time, waiting for directions. When I didn't respond like her mother, she became uncomfortable. "I don't know what to do." I asked her to lie on her back. Of course, she complied.

Again, I waited. Joann looked at me for more direction. Finally, she closed her eyes.

Her lips quivered, and tears filled her eyes. "I'm so scared. She left me. Mom was so upset that she left me in the house by myself. She was crying and just slammed the door and walked out. [Joann told me she was three years old.] I didn't think she was coming back. I waited and waited. I got hungry, so I climbed on a chair and opened a new box of Cheerios. I remember holding it in my lap all day. I was so scared." Joann sobbed and sobbed. I waited, giving her little one all the time she needed to release her fear and grief.

"After Mom came home, I did whatever she wanted."

Joann gave herself permission to move aside and allow a very young voice to teach her why she was so afraid to make a mistake that might disappoint or agitate her mother. Tears came with the realization that she had spent so much energy placating her mom's feelings and reactions, making sure she didn't leave again.

As the tears subsided, Joann screamed out the frustration of being trapped. She sat up, grabbed the hose, and lit into her mom for the wasted years of psychic imprisonment. "You scared the shit out of me. You were supposed to keep me safe. You were supposed to help me grow up, but you kept me a little girl. Please leave me alone and let me grow up. Please," she whined.

I asked Joann, "Are you begging your mom to let you grow up?"

Joann grabbed another phone book. With a new voice of a grown woman, Joann slammed the hose on the book. "I'm not a little girl anymore, and I'm done trying to please you. Get your own life. I'm not asking you; I'm telling you that I'm making my own decisions about my life, whether you stay or leave."

After her anger was spent, Joann picked up a pillow. With a gentle, loving voice, she spoke to a terrified three-year-old girl. "I'm so sorry that I have ignored you all these years, leaving you to deal with Mom. I now see why you are so scared. I'm so sorry. But I'm here now, and I will never leave you. You can't make a mistake that would make me leave you. It wasn't your fault. It was Mom's."

Joann picked up another pillow and spoke to her mother. "I know that you were scared, being a single mother. We have both been imprisoned by fear and anxiety. But it's going to stop now. I love you, but you're not going to punish me for being myself. You're not going to run my life anymore. And you're right: I am very sensitive, so I want you to stop scrutinizing and criticizing me. If you can't enjoy being around me, then you're going to see a lot less of me."

The anger Joann was finally able to express gave her the confidence to trust her inner voice and to risk setting loving limits with her mom. Her message was clear without a mismatch of tone and content.

It was also scary to let go of the long-established love-hate pattern of relying on her mother to tell her how to live her life. Months later, Joann told me that occasionally she would fall back into conforming to her mother's opinions or being triggered by the discordant tone of her mother's voice. Joann learned to reassure her little one and tell her she was no longer weak or incapable of living her own life.

As Joann replaced self-doubt and criticism with encouragement, she gradually broke free of the generational wound. She actually bought a new wardrobe by herself. She said she initially wanted to ask a friend to come along, but her little one told her she didn't want anyone to give her advice, at least this once.

Joann also said that gradually her mom was coming around to this new, respectful relationship of equals. Even Mom's anxiety began to abate. She was giving less unrequested advice to a daughter who seemed much less in need of it.

When we have a safe place to grieve, to dare to re-experience the depth of our losses, we are then able to integrate trapped, right-brain emotional information into our autobiography. Each time Joann communicated with her little girl, she reinforced their shared story.

In owning our anger and vulnerability, we can let go of the once-protective mantle of separateness. We can risk rejoining the human race because we have the power of our own truth to protect us, the humility of our vulnerability, and the wisdom to appreciate our universal desire for love and affirmation. We at once see the injured little ones in others while we set better limits with compassion and humility. The power of gentle self-protection enables us to risk asking for what we need because we can say no to more than what we ask for.

When I became a very busy physician, working twelve to fourteen hours a day, I would become irritated with my young children if they were having a really loud, fun time. I was unaware at that time how their fun was triggering a right-brain response of irritation and envy originating in my own childhood. My mother's mantra ("Do something productive") continued to haunt me. I could never admit, even to myself, that I felt a separateness from my children. Once I realized I had a small boy in me who was jealous of my kids (just like he was of the neighborhood boys running off to play without him), I could enjoy their fun and break the generational cycle of unconscious envy. While I didn't yell at my kids to do something productive or shut them up because they were making too much noise, I was nonetheless unavailable to them in their joy. I used the excuse that I was a doctor and I was tired, but it was more than that. We all missed out.

When implicit memories have easy passage through the hippocampus, we have ready access to enjoy pleasant memories and add perspective to unpleasant ones. The aroma of chicken soup bubbling on the stove even now creates an image of Grandmom's kitchen, of her plucking the bird, cleaning the carcass, and submerging it lovingly in the big, blue pot. I am once again reminded of her nurturing, loving hands. More importantly, I feel one of the most restorative and healing emotions: gratitude for all the blessings in my life.

Why bother excavating uncomfortable feelings and trying to make sense of them? In my case, those feelings were self-destructive because I drove myself in unhealthy ways, cheating my family of precious time together. In Joann's case, her anger came out sideways in passive-aggressive remarks. She wasn't the person she wanted to be. The more she treated herself with gentleness, the less she required it from her mother, and the easier it was to accept her mom for who she was and feel gratitude for what she did receive from her.

To compensate for the confusion of being flooded with unpleasant emotions, we may compulsively and inflexibly control our environment. Or we may just go numb, going through life on autopilot. Because we cannot risk being triggered again, we cut ourselves off from our feelings and the people who love us.

In my days in medical school, I spent a brief elective period with an infamous surgeon, who had a reputation of exploding in the operating room. He was a superb technician, dedicated and compulsive. He constructed his office, his calendar, and rounding times with meticulous care to eliminate as much stress as possible. As in every other aspect of his life, he dressed with great care. Although quite formal with his colleagues and students, he was nonetheless a nice person and in complete control of his intellect. He reserved plenty of time with new patients so he could answer all their questions.

However, if his day became unpredictable, he became anxious and irritable. If patients took more than their generously allotted time, he would take it as a personal affront and terminate the visit. He was skilled and meticulous in the operating room, but if the case went too long or developed unexpected complications, he would swear at the nurses and was even known to throw instruments. It was as if he had only two modes: in complete control or overwhelmed. Unfortunately, his anxiety manifested as anger at the people closest to him. Intuitively, he knew he lacked the emotional flexibility to deal with life's unpredictability. He attempted as best he could to create a stress-free world so he could be the person he wanted to be. It saddened me that he was most remembered for the times when his left brain couldn't control the flood of emotions from his right brain.

Some of us can be quite successful in living almost solely from the rational left brain, even if it hampers our ability to have intimate relationships. Others are less able to stem the flow of unregulated emotions. Taking the slightest comment personally, they create relationships that confirm their world view, living with people who either tiptoe around them or become so frustrated that they attack or abandon them.

I began making sense of my life when I stopped running from the childhood voices that were chasing me, hoping I would one day stop, turn around, and catch them as they jumped with joy into my outstretched arms. In return, they offered a deeper self-awareness and compassion that have made me a wiser adult.

Chapter 10

GOOD GRIEF

> Grief is forever. It doesn't go away; it becomes a
> part of you, step for step, breath for breath.
> —Jandy Nelson
>
> Should you shield the valleys from the windstorms, you
> would never see the beauty of their canyons.
> —Elisabeth Kübler-Ross

Early in my time of working with Elisabeth, I was part of a team offering workshops for children and adolescents. I had been teaching about grief for two years and believed I had a good grasp of this material. However, little Matthew, the ten-month-old son of our host, gave me a profound tutorial. His crib and my bed shared a common wall separating our adjacent bedrooms. I could hear every sound that came from Matthew's room.

Matthew's Birthright

On the first morning of our visit, Matthew awakened me at about five o'clock in the morning with his melodious song to the universe—or to an empty room, depending on your point of view. It was a delightful awakening, hearing this child greet the new day. After about ten minutes, I suddenly heard the thud of a toy being jettisoned from the crib. Within seconds, Matthew was in a full-blown tantrum, symbolically shaking his fist in protest at the same universe he had serenaded just moments ago.

Thinking he would awaken the whole house, as if he had never done this before, I tiptoed out of bed to rescue his toy, but in less than a minute, even before I reached the door to my bedroom, Matthew had stopped crying. By the time I had reached my bed, Matthew was once again regaling the universe as he played with another toy.

Unlike many adults, Matthew didn't say to himself, "Why get mad? It's not going to get my toy back." Nor did he, after his tantrum ended, sit miserably in his crib, unwilling to play with another toy lest it somehow suffer a similar fate. Little Matt just let his body do what it needed to do. After releasing healthy anger, he was right back to singing to the universe.

The following morning began much the same. After a while, I heard a rhythmic squeaking of the springs supporting Matthew's mattress and happy giggling as he bounced himself up and down. Then I heard a thud of what I presumed to be his skull hitting the wooden headboard. Untempered wailing followed.

Once again I tiptoed out of bed to rescue my new companion. Once again Matthew stopped before I reached his bedroom door. Climbing back into my bed, I waited to see what Matthew would do next. This time he took a bit longer, but after a few minutes, I heard both springs and child squealing again.

Acknowledging our feelings keeps us in the moment. In allowing his emotional reality to be expressed, Matthew could release his grief and return to a place of delight. Both his tantrum and outpouring of grief were instinctual. This is our birthright, the tools we are born with to process life's inevitable losses.

Unfortunately, many of us lose the ability later in childhood to own our feelings, grieve our losses, and return with gratitude and delight to the present. In denying our feelings, we chew on our past with resentment or ponder our future in fear. That is the price of lost grief. The difference between a healthy adult and a healthy infant isn't that the adult doesn't have temper tantrums. Rather, a healthy adult can set aside strong feelings long enough to find a safe and appropriate time to shake his or her fist in protest.

If we have lost the ability to grieve, losses layer one on top of another. As the pile grows, the stored-up emotion may become too big to explore and release safely. When new losses occur, we either withdraw in denial ("Me? No, I'm not upset.") for fear of losing control, or we become overwhelmed, triggered by old feelings. Instead of grieving, we surprise family and colleagues with emotional outbursts of uncontrolled crying or anger.

Diane's Grief

Diane celebrated her forty-third birthday alone. She just didn't feel like being with anyone. She was single and had worked her way up from teller to branch manager of a bank. She enjoyed close relationships with her colleagues, many of whom had worked at the bank nearly as long as she had. Diane was extremely competent and had increased her branch customer base by her genuine interest in its patrons. She also went out of her way to support her coworkers.

For several weeks, she had seemed preoccupied and irritable. Work became an obligation, and she had no energy for coworkers or her customers. She had withdrawn from her team, eating alone at her desk, and stopped initiating conversations. When a friend commented about her change in attitude, Diane became upset and defensive. But her friend persisted and told her she was worried about her. Diane apologized and agreed that she wasn't herself. She visited a therapist, who referred her to our workshop.

When Diane filled out our application, she listed her twelve-year-old dog, Jo-Jo, who died of cancer two months earlier, as her only major loss. She had been treated with surgery and chemotherapy for over two years, so her death wasn't unexpected. Although Diane felt she had handled Jo-Jo's death well, the timing seemed to fit with Diane's recent funk.

When Diane came to the mat, she showed us photos of her beautiful German shepherd/collie mix, recounting what a wonderful friend Jo-Jo had been. Except during work hours, they had been inseparable. Jo-Jo seemed to read Diane's mind, knowing just how to break a spell of sadness or irritability by depositing her leash in Diane's lap and dragging her off the couch. Diane talked about the last two years of cancer treatment and how at the end she had to carry Jo-Jo outside nearly every hour because of diarrhea. Yet Diane ended by saying, "Jo-Jo took much better care of me than I did of her." Then the tears came. For a while, I assumed Diane was crying for her friend, but as the tears became sobs, Diane's posture changed, and she seemed smaller and younger. After perhaps another full minute of sobbing, Diane was able to whisper, "The only person who took better care of me than Jo-Jo was my mom." Then even deeper sobs.

When Diane could get her breath, she told us her mom had died of cancer when Diane was twelve. Much like Jo-Jo, she had been sick from her disease and treatments for about two years. Her mom had been her best friend. After her death, Diane had a rough couple of years, especially since her dad wouldn't talk about her mom. Rather, he had rapidly replaced her with a woman he didn't even love. Diane learned she had to stuff her sadness and resentment and move on.

I handed Diane a pillow. This is the twelve-year-old girl who lost her mom and best friend to cancer. Diane rocked herself with touching gentleness. "I had no idea that you were still so sad about Mom. Any time you want to talk about her, I am here for you."

When Diane returned the pillow to me, she just shook her head. She was stunned by the completely unexpected grief over the death of her mom, which the death of her pet had triggered. She now understood why her friend had been concerned about her and that she hadn't been herself for the last few weeks. Then, out of plain curiosity, I asked Diane how old her mom was when she died. "Oh my God," she said, "Mom was forty-three. Forty-three and twelve, just like Jo-Jo and me."

It isn't uncommon for us to become sad or irritable around anniversaries of major losses, even though we aren't consciously aware of the date. Often it's a friend or relative's casual reminder of the anniversary that will bring us out of our funk.

We are born with an instinctive ability to grieve. Diane will be less afraid to grieve in the future, having learned firsthand that allowing deep feelings to surface helps us all to re-energize. Her unprocessed grief had shut her down, causing her to withdraw in cynicism from the life and people she loved. Blinding us from seeing what is on the other side of the hill, our fear of feeling and expressing grief can burden us with what seems to be an interminable and pointless climb.

We cannot put some of our feelings in a drawer, selectively being joyful while keeping a lid on the so-called negative emotions of anger, fear, and sadness. I didn't realize I was settling for a narrow range of feeling, fooling myself into believing I was experiencing contentment. Much like Diane, I didn't know what I didn't know.

Suppose a two-year-old came into a room, swinging a butcher knife. An attentive parent would naturally take it away. Not understanding the danger of the blade, the toddler would likely protest, erupting into a full-blown temper tantrum. A healthy dad would sit with him until the anger subsided, perhaps name the feeling as anger, and then explain that the sharp blade could hurt him, and then distract his son with another toy. Life goes on after a moment of grief.

Suppose Dad was unable to tolerate his son's anger, yanked him off the floor, and gave him something to cry about. What would the boy learn? Clearly, he would get the literal message that playing with the knife could result in his dad taking it away and that protesting would cause further harm. But even a two-year-old is capable of extrapolation. He would also learn that something was inherently wrong with his internal gyroscope. His spontaneous response caused his dad to yank him off the floor and hurt him. Even at two, he would learn that it's unsafe to interpret life's events in his own unique way. Instead, this toddler may become a watcher, siphoning off creative energy to protect himself from harm or exile by figuring out how others expect him to feel and respond to life's losses.

One might argue that there is nothing wrong with teaching kids to behave, but submission comes with a heavy price.

Kyle: Without Grief, We Become What We Hate

Kyle was the middle of five children. They lived in the country, and his mom had her hands full with raising the large clan. Kyle's dad, Harold, was a tough Korean War vet and a very busy VP at a small industrial company. He expected his boys to do what he said and when he said it. He didn't tolerate delay or disobedience. Kyle witnessed the beatings his older brothers received for the slightest hint of rebellion. He was afraid of his father. He was obedient.

As he got older, Kyle made sure he was strong enough to defend himself, but his fear never went away. Worse than his father's authoritarian rules were his endless political and social diatribes, filled with fear, hatred, prejudice, and sanctimony. Finally, Kyle couldn't take it anymore. Kyle fought back verbally, with screaming matches at the dinner table, hovering just short of violence. Eventually, Kyle became a "flaming liberal," his response to Harold's self-righteous domination.

Over the years, Kyle maintained his liberal beliefs, trying hard to be kind and open minded, as unlike his father as he could be. But he discovered he was more like his dad than he thought. At times, despite his efforts to the contrary, he was defensive and angry at work, especially if he was challenged. When he heard right-wing commentary on TV or from colleagues, he would react with utter disgust. Although the content of his beliefs was different from his dad's, Kyle's condescending certainty was so irritating that his wife began calling him "Harold," which absolutely sent Kyle through the roof or into deep shame. The shame manifested as rage or sulking withdrawal and depression. Still under his father's spell, he had become what he most despised.

Like many of us, Kyle's father took away his birthright because he had little tolerance for chaos. The natural expression of emotions by Harold's children must have awakened feelings in him he didn't want to deal with. As children, we give up that birthright rather than risk injury (physical or emotional) or exile. Survival trumps free expression. The price of unexpressed natural emotions is our reactivity and the accumulation of resentments, fear, envy, and self-doubt.

Grieving: No Right Way

When we grieve, all our natural emotions come into play. We shake our fist at the universe, rend our clothes in mourning, agonize over fears of future pain, and ultimately face the existential decision to live again. As our compassion for ourselves deepens, we praise our Maker for the exquisite bittersweet wonder that is life. And we dare to open our hearts once again, each time with more wisdom and abandon. That is the gift of grief.

Most of us find an appropriate outlet and pace for our grief, without any help or intervention. We were given the tools to grieve as we go, much like little Matthew in his crib. Others have found defense systems that work, surviving with relative balance. We choose not to open old wounds, because life is mostly good. Some wounds find a resting place with time and perspective, and we learn indirectly from them. We become softer just by surviving and by being surrounded with courageously loving people who treasure us despite ourselves.

Couples often grieve differently, one needing to express the pain while the other bleeds internally. This disparity can be very difficult when a major loss occurs, such as a child's death or major disruptions of careers or location. One spouse may feel pressured and the other abandoned by their different grieving styles.

Many years ago, a man brought his wife to see me to "make her talk about the fact that she is dying." In their forties, they were struggling with her progressive ovarian cancer. Clearly, he needed to make plans for himself and their young daughter. After his opening remarks, I turned to his wife, who responded with, "Yes, I have cancer; but I ate a good breakfast and greatly enjoyed sitting on my porch and looking at the mountains this morning." She was taking one day at a time, extracting the rich pleasures remaining for her. She wasn't denying her death but chose not to be dying twenty-four hours a day. However, her husband needed a plan to manage his anxiety around the overwhelming grief of losing the woman he adored. Once they recognized how differently they were dealing with this huge loss, they could make room for each other's needs.

Making the choice to sacrifice closeness so we don't feel the pain, we wall ourselves off form the vulnerable parts of ourselves as well as our loved ones. Occasionally, the window of grief is surprisingly thrown open, giving those we love hope for a breakthrough, only to close it again.

Charlie's Brief Moment of Tenderness

One of the oncology nurses asked me to see Charlie. In his midseventies, he was dying of chronic leukemia. Most of the time he was withdrawn, with occasional flares of anger. When the nurse asked whether he was depressed, he yelled at her for being stupid and kicked her out of his room.

Charlie wasn't warned that I would be coming to see him, so I was thrown off a bit when he asked me what I was doing there. I decided that truth would set us free. "Your nurse asked me to see you because she is worried about you. She doesn't quite know how to help you. Besides, you've been a pain in the ass."

Charlie gave me "the look" and nodded with relief that he wasn't going to have to play mind games with me. We talked about his cancer, concerns about the suffering to come, and some fears about dying.

When I asked whether he had any unfinished business with his only close relative, a daughter who lived in the Bay Area, Charlie seemed not to understand the question. I explained that many adults who had attended my workshops still longed for words they had never heard from their parents. Charlie began to cry, reached for the phone, and dialed his daughter. Through his sobs, he told her he was dying and asked her to come. As I left, I pictured his daughter dropping everything, walking out of her office, jumping in her car, and driving the nearly one thousand miles to Tucson.

I came by Charlie's room midmorning the next day, admittedly curious and hopeful for a heartfelt reunion. When I walked in, he gave me a squinting look that quite clearly said, *I don't know you, and you don't know me*. His daughter sat way off in the corner of the room, looking tired, sad, and distant. I introduced myself to both of them and asked whether there was anything they needed.

Both shook their heads no, and I left. The window had closed.

I believe that had Charlie risked saying to his only child all he wanted to say, he would have collapsed in grief for all the missed opportunities and wasted time. But Charlie was too sick and weak to expend that energy.

I circled back several times until I could speak with his daughter and tell her about the love I had seen in her father's eyes and the enormous regret that had impelled him to call her. At the time, she was too hurt and exhausted to appreciate it. Her window had also closed.

One of the consequences of unresolved grief is that it can prevent us from recognizing our parents' pain and from remembering the precious good times of our childhood. I hope Charlie's daughter has been able to appreciate what I saw in her father's eyes.

It's possible to reclaim our birthright, even if it was taken from us years ago. For us thinkers (as opposed to feelers), it helps to have a list of emotions to refer to. I have found myself more than once asking, "Let's see ... am I mad, sad, scared, happy, or jealous?"

In earlier versions of this book, the three appendices were written as chapters 11–13. Because they are more didactic in nature, I decided to move them. We have continued to teach this material in our workshops for over thirty years, because they provide a very useful guide to recognize old patterns of behavior that prevent us from living in the present moment.

The first appendix describes and expands on Elisabeth's simple explanation of our five natural emotions, their healthy purpose and expression, and their many distortions. The second appendix presents our version of Dr. Stephen Karpmann's triangle of dysfunction and the games we play to stay in relationships while avoiding true intimacy. The last appendix offers a path out of the triangle. (Dr. Karpmann's latest book is also listed with other additional resources in the final pages.)

If you are someone who finds didactic teaching helpful in the middle of a story, I recommend that you break off now and read the three appendices. However, if you prefer to stick with the story, save them for the end.

Chapter 11

HIDDEN AGENDAS

> Where love rules, there is no will to power, and where power predominates, love is lacking. The one is the shadow of the other.
> —C. G. Jung

After my first workshop, I decided to apply for the two-weekend training program of the Elisabeth Kübler-Ross Center, which emphasized the skills needed to facilitate mat work. I believed it would improve my ability to hear what my patients were saying and what they were unable to say.

The training program taught how to facilitate the externalization of emotions. Trainees took turns practicing on each other, giving each of us plenty of time to do our own work. My little ones watched carefully to see who was safe and who gave them the space they needed to discover what was inside them. Many of us wanted to facilitate just right, which often meant we were doing most of the talking and pushing each other to hit phone books or scream out our fear, when what we really needed was time to allow the childhood knowledge and feelings to bubble up to the surface. My little ones confirmed what I most appreciated about Elisabeth: patience. As it turned out, I loved the quiet, sacred space surrounding the mat, where stillness, presence, and safety promoted poignant reconnection.

After the second weekend, I was surprised and pleased to receive an invitation to be a trainee at the next Life, Death, and Transition (LTD) Workshop. Although it was inconvenient to leave my medical practice for a week, I knew in my heart that this work would change my life. Looking back, I knew my little one wouldn't have accepted any of the rational explanations why leaving my practice was irresponsible, fiscally unsound, and generally impractical. He had tasted a moment of deep connection and wanted more.

At the LDTs, which were large workshops, we had four or five staff and two trainees. Being a trainee, I was told to watch and learn but not to presume to say anything during Elisabeth's presentations. I was very happy to sit back, say nothing, and soak it all up.

During my second workshop as a trainee, Elisabeth turned to me and ordered me to tell the group about doing mat work at home with young children in the house. (Elisabeth was very intuitive, almost scary at times. I had seen her take away the notes of a staff member in front of ninety participants just as he began his presentation on natural and distorted emotions. Managing to meander through it, he was forced to use personal examples and speak from his heart rather than from his intellect—which was exactly what Elisabeth wanted the group to hear.)

Her unexpected request left me confused and temporarily speechless. Although Anne, who had loved her first workshop and was about to embark on the training weekends, and I had set up a mat in our guest room, I hadn't mentioned this to Elisabeth. Wondering how she knew, trying to figure out what she had in mind, and whether I would be stepping on anyone's toes by talking, I was mostly telling myself to be very brief. I was censoring myself.

One of the qualities that drew me to Elisabeth was her fearlessness. She would come on stage in front of a thousand people and trust what would come out of her mouth. She seemed to speak to one person at a time, as if each of us was in her living room.

From some rebellious place, I made an instantaneous decision that if I were going to do this work, I wouldn't allow my perfectionism to silence me. It was time to take some risks and trust my gut, which in retrospect meant I would allow the voices I had suppressed for so many years to speak through me. I took a deep breath.

With that, I turned toward the participants and described what had just happened at home a few days before.

Lawrence J. Lincoln, MD

Our Son, Matt, Does Mat Work

In our guest room, Anne and I set up a mat on the floor with a hose, phone books, tissues, and a pillow. Matt, age eleven, and Rachael, age nine, passed by the room every time we entered our home from the garage. As expected, they had asked about the purpose of the mattress and the thick, red hose sitting next to the yellow pages. We patiently explained that these were tools to get out our frustrations. Later, they commented that the tools seemed quite effective. After spending a few minutes in the guest room, we were much calmer and more fun to be with. Several years later, Matt and Rachael wouldn't so subtly recommend that we take some time on the mat and even put them out on the phone book if we needed to.

One afternoon, Matt asked me whether I would show him. I brought him to the guest room, closed the door, and put on the gloves to demonstrate the use of the hose on the phone book. I explained that it was important to identify the person you were upset with and talk to him or her aloud while using the hose. I also taught him about privacy and confidentiality.

To my surprise, Matt walked to the mat, put on the gloves, and began speaking to the phone book. I quickly slid against the wall, out of his vision. I wouldn't facilitate my son. I can't remember the specifics of his work, but he was clearly talking to his dad as he whacked the hell out of the book. As his anger melted away, tears came.

Matt is no fool. He was getting a two-for: getting out his anger and making sure I heard it, knowing full well I wouldn't speak about it afterward. It was his private and confidential work.

When Matt was finished, I figured he would storm off the mat, throw open the door, and rejoin his mom and sister, leaving me to stew over the intensity of his pain and deal with my guilt for not being the perfect father. Instead, he put down the hose, slowly and methodically removed his gloves, then crawled off the mattress, headed across the tiled floor, and climbed into my lap. He curled up against my chest and let me gently rock him. Nothing needed to be said. Finally, he looked into my damp eyes and told me how much he loved me. I squeezed him tight.

I learned that day that there would always be a bridge of love over any valley of hurt and resentment Matt and I might traverse. I also began to consider that witnessing each other's pain might create spiritual bridges all over the planet. What would happen if we could really hear the pain others carry and understand how much childhood experience has affected our political, religious, and sectarian rhetoric? Currently, conversations often dissolve into banter, accusation, defensiveness, and the need to win an argument. Rarely do we engage in true inquiry (tell me more, or how has your life experience caused you to carry these beliefs?). Had I defended or justified myself to my son, we might have had a good talk between father and son, but it would have been much less likely that Matt would have crawled into my lap, a memory I still cherish thirty years later.

When we take the time to ask, "Who are you today?" we invite unconscious voices to participate. I wonder what would happen if we had the patience to listen to the unheard voices of our enemies with loving curiosity rather than defensiveness. Perhaps we are too afraid to discover that we have more in common with our enemies than we care to admit and that they are equally human. I believe it would then be much more difficult to engage in violence.

After three workshops as a trainee, Elisabeth invited me to join the staff and told me I could attend as many workshops as I wanted. I spoke to my partners, who agreed to cover me. I immersed myself in this new work, traveling nearly one week each month across the United States and Canada. I wanted to spend as much time as possible watching Elisabeth facilitate mat work and listening to the wisdom in her stories.

Fortunately, Anne was just as excited about the work, encouraging me to do all I could despite the financial costs and time away from home. Later, she told me that the boy she fell in love with was back, and she wasn't about to lose him again. But long, intense days at the workshops, followed by playing catchup with my medical practice, frequently left me irritable.

Instead of paying attention to neglected voices inside, I began to chastise myself and them. After all, I was doing what I loved with the support of my family. If I wasn't happy now, something was wrong with me. Intellectually, I knew better. But I was becoming a workshop "leader." It was okay if others had issues, but I should have my shit together.

Little did I realize that I wasn't so subtly telling my little one to buck up, be strong, and once again rise above his needs. After all, he'd had his turn at grieving, had told me his story; but now I was doing important work, and others needed my attention. I was treating myself yet again the way he'd been treated long ago. Basically, it was time for my little one to grow up, be happy and very grateful for all he was given, and stop complaining, whimpering, and dragging me down. Eventually, as Matt had done, he would let me know how little he appreciated my unconscious plans for him.

It is much easier to see how *other* people have hidden agendas than to look in the mirror. After staffing several years of workshops, I could readily see how some participants, despite their stated goals of learning about themselves, actually came for other, less conscious, reasons. Some came to get fixed, and others came to bury the past (along with their little ones) so they could get on with their lives; still others came to be cured of *all* the negative emotions of anger, sadness, and fear. Sometimes I saw that it was the little ones who brought the adult to the workshop to receive love and attention from others, because their own adult was either unable or unwilling to care for them.

After about six months of leading the externalization portion of the workshop, Elisabeth unexpectedly requested that I lead an entire workshop. I wasn't prepared to do this, but I deferred to Elisabeth. I was rewarded with a painful but valuable lesson about my own hidden agenda as a workshop leader.

My Trial by Fire

In late 1986, Elisabeth was scheduled to begin an overseas tour, including several lectures and a series of workshops. She had invited me to be part of her staff and lead the two days of mat work, after which Elisabeth would teach and interact with the group, telling her illustrative stories of grief and love.

I had listened to Elisabeth weave her spell about a dozen times, taking notes just in case; years later, I would be asked to lead an entire workshop. Thousands of tickets to her lectures had been sold, and the LDTs were full. About ten days before our flights, Elisabeth got an intestinal bug and canceled her appearances. The organizers were panicked at having to refund all the lecture tickets. I called Elisabeth and tried to change her mind, and she gave me hell for thinking more about the workshops than about her health. Then she told me to go and lead the workshops myself.

I declined. She insisted. I was nowhere near ready to lead a complete workshop. I finally agreed so long as everyone attending a workshop was told Elisabeth wouldn't be coming. The organizers made the calls, and a few attendees requested a refund because they only wanted to experience Elisabeth. I could now go with a clear conscience and assume the other participants were there to do their grief work.

I suppose that secretly I was excited about the opportunity. Even if I wasn't ready, I would put on a mask of competency and experience. I didn't check in with my little ones about their needs, desires, or concerns about leading. I just agreed to do it.

The first workshop of the tour began smoothly with the usual introductions, followed by the interpretation of impromptu drawings and the teaching of natural and distorted emotions. Then, sitting on a pillow in front of the mattress, I began to facilitate the grief (mat) work. The first participant shared his story, expressed some emotion, and seemed finished when he stepped off the mat. I was slightly distracted by whispering among a group of about a dozen psychotherapists, who sat together directly in front of the mat. The muttering by the group of professionals became more intense and distracting during the next participant's sharing. I began to feel irritated and judgmental about so-called therapists who were talking rather than listening to the person telling her story, and the more irritated I became, the less I was listening. I kept telling myself to stay focused on the participant. Finally, as the second participant finished, I decided to request that the group maintain silence during the mat work, but before I could say anything, one of the therapists yelled out, "You're incompetent."

When Elisabeth facilitated mat work, she said very little. She was a master at uttering one or two phrases that would drop someone into feelings. Mostly, she listened. Her unspoken message was, "This is your work. You are safe to tell your story and do what you need to do. I'm here with you." Learning from Elisabeth, I also intervened very little but clearly not enough for this group of professionals.

Their words were like a knife in the gut. I was slapped with self-doubt and definitely became angry with my accusers. I could feel myself blushing as I looked at the group's spokesperson. I wasn't going to show them my underbelly. I responded with my best emotionally neutral voice. "You are welcome to come to the mat and put me out on the phone book." She declined my generous offer. I parried by requesting that they give their undivided attention to those who chose to come to the mat. For the rest of that day, I facilitated one person after another, working hard to stay focused and keep my internal voices quiet. I needed them to be as quiet and respectful as those therapists

None of the group of therapists budged from their spot during the first long day of mat work. They were quiet and respectful of the other participants but didn't come up to do their own work. I could tell they didn't trust me, or even if some of them did, they wouldn't break rank. I was glad when the day ended. During the staff meeting that night, I let off some steam about them and received support from the team, who wanted to defend me. Mostly I maintained my workshop leader persona with the staff.

Had I known then what I know now, I would have invited my cacophony of inner voices to voice their feelings. I would have gotten and given an earful.

"Those arrogant assholes, talking over other participants and judging my work." "What did you expect? That everyone would swoon on your every word like they do with Elisabeth? You're not Elisabeth! Look who's arrogant."

"You're making a jackass of yourself in public and in front of professionals, experts. You're a fraud."

"You didn't ask me about leading this workshop. I would have told you I was too scared to lead a workshop. Now I'm ashamed of myself. Humiliated."

"Maybe it's not so bad. The participants who came to the mat today seemed like they got something out of it. Why don't you ask the staff if you're doing a good job?"

"No way. I'm not going to ask them. Even if they tell me I'm doing a good job, I won't believe them; and I can't take any criticism right now. So, all of you just shut up so I can be a workshop leader. I don't need anything from anybody."

When I climbed into bed at two o'clock in the morning, I really wanted to pack my bags, fly home, and punish myself for the hubris of believing I was competent enough to fill Elisabeth's shoes. My inner voices were angry with me (I was angry with myself) that I had set them up to fail. But I had maintained my personae during our staff meeting and let them pour out their judgment on the ungrateful group of therapists. The fact was that I wanted the recognition of being a great workshop leader but was ashamed of my need for recognition. So I let the staff make it all about "those arrogant therapists."

At a recent workshop, a participant asked me how I knew the age of a particular inner child. He declared that he had been sad and angry most of his life, so he couldn't separate the distinct voices. I requested that he close his eyes and ask himself when he remembered the earliest time he felt sad. He was able to describe an event when he was four or five. Then I asked him to recall when fear, then anger, and joy became predominant feelings. He told me the fear had been present as early as he could remember, but the anger really had a life of its own around age nine. He wasn't so sure about joy. Mostly he was happy when he was in the woods behind his home. I then explained that I arbitrarily defined my inner children based on the earliest time a predominant feeling appeared. Obviously, all the different feelings have existed my whole life, but I find that separating out specific ages of inner voices allows more clarity in my introspective dialogues. I then asked the participant to use his imagination and speak to a scared, very little boy, a sad four- to five-year-old and his angry nine-year-old. He very easily entered a dialogue with each part of himself and somewhat surprisingly discovered that each voice had different information to give him about his early life. At the time of my first leadership experience, I wasn't so clear about who was who inside me.

I tossed and turned all night and fell asleep at about five o'clock in the morning. When I awoke, I felt sad. I took a moment to check in with myself to find the source of this feeling. I imagined a young child in my mind and waited. He told me he was sad because I was ashamed of him for wanting a standing ovation. I wanted to tell him it wasn't so, but he was right. I was acting as if I were leading the workshops only to help others the way Elisabeth had helped me and that I didn't want or need the gratitude of participants, let alone positive recognition. In fact, I thought those needs made it dangerous for me to be a workshop leader, because I might manipulate the participants for my own gratification. I waited for his response. After about fifteen seconds, the little guy asked me whether I wanted him to go away.

Once again, I was treating myself exactly the way I had been treated. Orphaned at a young age, my mom grew up in a foster home where her personal needs would only cause her pain. She learned to submerge her fear, grief, and personal needs—and simply move forward. She taught me well. If I had no needs, I couldn't be hurt or disappointed, I couldn't fail, and I couldn't hurt anyone else with my selfishness. Yet I was listening to the young boy I had met only about two years ago tell me he wanted to be seen and cheered. Was I to banish him again?

No. Of course he wanted to be seen as gifted and talented. I apologized to him for silencing him once again. He wasn't bad or selfish for needing attention, and this need didn't diminish his desire to help others. So, lying in my bunk thousands of miles from our home, I gave my inner little boy his first of what would be many silent standing ovations. I also told him he couldn't go away, because he was my best consultant on sadness. I needed him to whisper in my ear when he saw that a participant was sad or ashamed, or needed to be seen and appreciated. My little one responded by saying he was too scared to facilitate in front of the psychotherapists, who said he was incompetent.

I promised that I would silently reassure him all day long, no matter what those professionals were saying about me, and that I would give him mini ovations each time he helped me to see the inner child of a participant. Finally, I told him he had just taught me that his desire for recognition didn't make him unsafe so long as I took the time to give him what he needed. It was up to me to keep him from getting love and recognition in all the wrong places. I felt him smile and take a few dramatic bows during my silent applause. Then he got quiet for a moment and said, "That's all I ever wanted."

As I got my clothes on, I laughed aloud at how seriously I had taken the criticism I had received the day before. I knew I wouldn't be alone for the coming day of mat work and that I could provide a safe container for the little ones inside those therapists to do what they needed. I went to breakfast with a smile on my face.

After singing, I once again opened the mat. A woman came to the front and told a very poignant story of loss that touched the whole room, including one of the therapists. Trying and failing to hold back her sobs, the therapist was overwhelmed with her own childhood grief. After the first participant finished her work, the therapist literally crawled onto the mat.

I sat quietly, giving her little one the time and space to finish sobbing and tell her story of betrayal and neglect. Although I suspect that the therapist remained skeptical of my abilities, her little one had been watching me closely for a full day. She allowed me to talk with her. At one point, she reached out for my hand. I heard sobbing from some of her colleagues at the sweet tenderness of the moment. Then, one after another, the professionals came to the mat to do their own work, in many cases experiencing their little ones on an emotional level for the first time.

On the last morning of the workshop, the woman who had called me incompetent came over to apologize; and what she said stays with me. "When I heard that the famous Elisabeth Kübler-Ross was presenting a workshop, I told myself that I would attend to improve my professional skills. But deep inside I wanted Elisabeth to take my broken little girl and whitewash her clean. I hoped I would leave happy and whole forever. I was angry that Elisabeth was not here to work her magic. The angrier I became, the sadder my little girl felt. She saw that I didn't really like her for who she was and that I just wanted her fixed. I now know that it is up to me to do my work and accept her for who she is and not who I wanted Elisabeth to make her." She then thanked me for holding steady in the work. I thanked her for her kind words and felt my little one giggle.

Many of us carry the same unconscious agendas for our little ones that our parents did. Sometimes, despite our parents' best intentions to spare us future pain and rejection, their agendas instead confirm to us that we aren't acceptable for who we are or what we really care about. We learn to hide our true selves from our parents and sometimes even from ourselves. Even at a very young age, we create a persona that allows us to look normal and is acceptable in the eyes of our caregivers. And we buy self-protection and love by banishing the whisperings of our hearts. But it takes energy to silence our inner yearnings.

As much as I looked in the mirror and said I would treat my biological children differently (and in many respects, I did), I continued to treat myself with the same hidden agendas: *Be tough ... Take care of yourself because no one else will ... Push, push, push ... Don't let anyone see you are hurting ... The only way to be safe is to excel and be better than everyone else ... Don't give them ammunition because you are a Jew ... It's okay to support others, but* you *don't show weakness or neediness.* These internalized messages were powerful drivers that pushed me to succeed, but at the end of each day, a small voice kept asking, "What about me?"

I have learned that, at least initially, my little one tries to get my attention with a gentle internal tug on a shirt sleeve. When I ignore him or make false promises, the little guy's anger at me spills over into my adult life. I become standoffish, answering questions with as few words as possible. Easily irritated, I notice that others are apologizing for interrupting me and tiptoeing around me. From one moment to the next, they can't be sure which Larry they are dealing with. I start looking for food to console myself. The little guy wants some kind of nurturing, and he'll take sugar if love is withheld. When anger and sugar fail, he becomes despondent, hopeless; and he begins to shut me down. His low-level despair may manifest as cynicism, withdrawal, and simmering judgment.

Finally, when others comment that I "look tired," I know it's a very late clue that I have ignored many requests for self-attention.

If someone asked me whether saying one prayer would create a lifetime relationship with God, if one strenuous workout could produce lifelong fitness, if one yoga class could forge a permanent mind-body synergy, if one vegetable juice could guarantee a lifelong ideal body weight, or if one meditation session could create permanent tranquility, I would laugh at the ridiculousness of the question. Yet part of me expected I would be cured after my first workshop, that I could put away my past and move on.

I was thirty-seven years old before I met the voice I had banished. I suppose I assumed that giving him space at the workshop or doing an occasional piece of externalization would take care of things, that he would be happier and let me go about my busy life. I didn't learn for many years that I needed to make the same level of constancy and commitment to my inner children as I did to Matt and Rachael. My little ones would act out their anger and nearly shut me down many more times before I learned.

Truth be told, I banished my little ones because I not only disapproved of their vulnerability, but I was afraid of them. A grown man, I was scared of the emotions of little kids. Ironically, my inner kids felt the same way about me.

When adults show persistent disapproval or conversely shower their kids with inappropriate praise, kids learn that love is, at best, a commodity bought with the right behavior. The end result is a mix of resentment, self-doubt, mistrust of adult motives, and confusion. My little ones had no intention of "performing" at my workshop so Dr. Lincoln would feel better about himself and go on ignoring them while he worked that much harder. They weren't about to make life easier for me.

My little ones had lost faith in the unconscious adult I had become. Although very hopeful (bereft little kids hang on to even a morsel of attention, which is why they can be so easily manipulated), they remained skeptical that one five-day workshop had permanently changed me. Like all kids, they wanted consistent, loving connections over time. Once our relationship had been rekindled, they wanted more of me and became militant when I relapsed into habitual old patterns.

My first hint of uprising came fairly soon after my first workshop. I was excited to learn more about myself. I drove to a local bookstore and inquired of the location of the self-help and psychology section. As I perused the shelves, the first title that leaped out at me was *Healing the Child Within*. Suddenly, I found myself walking out of the bookstore as I heard an angry, rebellious voice mutter, *I don't need to be healed—there's nothing wrong with me.* I stopped just outside the store. Then I heard from another more temperate, younger voice: *We don't want you to heal us. We don't need to be managed. We don't need to be fixed, calmed down, or changed. We want you to hear us, see us, and love us for who we are.*

The little guy had no intention of reading books that even suggested he was impaired or needed to be changed. What children need and want is simple. No hidden agendas; just listen, support them, and keep them safe. I thought I had learned my lesson many times, but more than twenty years would pass before I really understood.

Much like when a child (inner or biological) demands to be heard, the clamor of the masses can lead to similar upheaval. Hong Kong residents persist in their desire for democratic self-rule twenty years after its return to China by the British. The Arab Spring erupted with the call for a new order. Unfortunately, hope ceded to sectarian violence or a return to authoritarian rule. Often strong leaders become fearful, shutting down protests with regressive force. In Rwanda, President Kagame, having survived and ended the holocaust of 1994, continues to suppress dissent. His fear of another violent insurgence certainly has a basis in past events. Perhaps his commitment to political stability, abolition of corruption, improved infrastructure, education, and health care for all Rwandans will dampen long-standing mistrust and hatred between Tutsi and Hutu. It remains to be seen whether the decision to limit dissent will lead to reconciliation or permanent dictatorship. President Kagame walks a tightrope as he changes the constitution he created so he can run for a third term as president. I believe the outcome will hinge on whether he can earn the trust of the Hutu majority or whether his appeal for "one Rwanda" will be seen as his hidden agenda to maintain power and control by his minority.

I suppose my agenda for my little ones was for them to be happy, grateful, and quiet so I could be the successful, highly competent person I wanted to be. I especially wanted competing voices with differing needs to be silent. How would I know what I was supposed to be when I grew up when I kept hearing several "little ones" making their separate demands?

The loudest internal voice is the determined six-year-old, who wanted to prove to those neighborhood kids he was better. He rarely relaxes and only when all his work is done. Alas, there is always another thing to do. Even now, on most mornings, his is the first voice I hear. "Okay, rise and shine and get busy. We have a lot to accomplish." This one awakens me in the middle of the night making his to-do lists. I hear his mind going, even when I awaken briefly to change position or use the toilet. He collapses into bed at night from both physical and mental exhaustion, falling into catatonic sleep almost instantly; but after several hours, he is ready to go again. Before my first workshop, I would on occasion go for a five-mile run at two o'clock in the morning just to burn off his excess energy. Now I have learned to acknowledge his need for fame and fortune, thank him for all the years of hard work, and promise I will review his list when the birds start singing and the sun comes up.

A quieter, though equally omnipresent, voice is that of the five-year-old, who went into hibernation after the smothering. He remains shy, timid, and very loving. He worries about other people and wants them to feel safe and appreciated. He wants me to slow down and pay attention to him. He would like to read a book, go to a movie, or talk with a friend one on one. He loves his family and wants them to be happy and playful, but he doesn't know how to play either. He loves to be seen and appreciated for his quiet wisdom and open heart. He wants to travel to distant lands—not only to see how others live and what makes them tick but to leave our busy world behind. He travels light. Scared much of the time, he yearns for a peaceful, caring world. His predominant emotions are fear and sadness. He doesn't want me to watch the news because it is so discouraging. Sometimes out of the blue he tells me he is sad without even knowing why. He just wants me to say that I hear him and that his sadness is okay.

My adolescent was happiest going to high school and training hard for sports, especially wrestling. He felt challenged and competent and, perhaps most important, inspired by teachers and coaches. He still dreams of being headmaster of a school, creating excitement and joy for students, and cheering on a dedicated faculty. He wants to make a difference in young lives. He is sentimental and a dreamer. He can still wake me in the middle of the night, dreaming of an imaginary wrestling match or training hard for another season. He loves this individual sport. He wins or loses based on his performance without having to count on, or be responsible for, anyone else. He craves an uncomplicated life. I don't have the heart to tell him otherwise.

I have a chorus inside, each singing a different song. They are all very serious. We could all lighten up a bit. No matter what I choose to do, someone inside is left behind. No matter how much I enjoy my day, however many people I help, someone tugs at my shirt, asking, "What about me?" When I put my feet up with a good book in my hands, I feel my little super achiever become restless. I believe these competing voices are the source of what I call "existential yearning," that empty hole inside many of us that can never quite be filled. No longer believing it is a deficiency in me, I recognize it is part of being human.

I have fewer hidden agendas. I respect that inside of me are competing needs. We all respect what the other wants. We take turns with our dreams. Now that I'm in retirement, I feel the younger voices tug at me as if to say, "Now what?" I shrug and reply, "Don't look at me! I'm just the adult. I'm retired." They look at each other and shake their heads. We all laugh.

Remember, when I write about my "little one," it may be any one or several of these voices. My daily spiritual practice of listening to them, encouraging the quiet ones to speak, and answering their questions has led to more clarity and safety in my outward relationships.

After my workshop, I believed that if I could remain open hearted, what career I pursued wouldn't matter. I gave myself Zen lecture number 123: *I should be equally happy doing medicine, baking bread, teaching school, being a workshop guru, or sweeping streets. Since I have committed so much time to becoming a skillful infectious disease specialist, I might as well be happy in my chosen career.* But one nagging internal voice didn't buy it.

About twelve years ago, after a particularly brutal on-call weekend and two fifteen-hour workdays, it all came to a head. The workload and my reactions to it made me equally exhausted. When I finally had time to sit quietly and listen, a voice unloaded with, *You really don't want to know how I feel.* (How many adolescents have said those exact words to their parents?) Apparently, I wasn't really prepared to hear what he had to say, but the workshop guru responded, "Of course I want to hear how you're feeling."

Okay—I hate medicine. I always have, and I always will. I hate the hours. I hate that I never know when we will be able to get home and do something fun. I'm tired of listening to everyone else's problems and worrying whether they are going to get better. I hate it when you come home and have to answer all the pages. I hate it when you have to go back to the hospital. I hate it that you worry about your patients more than you worry about me.

In my most understanding and logical voice, I tried to explain to him that this was the nature of clinical medicine, that we had survived it for nearly thirty years and that we would survive the next years as well. I lectured him that when people are sick, they need a lot of reassurance and support and that it was a privilege to provide it for them. I reassured him that his fear, that we would never finish the day and never have time to play, was unfounded and exaggerated, since we did have time to exercise nearly every day, to take regular vacations, and to see friends on the weekends. I was certain that logic would prevail and that my reassuring words would soothe the little beast. I waited for his calm response, certain that our nice, little internal dialogue would resolve the frustration that kept appearing during my time on call.

No more explanations! You're not listening! I hate medicine. I always have, and I always will. No more lectures, no more self-righteous BS about the beauty of service. On my (and your) deathbed, I'm still going to hate medicine.

He wasn't buying my pep talk.

"All right, all right, I get it. I apologize for trying to make you feel something that you don't. I'll never ask you to like medicine again. You don't even have to come to work with me anymore—just when and if you want to. But do you understand that I like some parts of medicine and that I have responsibilities and commitments to my patients, my partners, and our family?"

I am continually amazed at how wise our little ones can be. They are capable of enormous acts of connection, kindness, forgiveness, and ethical wisdom. My irate little guy answered, *It's okay that you like what you do, just so long as I can dislike it. I know that a lot of people depend on you, including Anne, Matt, and Rachael. I also see how you help people, but I've been helping and worrying about other people all my life, which is a lot longer than you have been a doctor. I want you to worry about me now. I'm mad that you put everyone else ahead of me. You can go do your work, but I'm not coming with you anymore.*

I smiled at his clarity.

During my facilitation of mat work, I have often requested that adults, while they are holding the pillow representing their inner child, practice a dialogue by asking their little ones specific questions. Initially, I often hear an immediate, almost reflexive response, such as, "Of course, he likes my wife." I reflect on how much kids hate it when grown-ups (especially their parents) speak for them. "Ask the same question again," I'll say, "but this time close your eyes, sit quietly, and patiently wait for the answer from your little one." It is uncanny how often the answer is different from what the adult believed it to be. Sometimes the answer is upsetting, and other times it is so filled with clarity and wisdom that it is mind blowing. I've had adults tell me that they had no idea Yoda lived inside them.

It is a gift to see high-powered adults leave a workshop with newfound respect for the wisdom and clarity that comes from the inner children they have unknowingly banished. The type of obligatory attention that gets kids off their parents' back doesn't satisfy their need to be seen and heard. Kids know when they are being appeased, manipulated, or managed. They aren't circus animals. It is pure pleasure to witness the look of wonder and respect from an adult for his or her newly discovered inner child, the look that says the child is important to the consciousness of the world.

Before climbing out of bed the morning following our conversation, I made it a point to ask my adolescent whether he would like to join me for work. When he declined, as I knew he would, I wondered whether it was possible that he could symbolically stay home while the rest of me saw patients all day.

I was amazed by how much easier the day flowed. Although I was just as busy, my resistance to the helter-skelter of infectious disease had lessened. I was able to take things as they came without clenching my jaw, to do my work much more efficiently without the frustrated chatter in my head. I managed to slow down the interactions with my patients. Although I still anticipated, with apprehension, my long weekends on call, I didn't experience the dread my adolescent had. I actually began to enjoy medicine again.

What I internalized was that children want their feelings to be acknowledged and respected even more than they need to get their way. My little guy understood that he and I had competing needs and that life isn't black or white, either all work or all play. So long as I took time to check in with him before my day started, he was content to stay home and allow my day to unfold.

I developed a brief ritual of resting my hand on my abdomen as a way of letting the little guy know I remembered he was at home. Often I could feel him smile when I took those two seconds to acknowledge him. Sometimes he would say that he hoped I would get home soon. Sometimes he would actually give me support and make me laugh by exclaiming what a completely crazy day he was watching me have. My laughter was my thank-you to him, my gratitude for his seeing me as well. We had become allies.

One morning, several months after our conversation, a voice inside surprised me by accepting my invitation to come to work. He told me he particularly wanted to talk with one of my patients. He could see and advise me about the fear and frustration of a young athlete who had developed a postoperative knee infection. In my previous visits, I had focused on the knee and the bacterial cultures, explaining my choice of antibiotics.

On the third morning of my care, with my little guy along with me, I examined the knee and expressed my pleasure that it was looking less swollen and inflamed. Then I simply asked, "How are *you* doing with all of this?" My young patient poured out the grief of shattered dreams for a promising athletic career as well as the loss of a healthy, strong, and graceful body. Many days later, during a follow-up office visit, the athlete commented to me that I was the only doctor who had actually asked about more than just the knee.

Inside, I knew it wasn't Dr. Lincoln, the infectious disease specialist, who had asked the question. I just nodded and quietly thanked my expert consultant for his sage council. In this case, it was my seventeen-year-old.

On the last play before the end of the first half of a high school football game, I tore two ligaments and the medial meniscus of my right knee. In those days, I wore a cast for six weeks following my surgery, ending any hope of competing for a state wrestling championship in my senior year. Eager to cheer me up, no one asked me how *I* was. As it turned out, I never fully recovered my strength, balance, or quickness. Although I went on to wrestle in college, the injury was just a reminder of what I had lost. Now my adolescent was able to heal a bit by supporting another athlete.

My little one still doesn't like medicine, but he likes a lot of the people we meet during our day together. He still takes mental health days when he needs a break, and he has taught me to do the same, not by harassing me but by offering an example. We've become a good team.

Don's Hidden Little Boy

Don was in his early fifties. The youngest of three children, he had left home as soon as he graduated from high school. He had experienced ridicule by schoolmates, who called him "sissy" and later "faggot" well before he acknowledged to himself that he was gay.

Don was an extremely talented and very successful attorney. He had been in a devoted, fifteen-year relationship with his best friend. Everything was great except their physical intimacy, because Don froze with any unexpected touch. His partner felt rejected but didn't want to hurt Don with repeated attempts at intimacy. They both wondered whether Don's reaction to innocent and loving touch was due to repressed childhood sexual invasiveness. Don had no memories before the age of ten.

Fearful that his partner would eventually leave him or find gratification outside the relationship, Don entered counseling. Very much a problem solver, he attacked therapy with the same energy and determination by which he faced all challenges in his life. He tried talk therapy and underwent hypnosis and several other techniques to help him recover childhood memories. No information came to him. His therapist referred him to a workshop.

When Don sat on the mat, he told me he didn't think his little one existed; or if he did, he wasn't communicating with Don the way he had seen others do at the workshop. I asked Don whether he had anything to say to his withholding little boy. He grabbed the hose, reached for a phone book, and told Donnie he was tired of his silence and demanded that he tell what had happened to him. He accused his inner little boy of ruining his relationship because he froze when his partner touched him. Enough was enough. It was time for him to talk.

When Don finished expressing his anger, I asked him to put himself in Donnie's shoes. Don immediately answered that he was telling Donnie to speak up for his own good. (How many times have parents told their kids that they were acting a certain way for their own good?) I then asked Don, "If you were a little boy, would you talk freely to an adult who was angry enough to beat the truth out of you?"

Don's mouth fell open. He looked at me and, shaking his head, said that was just how his father had treated him, with threats, demands, and beatings. He picked up the pillow and held a little boy, whose only communication was silence. With tears in his eyes, Don spoke very gently to his boy in hiding. "I am so sorry to treat you the way they did. I see how scared and mistrustful you are to have to remain so quiet. You must think that I care more about knowing the truth than I do about you, and you are right. I never considered what it must be like for you to be hurt so many years ago and then dragged to workshops and therapy so you could be forced or tricked into telling me what happened.

"I guess I've wanted to know so I could finally feel better and leave my past, and you, behind. It's been hard for me to carry around such a depressed little boy, but today I see that you just want to feel safe and not be discarded once this workshop is over.

"I want to tell you that you never have to speak about the past if you don't want to. I see how trapped and scared I have made you feel, and I won't do that anymore. We can just sit quietly together." Without realizing what he was doing, Don rocked his little boy with patience and gentleness. After a while, Don looked up at me. I then asked how his body felt. He took a few seconds to experience himself. "I feel calmer than I have felt in a very long time."

I spoke to Don months later. He hadn't found any memories about sexual abuse, but he had begun to recall violence at home. He had a sense that his father had been furious that his son was so gentle and had been determined to toughen him up. Don then told me that he had continued to hold and reassure his little boy every day. Recently, after asking his little guy's permission, Don told his partner about him. Afterward, his partner asked Don's little boy if he could hold Don, and his little boy said yes.

Matt and Rachael repeatedly challenged us to choose to love the children we had as opposed to a dream we had for them. They have been our best teachers regarding what our priorities really are. Listening to my internal little ones and hearing the hidden agendas they so doggedly have pointed out to me have made me a better parent, better mate, and better friend. My little ones continue to demand that I make conscious choices about my priorities ... and choose love. Our internal dialogues will be a lifelong process.

Chapter 12

THE EXTERNALIZATION PROCESS

*When we are no longer able to change a situation—
we are challenged to change ourselves.*
—Viktor E. Frankl

The externalization of emotions, mat work, is one of many useful techniques to release stored-up feelings; but it must be more than just a release of anger and grief, a condemnation of those who abused or neglected us, or an opportunity to convince ourselves that our world view is the right one. Otherwise, pounding phone books is no more than a proclamation and glorification of victimhood.

As children, we test the waters of self-righteousness. "Mommy, Carla hit me. She's so mean!" We think we want our parents to take sides, to love us most of all, until it happens. We learn that the price for getting attention by being the injured party is to suffer from the inner knowledge that this form of parental love will always be at someone else's expense. If mat work stopped with the proclamation of our injury, it would be a disservice to our little ones.

Mat work isn't just about who can make the most noise, destroy the most phone books, or tell the worst story of injury or neglect. The true work is about developing an internal relationship that leads to accountability for our thoughts, words, and actions.

Injured children don a mask to look normal to the outside world. My mask was one of gentleness to wall off my anger and believe I wasn't like them, the bullies. It was also one of calm to bury my fear and anxiety. Finally, my mask was one of competence to rise above those who hurt me. I was a nice person, after all. I imprisoned my sad little boy because I didn't want to be a sissy ever again. I sequestered my terrified little one so I could function in a stressful world, and I put double walls around my needy one so he wouldn't humiliate me with his groveling. I was calm, centered Dr. Lincoln—until I wasn't. Once triggered, I was a self-righteous little boy in my martyrdom and judgment. Those banished little boys needed a wise parent who could bring them in from the cold and teach them that their hurt feelings don't justify hurting or condemning someone else, even silently.

Mat work was the vehicle for my little ones (my trapped right-brain emotions) to teach my adult self (my cognitive left brain) what had really happened to them. It was unexpectedly useful to re-experience the raw intensity of my childhood feelings to get my adult attention. I look back and realize how amazing it was for my little one to see that, even as he was in the midst of terror and murderous rage, a part of me was simultaneously watching and taking it all in. It was as if my left brain, or wise parent, finally could say, "I get it. No wonder I was so scared and became so driven."

The ninety witnesses at my workshop were very meaningful for my little one, because their silent presence made the remembered experience even more real. When I looked up from my mat work, I saw in other peoples' eyes that I needed to take my little ones seriously. Also, my little one needed to watch mat work for one long day to see that releasing intense emotions doesn't lead to psychic disintegration but rather restoration. When he observed that there could be a resting place for pain, he felt safe enough to take the leap of faith and come to the mat.

I don't want to minimize the value of releasing all that pent-up rage and grief. I felt much lighter and much less afraid of my feelings. However, I don't believe the lightness would have endured had I not taken the next step and begun the process of integration, creating a more attentive, strong, and wise internal parent.

I had met the timid little boy who was banished for being scared and humiliated as well as the quiet hard-ass who came out of the ashes. Now they were my responsibility. I couldn't use them as an excuse for bad behavior, such as sulking martyrdom, lashing out or withdrawing from loved ones or colleagues, or looking for love (attention) in all the wrong places. Now that I knew who they were, it was on me, my grown-up self, to be accountable to them and for them.

Occasionally at the end of an especially deep piece of mat work, a magical moment happens. The work may begin with anger or fear, progress through screams of terror, followed by roaring, pounding outrage onto the phone books to a point of near exhaustion. When all the years of pent-up, compressed rage have been released, the participant's ability to hold back the years of grief is gone, and the sobs of a hurt child come pouring out for what he or she never had and always wanted. Finally, when the grief for all the wasted years has run its course, there comes a profound stillness, as if God (however one defines the force and mystery of creation) is cradling a child in his arms, and love has filled the void where pain resided. Each time, as a facilitator, my eyes fill with the mist of gratitude that I have been privileged to bear witness to such a moment, when there exists only one word—love. Almost always, this moment of primal connection to our source is transformative.

Learning to parent ourselves, being truly accountable, is a lifelong process. On occasion, old feelings still get triggered to the point of needing to do mat work. Usually I start with the current trigger, but almost always this leads me back to another layer of childhood grief or shame. I am honored each time I receive a new piece of information from my little ones, because it means I am becoming a more trustworthy and effective parent.

We don't push the participants at our workshop. The little ones must feel safe enough to reveal themselves. They get to set the pace, not the grown-ups. Some participants watch the entire weekend. For some, it has been empowering to refuse to come to the mat, perhaps for the first time in their lives feeling safe and strong enough to say no to someone in authority. Others have been sobered by the insight of how scared their little one must be, to be unable to tell their story even in such a safe setting. Even sitting in their chair, shedding quiet tears while witnessing others do their work, allows for deep insight and a welcome release of grief.

Externalization isn't for everyone. In my case I needed to experience my raw emotions to shatter the walls I had constructed around my past and peel off the mask of calm confidence I presented to the world. However, a rare participant chooses to leave the workshop because he or she isn't prepared for the intensity of emotion and the panful stories. We encourage them to stay for the final day of teaching, which clarifies the reason for the mat work and may provide a road map for future growth. However, if someone still feels he or she wants to leave, we make sure that the person leaves safely, as an adult.

Occasionally, we receive an angry letter that the workshop disrupted carefully constructed defenses. In fact, upheaval is true for most participants. Most, like me, are extremely grateful for the disruption. A few don't have the support to consolidate the benefit of the experience. However, we recently received a letter from a participant several years after her workshop, who was originally angry and disappointed; but she wrote that the experience of the workshop stayed with her. At first, she grudgingly noticed that fresh memories and insights began to clarify behaviors that kept her isolated and unhappy. After many months, she began to dialogue with her ten-year-old, who now felt safe to let herself be nurtured. We cannot control the timing of a participant's experience.

Anne and I offer to connect with the therapists of participants before and after the weekend. We have seen how valuable a gifted therapist or a safe support group can be during the postworkshop period, when emotional swings often occur. Many participants comment on how much better their therapists have become after the workshop.

Although we are pleased when participants leave our workshop in a good place, our goal for the weekend isn't to make all of them euphorically happy and push them out the door on a spiritual high. That intention would be unrealistic, unsafe, and manipulative. The workshop is meant to provide the tools for the inevitable hard times that inhabiting a physical body guarantees. Emotional repercussions are predictable after an intense experience. Those who leave on a high or leave feeling scared and lonely won't stay that way. That's life. Our hope is that the insights and compassion from the weekend will help all of us to be more introspective and gentle with ourselves as so-called unwanted, negative feelings resurface.

For many years after we began our Tucson workshops, we had a weekly support group for former participants. It was an invaluable resource to remind each other to trust the process of allowing feelings to come. Often we condemn ourselves for being triggered and losing control, or we punish those around us for awakening our imprisoned little ones rather than seizing the opportunity (as painful and humiliating as it is) to get to know ourselves better. Being triggered, or, as Elisabeth says, "reacting longer than fifteen seconds," can be the catalyst for deeper understanding and self-forgiveness as well as tolerance for the triggered little ones in others. Ideally, these are the tools we impart to our participants.

The Growth and Transition Workshop is now completing its thirty-first year. Initially, the weekend workshops, modeled after Elisabeth's LDTs, were filled with hospital staff; but gradually they have opened to all comers throughout the United States. Many therapists who know of this work have referred their clients. After we returned to Tucson in 1987, Anne assumed the organizational duties for Growth and Transition, and we have been coleaders ever since. We have also been fortunate to have the assistance of many other talented staff of the Elisabeth Kübler-Ross (EKR) Center to help us with our weekends.

As Elisabeth's health and energy waned, the EKR Center closed its doors in 1995. Elisabeth suffered a series of strokes, leaving her disabled and often frustrated with her dependency. She died in 2004.

Until about seven years ago, Sharon Tobin and Shannon Steck continued their Safe Harbors workshops for survivors of childhood abuse. Others continue to offer weekend programs as well. Knowing we were all aging, Anne twisted my arm and created the curriculum to offer a training program that would teach the facilitation of mat work as well as the intricacies of creating and leading a Growth and Transition weekend. I recently assisted Anne with her second training, which is helping spawn another generation to carry on Elisabeth's work.

During our two years in Delaware from 1985–87, I traveled extensively, including to Australia and New Zealand twice a year, to lead workshops and train local staff. It became clear to me that if I wanted to do this work full-time, I would have to travel two hundred days a year. It was heady work to be a catalyst for personal transformation and be revered as a good teacher. As I mentioned in the last chapter, I loved it—perhaps too much.

I became worried that I wasn't safe within myself to carry the projections of the wise, gifted protégé of the world-famous Elisabeth Kübler-Ross. I didn't trust myself to carry that kind of admiration and adoration without the risk of unconsciously using others for my own gratification.

I talked to Elisabeth about this one night, and her response was classic EKR. "I'll tell you when your head gets too big." But her words didn't change the mistrust I felt for my needy one inside, who craved his standing ovation. He could be a danger to others and the source of public humiliation for me. Only I could be accountable for myself. I had to back off. Coupled with my priority to be available for Anne and our teenagers, we decided to return to Tucson in 1987. Anne began her counseling practice, and I resumed my infectious disease work. I reduced my workshop schedule and traveling.

Here is a quote attributed to Nelson Mandela, but Marianne Williamson (*A Return to Love*, 1998) actually wrote it:

> Our deepest fear is not that we are inadequate. Our deepest fear is that we are powerful beyond measure. It is our light, not our darkness, that most frightens us. We ask ourselves, who am I to be brilliant, gorgeous, talented, fabulous? Actually, who are you not to be? You are a child of God. Your playing small doesn't serve the world. There's nothing enlightened about shrinking so that other people won't feel insecure around you. You were born to make manifest the glory of God that is within you. It is not just in some of us; it's in everyone. And as we let our own light shine, we unconsciously give other people permission to do the same. As we're liberated from our own fear, our presence automatically liberates others.

It would take me several more years to feel safe within myself before I would let myself shine. Although I understood intellectually that all children crave attention and approval, I still felt shame that my needy little boy wanted it so much. He was grieved when we returned to Tucson and resumed my medical practice. He was never happier than when I worked with Elisabeth full-time, especially on his sojourns to Australia and New

Zealand. The mixture of transformative work and delightful play with the incredible "down under" staff was a highlight of his time with Elisabeth. Still he was in complete agreement that Anne, Matt, and Rachael came first. His priority to our family built my trust that my needy little boy wouldn't put himself above the people he loved and would indeed be a safe workshop leader.

Despite our dramatic and poignant initial meeting at my first workshop, my little one and I retained varying degrees of suspicion, distrust, and fear. It would take years of consistent dialogue before we trusted each other fully. I could reassure him repeatedly of his innate goodness, but it took time for him to believe me. After all, I had curtailed our work with Elisabeth because I didn't trust his neediness. I had to demonstrate to him that I wouldn't abandon him if he were in distress, condemn him when he was overly competitive or compulsive, or lose patience if he became irritable, needy, or depressive. I had to demonstrate that I would always be accountable to him.

What does being accountable to my little one mean? That I check in with him daily, making time to empathize when he feels out of sorts and celebrate when he's happy, joyful, and proud? Being accountable to him means I don't make promises just to shut him up, judge him for his negative feelings, or taunt him to get over his pain and move on. At times I continue to imprison him with my busyness or lose patience with the repetitive nature of his triggers. But when I ignore him, I inevitably pay for it.

Occasionally, my little ones have demanded to do mat work, putting my adult out on the phone book for treating them just the way my busy, preoccupied parents did. But when I have used my dear mom and dad as an excuse, my little ones have really let me have it. There came a point in my examined life when I had to take responsibility for my present and future. My little ones basically told me, *You've heard our stories. You've told us you believe us and love us. Now it's not about Mom and Dad anymore. It's on you! No excuses, no rationalizations. You show up for us, or life will be unpleasant.* They kept their promises much better than I have.

Before a big presentation, I still might experience some fear or performance anxiety. If I'm not accountable to my scared little perfectionist, I go into my talk preoccupied with how I am doing rather than what I want to say. On the other hand, if I take a moment to sit with him, acknowledge his desire to give a great talk, assure him that his nervousness makes sense given the high expectations he has of himself, and then give him my standing ovation for his gentle heart, his ability to synthesize and speak simply about complex concepts, and his desire to inspire others, I am always amazed by how I feel him smile. I take a deep cleansing breath and enjoy what is to come. When I am accountable to him, he no longer needs to seek approval in the wrong places. In return his insight and love of others are available to me in real time. I am then able to be "in my body" for my presentation.

Over the years, he trusts that when I inevitably ignore him again (bad habits die hard), I will return, apologize, and get with the program. In turn, I trust that he is safe to enjoy a standing ovation without having to manipulate others for it. I know he understands Mandela's words that the light shines in all of us. Being accountable to him has softened his competitiveness. More than ever, he cheers others on and rejoices in their luminosity.

The imagery of the inner child helped me to visualize myself by remembering Matt and Rachael at that age. It was and remains much easier to generate compassion for myself as a small child than for a neurotic old man. While my love for Matt and Rachael helped me to find compassion and forgiveness for myself, I didn't expect how my deepening relationship with myself improved my ability to be a good dad. Attuning to myself taught me over and over again how to listen, be present for, and trust those I loved. More importantly, I was able to risk being vulnerable with my kids to tell them how much I loved them.

Telling My Son Who He Is to Me

I had been leading workshops for five years, including teaching about near-death experiences as well as cultivating inner relationships. By then our son, Matt, was in full-blown adolescence. Our sweet little boy had turned into an angry teenager, determined to break as many chains to his parents as he could. Anne and I could do nothing right. It was scary and painful. We had many bitter conversations that often ended in frustrating power plays. Anne and I wondered when the disagreements and our fears for our son would end.

I was away at a workshop, teaching about what the light requests of those having a near-death experience. One typical request is to review all the times they could have expressed their love to someone and didn't. As I explained to the participants that the pain and suffering caused by these missed opportunities are enormous, it dawned on me that if I died that day, I would experience enormous regret for not telling my rebellious son how much and why I loved him. I had already learned from my little ones how much joy they received when I saw them fully. Yet trapped in the nightmare of father-son adolescence, I responded to Matt with anger, frustration, or withdrawal much too often. For many months, I hadn't given my son what I was learning to give myself and teaching others to do. Once the lightbulb went on, I couldn't wait to finish the workshop and fly home.

When I arrived home, I exchanged welcome-home hugs with Anne and Rachael, and I proceeded down the hall to Matt's room. He was lying on his bed, reading a book, and listening to alternative rock. When I knocked on his door, he jumped out of bed to face his intruder with a stern look and fists partially clenched. I walked slowly across the room and reached for the collar of his shirt. I was much closer than the socially accepted distance between men as I stated, "I'm here to tell you who you are." I recall that Matt's muscles tightened; he believed he was about to hear something like, "You are a self-centered, ungrateful ..."

Instead, I told Matt what it was like to see him come into the world, to discover his unique gifts of attention and precise articulation of language, his commitment to fairness and equality, his ability to appreciate other points of view, his devotion to and love of his sister, and his insistence that I engage fully with both intellectual barrels if we were having a discussion or playing a game.

Tears ran down my cheeks as I allowed myself to feel the deep love and respect I had for my son, how precious he was to me, and how scared I was for him—but I held onto his lapels and kept talking. Finally, I ended by saying, "You cannot possibly know how precious you are to me. I hope one day you will treasure a child, and a teenager, the way I treasure you. When I am an old man and about to leave this earth, there is no man that I would trust to care for me and protect me more than you."

Through my monologue, Matt's fists gradually opened, and his eyes moistened. The words I used made it clear to my son that I knew who he was and that I was describing no one else on the planet.

The love got through. Since then, he has never had a moment of doubt about how I feel about him, and the trust between us continues to deepen and enrich our relationship. I don't believe I understand how love is capable of penetrating doubt and pain until I learned to parent my hibernating little ones.

About eighteen months later, I was driving Matt back to his college dorm after his weekly visit for Anne's Sunday dinner (and two bags of laundry). Normally, he would jump out, grab his books and his laundry, and holler a "Thanks. Bye. Love you." This particular evening, he asked me to pull over and park the car. When I turned off the ignition, my son slid across the front seat, took my collar in his hands, and then proceeded to tell me who I was to him.

I learned that I must not take love for granted. Although I had a close, tender relationship with my young son, I hadn't established this closeness with Matt as he moved through adolescence. Once again, I had to reach out to him and take time to discover who he was. We had many wonderful conversations following our reconnection, which continued to cement our closeness. Love must be fed and watered, like any living entity.

Currently, our two-year-old grandson, Henry, has predictably entered the so-called terrible times. He screams out his frustration and says no, even when he means yes. His parents must now rediscover their new son, who is replacing the almost-always sweet, happy infant he recently was. Similarly, Anne and I must feed and water the "old guys" we are becoming. Otherwise, we risk that our love will become stale bread.

One would think that such tender moments would break the cycle of all future generational dysfunction. In fact, the accumulation of these moments does make a huge difference. But each generation must do its own work as it moves through different phases of life. Recently, Matt, who now lives and works in Bangkok, called to give me more feedback about the first twelve chapters of this book. Our conversation turned to parenting. Matt said the first year or so of his girls' lives was relatively easy, giving them vast quantities of loving attention to create secure attachment, without much concern of spoiling them.

Now, as Scout is four and Zoe is two, Matt said the road map has become much more complex. Trying to find the balance of giving love and support without spoiling and overindulging unwanted behavior has been tricky.

Matt and Lindsay are great parents. They have what seems like infinite patience and are well along the learning curve of setting healthy boundaries for their girls. But, like most parents, sometimes they've just had enough of child rearing. On recent visits, I have occasionally seen Matt move from loving, engaged spouse-father to jaw-clenching, ticking time bomb.

The first time I saw it, I thought I was in a time warp. I was seeing a replay of myself from years past. Last night, I mentioned to Matt that when I noticed him go on overload, it brought back moments of regret for me. Even via FaceTime, I could see Matt wince that I had noticed this, but almost immediately he put down his embarrassment and wondered aloud what that was about for him. Then I saw tears fill his eyes. "Dad, I saw you constantly busy. My little one adores you, so he thinks he has to go nonstop, too. But when he's had enough, he is saying that he wants my attention and for me to stop giving it to everyone else."

Generational patterns continue to survive and occasionally haunt us Lincolns. It is amazing to me that Matt's overload happens so rarely for him. I don't think I had such patience or endurance. Each phase of life presents new opportunities for growth and self-discovery. That night I was privileged to witness a deepening connection for my son with his neglected little boy. I suspect Matt will check in more often with his little guy, acknowledging with love and compassion a boy's need for his dad's attention. This process will bring him closer to himself, to his family, and to his very grateful father. Despite all my years of spiritual practice, I cannot do this for Matt. Of course, I can listen, ask questions, and love my son; but each generation must find its own language and forge its own internal relationships. Hopefully, Matt will achieve this earlier in his daughters' lives than I did for Rachael and him.

Chapter 13

ACCOUNTABILITY

It is wrong and immoral to seek to escape the consequences of one's acts.
—Mahatma Gandhi

Although you should not erase your responsibility for the past, when you make the past your jailer, you destroy your future. It is such a great moment of liberation when you learn to forgive yourself, let the burden go, and walk out into a new path of promise and possibility.
—John O'Donohue

The Source of Willie's Infidelity

Willie's couples' therapist referred him to our workshop to deepen his understanding of his repeated infidelities. He came from a prominent and successful family. His parents were leaders in their church and respected in their community. On the surface, they looked perfect.

Unconsciously trying to reproduce his childhood family, Willie modeled what he knew. He and his wife were active in the church, setting an example of decorum for other families. But when his oldest son discovered him cheating with another woman, Willie's secret life blew the facade apart. Gradually, Willie confessed to a string of affairs and entered treatment and couples' therapy.

In therapy, Willie began to piece together a childhood of neglect. Although constantly helping others through her volunteer work, Willie's mom was cold and critical at home. Willie couldn't remember anything more than a perfunctory hug from her, and that only happened when the family was in public.

Willie's dad worked long hours, ending his day with several cocktails before and after dinner. He was a happy drinker and told a lot of jokes and stories, many of which were spiced with sexual innuendo. When he was sober, Dad had high expectations for his children. He preached about family values but spent no time teaching his children life skills. Willie and his siblings received praise for how they looked and performed in school and in sports. Any recognition each child had of his or her own unique character or way of being in the world came in the form of playful, public ridicule for his or her deviation from the norm. "Willie is such a show-off. Willie is so stubborn. His clothes are a mess before we can even get him to church." His parents never expressed any joy about Willie being Willie. Love meant conforming to the family culture.

During adolescence, Willie had his first taste of attention and affection in his relationships with girls in his class. His spiritual need for connection became linked with sexual gratification. As an adult, whenever he felt the hollow, empty feeling he later learned was the loneliness of early childhood, he would go on the prowl, trying to reproduce the wonder of his first sexual experience. It didn't help that he had chosen a life partner who was as distant as his mother.

In sharp contrast to his lonely, withdrawn early childhood, Willie described the thrill of the chase, the dance of seduction, and the physical consummation of the affair. But he especially liked the power and self-importance of making women feel good about themselves, something he was unable to do for his mother and his partner.

Listening to other stories at the workshop, Willie could appreciate for the first time the reason for his pervasive feeling of emptiness despite all his worldly success. Yet the first words he uttered on the mat were, "My parents didn't abuse me as a child. They didn't beat me. I had a roof over my head and three squares a day. I had lots of toys as a kid and a brand-new car when I turned sixteen."

Willie's loyalty to his parents fed his self-doubt, minimizing his own needs and feelings. I reassured Willie that his parents had done the best they could and that it was clear he loved his mom and dad. Whatever had happened on the mat never had to be repeated to his parents. If he would give himself permission, adult Willie could learn a great deal from the little boy who had been seeking love in all the wrong places.

Willie lay down on the mat, staring silently at the ceiling. Since he wasn't engaging me, I waited. Minutes elapsed before a little boy began speaking. "I spent hours in my room alone, lying on my bed. If I made noise, I got into trouble. I barely remember my childhood. I just did what I was supposed to do."

He choked out the next words. "She never came to check on me." Willie's body silently shook as years of grief poured out while at the same time he held in any sound that might upset his mom and dad. He had been a very good, very quiet little boy. Finally, grief moved to frustration, and Willie screamed out the wail trapped in his chest. Although Willie released a bit of anger at his mom and dad, it was the depth of his sadness that surprised and touched him.

Placing a pillow on the mat, I turned to adult Willie and asked whether he would like to go check on a small, little boy lying rigidly on his bed. Willie reached for the pillow. "I won't leave you alone again. I see that it wasn't safe for you to call out for help, but I will pay attention and come find you when you are feeling sad and lonely."

Willie returned to our workshop two more times over the next few years when he felt himself sliding toward a relapse and flirting with women he hardly knew. At the next workshop, he learned more about the emotional emptiness of his childhood and made an even deeper connection with his little boy. In subsequent therapy, he could introduce his neglected little one to his wife and request that she nurture him with a hug and kind word at least once a week. Willie promised not to cheat on his wife while they sorted through his past betrayals.

In his introduction at his last workshop, Willie admitted he had no idea how to be a parent to himself. Lacking healthy role models, he read books his therapist recommended but learned the most from listening to very specific requests from his little one. Little Willie told him about the kind of mom he dreamed of: one who would nurture him and smile with delight when she saw him, one who would surprise him with his favorite meals because she actually knew what he liked to eat, and one who would make sure Willie knew he was both lovable and loved. Willie was quite surprised that his little boy could construct such a clear image of the mother he wanted.

Little Willie also coached adult Willie on being a good dad, going beyond risqué jokes to actually playing sports and games with him, asking him questions about how his day went, and bragging about his uniqueness rather than making fun of him. Willie apologized to his little one for forgetting to check in with him after previous workshops, noting that he was busy and preoccupied just like his father. In return the forgiveness and encouragement Willie received from his little boy moved him.

During a second mat session, Willie met his adolescent. Initially suspicious and outwardly angry, the adolescent didn't want to be dealt with. He was furious at being accused of acting out. On the mat, the adolescent's anger was rapidly directed at his mom for ignoring him and at his dad for eyeing the girlfriends he brought home and trying to take center stage with off-color jokes. He continued to blast his parents for their lack of attention. "At least my girlfriends wanted to be with me. Tears poured out of the angry, rebellious teenager. Without any prompting, Willie reached for the pillow and rocked his lonely and confused adolescent.

In his conversation with the internal adolescent, Willie expressed his gratitude for the young women who gave the boy the nurturing and attention he'd always wanted. Willie told him it was natural to enjoy the sight of a beautiful woman but no longer appropriate to use women to try to fill the emptiness of his childhood or to feel powerful and important. Willie then told me about this handsome young man, who also was creative, artistic, thoughtful, and courageous. For the first time, his adolescent listened to an adult praise him for who he was as opposed to who he was supposed to be.

As part of their conversation, Willie asked his adolescent whether he loved Julie and wanted to stay with her. "Sometimes I want to leave, especially when she seems angry or pushes me away. But I am learning that Julie does that because of how she was raised. Besides, she is really trying hard. I know that she loves me."

As Willie learned to provide a new internal father and mother for himself, the urge to chase other women became more manageable. When he felt the old feelings stir, Willie spent more time with his adolescent, giving him a chance to express his frustration and hurt. As a result, Julie took less and less of the blame for these old feelings, and Willie could thank Julie for mothering his little ones. As Julie felt less of the adolescent anger directed at her, she felt safer and softer as well.

The last mat session developed into a very important three-way conversation that included the scared, lonely little boy; the adolescent; and the grown-up Willie. It began with mutual condemnation.

Little one to adolescent: "You're causing all the trouble with Julie, getting her upset just like you did with Mom and Dad. If you keep going after other women, Julie is going to leave."

Adolescent to little one: "You were the Goody-Two-shoes, sniveling in the bedroom, waiting for Mom to come. What good did it get you? Nothing! If no one pays attention to me, I'm going to find someone who will, and to hell with the consequences. At least I'm not a wimp."

Little one: "You're right. I am scared and weak. I wanted someone to love me and care about me. I tried to be as good as I could, and it didn't help. We both wanted the same thing. We just tried to get it in different ways. At least you got some attention. They ignored me, and you made them mad. You're braver and stronger than I am."

Adolescent: "I just look braver on the outside. You tried really hard, but Mom was never going to care about us, and Dad was clueless. Besides, the girls I dated really liked you more than they liked me. They saw how sweet and gentle you are, and they didn't want to be around me when I started to get mad like I did with Mom and Dad. The same thing happens with Julie."

Adult Willie: "I am so proud of both of you, how wise you both are. You've taught me so much today. I also see how much you both needed attention and tenderness, and tried to get it the best way you knew how. It's up to me now. I'll do my best to find you when you feel lonely and to protect you from hurting yourself—and Julie, I promise I will try to do better. Kick me in the butt when I forget."

Amazed by the insights and compassion his little ones revealed to him, Willie had stopped condemning himself. His self-respect blossomed. The interaction between adult and child voices was mutually beneficial. He learned how to be a better parent to himself and his sons, a better spouse to Julie; and perhaps most importantly, he began to appreciate untapped wisdom that was hibernating within.

With reconciliation of the voices inside came a huge reduction in shame. Willie could talk about his inner process with Julie and some close friends. Over time, Julie began to trust and admire this new man she was meeting. Willie later wrote to tell me he was sponsoring other men in his twelve-step program for sex and love addiction because he wanted to pass on his gifts.

We look in the mirror and swear, "I won't be like them (Mom or Dad)." We might even treat our friends and our kids the way we want to be treated. But in the end it is ironic that we continue to abandon the most tender and fragile parts of ourselves just as our parents did. From a sense of unworthiness, we deny ourselves the care and attention we readily offer others.

Children who are condemned may act out to confirm what their parents accuse them of being. I've heard more than one woman confess that after their fathers called them "sluts," they abandoned themselves and with enraged resignation went about proving them right. We prostitute ourselves for love or a morsel of attention because even negative attention is better than none.

We may have an inkling of the feelings we have stuffed, but ironically, years of compression have made them too powerful to own. At every workshop, I hear phrases such as "I'm not going to go there," "I won't open Pandora's box," "If I start crying, I'll never stop," "If I really let loose, I could kill someone," or "If I start to scream, they'll put me in a straightjacket." So we keep doing what we originally did, but it takes more and more energy to keep a lid on Pandora's box. As we accumulate more loss and stress, our intense feelings have a life of their own, overflowing at inopportune times.

Parents are supposed to teach their kids that everyone has strong feelings when they are hurt, and the intensity of those feelings doesn't give us permission or special authority to act on them. When siblings fight, healthy parents listen and validate both realities in the disagreement. At the same time, they prevent infliction of physical injury. Children learn to express their feelings safely without retaliation and see that the storm will pass. They learn to fight fair.

We may deny that anything is bothering us and judge others for being dramatic and too sensitive. We rise above our feelings—until we are triggered. Then the unexpected intensity of our compressed emotions gives them added and misguided authority. I have every right to tell a patient off when he or she calls me during my dinner to tell me about his or her sore tongue; or to yell at my kid for being lazy, selfish, or ungrateful. I am justified in blasting my horn and screaming at a commuter who speeds up rather than lets me change lanes. When my self-righteous anger passes, I become my controlled, nonfeeling self. Since I'm not accountable for an enraged voice in me I haven't even met, I project my intense anger outward, validating that it is always *someone else* who causes me to feel the way I do.

All over the world, men and women react from triggered, intense, and suppressed feelings as if they are the truth. I believe these stuffed feelings of grief and anger are the source of misunderstanding, hatred, violence, and tit-for-tat revenge. Childhood trauma and neglect produce behaviors that confirm our childhood world view. We don't seek to look at the world through another's eyes because we have already condemned them. When our "enemies" respond in kind, their behavior proves they are just who we believe them to be. We take no responsibility for feeding the flames.

Our two granddaughters, Scout (age four) and Zoe (age two), are good buddies most of the time. But I've seen Zoe pull Scout's hair in frustration. Scout retaliates, acting out the jealousy of one displaced by a baby sister. If I protect Zoe, Scout's jealousy is confirmed in her eyes, and she acts out again. At this point, I may feel myself wanting to pull away, not rewarding negative behavior with more attention—a reaction that again confirms Scout's world view. It is up to me to find a way to break the spell, letting Scout know she is equally cherished and setting limits around the violence. It's a delicate dance. Even grandparenting can be hard!

Is the pattern so different between the Israelis and Palestinians? Each side blames the other, denies their reality, and insists that the character flaw in the other makes reconciliation impossible. Rockets sail from Gaza into Israeli settlements while Israelis usurp property on the West Bank or respond with greater force in Gaza. Each group labels itself the victim and the other the perpetrator, nearly fusing the two roles together. Continually confirming their own world view, they sanctimoniously dehumanize each other. Unfortunately, the Middle East has no healthy parent to intervene in the cycles of revenge that scar the many souls who commit violence on their brothers, no King Solomon to prevent the two sides from pulling the baby apart.

Without successful grieving, we remain armed and armored, either condemning ourselves or blaming and attacking others. Being right trumps (no pun intended) compassion and reconciliation, and the need for power eclipses the courage to break the spell. Reacting to the perceived thoughts and behavior of others, we are never really accountable for our own. It is always someone else's fault. We become what we originally hated, while self-righteousness blocks us from seeing it.

Unwanted children, desperately in need of loving attention, wait years in the hope that someone will rescue them from their prison of shame and neglect. Our inner children wait silently, sometimes for years, for this taste of unconditional acceptance. At our workshops, men and women repeatedly revisit the torment of their early lives until their adults finally take it in, accepting and honoring their childhood reality. Our left brains may try to deny our right-brain impressions of the past as false memories. Victims of childhood abuse and neglect, especially when the source of the abuse comes from those they love, often tell themselves that their memories are overly dramatic, that they are being too sensitive, and that the treatment really wasn't that bad. They repeat the same phrases they heard from grown-ups years ago. Other workshop participants resist sharing their stories because their pain doesn't compare. Yet they cannot deny that something brought them to the workshop.

I kept my inner work private for many years. I didn't walk around outside the workshop, carrying a stuffed animal that represented my inner child. I don't use inner child language in my daily commerce. I didn't accuse my parents of abusing me. I knew they did the best they could and that their experience of my childhood was different from mine. This was *my* work. What was most important wasn't vindication or retaliation but the private loving relationship I developed within myself.

At least once every workshop, someone will say, "I can't hit my mom. She is so frail. I don't want to hurt her." I explain that we use a phone book because one of the most important rules of the workshop is that we don't hurt anyone, including ourselves. This process has nothing to do with our parents anymore. This is about a personal relationship within ourselves.

Our little ones need to tell us and sometimes show us what it was like for them so they can hear us say, "Oh my God, no wonder you feel the way you do!" Suppose a three-year-old boy climbed onto a table and fell off, banging his head and shoulder on the wooden floor. Screaming in pain and fear, he awaits the arrival of a parent. When his mother arrives, he tells her what happened. Instead of showing him tenderness and concern, she tells him to stop crying and says he isn't hurt, that it wasn't that bad. Even at three, the child would internalize that there must be something wrong with him; he cried for no reason.

But suppose, desperate to be believed and consoled, he reenacted his injury and hurled himself off the table again and again until his mother finally rushed over to him and said, "I believe you. You don't have to hurt yourself anymore to convince me. I'll stay with you and keep you safe."

We would be horrified if a mother allowed her son to hurl himself off a table repeatedly. Yet men and women return to workshops to reexperience again and again the torment of childhood molestation, physical beatings, and emotional abuse. Occasionally, I have wondered why a repeater would allow his or her little one to reexperience the trauma more than once. Is it self-punishment? Is the little one getting needed attention by reliving painful events in front of compassionate witnesses?

It takes commitment and great endurance to slog through endless bouts of dysregulation to build an internal parent capable of holding volumes of pain and torment. Repeated triggering of rage, despair, and shame drain the vital life force necessary for repair. Some lack the discipline or support to build an internal parent. Discipline, hope, patience, and much support are essential.

I believe the main reason little ones must relive their pain is because it takes time for the left brain to take it in. Grief requires telling our story many times. With each telling, the truth of it penetrates our left brains more completely. Another way of saying this is that little ones put themselves through repeated anguish to teach the adult what happened to them and to hear the adult finally say, "I believe you. You don't ever have to jump off the table again."

My experience has been that when an adult accepts his or her own childhood reality (what actually occurred often cannot be verified and is ultimately less important), the child has no further need to go through the raw pain of the past. In fact, the adult protects the little one with tender attention. Additional pieces of past experience may need to be explored but usually with less pain and fear, especially when the intention is to make more sense of the adult's life and thus become more loving and available for the little one.

At some point, it's no longer about the perpetrators of our past. This isn't to say we should condone intrusive or neglectful behavior; nor should we forget about the past. Part of my present accountability to my little ones requires that I speak out about current injustice with clarity and humility.

When I'm accountable to my little ones, it's up to me to hear when they are in need and speak for them when they are too ashamed or scared to ask for help themselves. As a parent, I need to intervene so my driven six-year-old doesn't burn out. I need to reach out to the quiet, scared five-year-old who disappears so easily. I need to demonstrate to a tiny infant that he or she is worthy of loving, gentle holding. And I need to laughingly, lovingly acknowledge that my socially challenged adolescent is much more comfortable in very small groups because he has no idea how to do small talk and is envious of those who can. Each time I ask for assistance, my little ones feel how much I care and love them. In turn, they have the space to take risks they otherwise wouldn't. They know that even if the outside world rejects them, they always have me.

When I am accountable to them, they show up in my life. They are experts at spotting others in need, fear, anger, or despair. They have taught me to be present for others without having to fix them, and they also see the incredible humor in our shared humanity. When I'm mindful of the voices inside, my judge loses power. When he calls me stupid, I hear a chorus of voices ring out, "We know. Isn't it great?" Humanity and humility overshadow my perfectionism and arrogance.

My lifelong process has starts and stops. I lapse into bad habits of addictive behavior, ignore internal needs, become preoccupied with fear and self-doubt, and lash out or withdraw from those I love. The process is humbling. Fortunately, it gets easier to accept the help offered, make amends to those I hurt, including my little ones, and recommit to checking in with them regularly.

Soon after I began writing this book, I asked my little ones what they would need to feel I was accountable to them. They told me they wanted me to make them my priority, to make them a part of my spiritual life.

They requested that I check in with them morning and night, before we started our day and when we ended it. Over the years, I have established a ritual that works for us. This is my spiritual practice, my specific form of mindfulness and prayer. Clearly, there are many other paths and techniques to cultivate self-awareness.

When I check in with myself, I ask whether anyone inside has anything to say. (Of course, this is all nonverbal). I wait, scanning my feelings and finding images of various ages I can identify inside. If it has been a particularly stressful day, I may hear how an event has touched a part of me, perhaps triggering old anger, fear, or sadness. Often a little one will want to celebrate a special connection that happened during the day. Sometimes I will hear a voice just say he is sad, without any particular reason, and that he just wants me (and the other ages inside) to know it. Sometimes if I am aware of a particular event that upset or touched me, I might ask them to comment about it. When I am finished asking questions, I offer to answer any questions my little ones have. Sometimes they mimic me by repeating the same questions, letting me know I can be a bit of the grand inquisitor. Sometimes one of them will tell me to shut up and go to sleep because everyone is tired, and we're all good with each other. It tickles me to feel their sense of humor and general irreverence of this holy time with them.

Quite often we finish with prayers of gratitude for our wonderful and abundant life, for the incredible opportunity to be of service, and for our children and grandchildren. We end by asking each other whether we want to pray for someone in particular.

The discipline of this twice-daily ritual has helped me break the spell during stressful moments in my day. Even during exercise, I check in to see where everybody is. On some days, when I am doing an intense workout on a stationary bike, it's clear that my competitive six-year-old is pushing the limits of endurance. On those days, the others laugh and hop on for the ride. On other days, there may be a general protest, and so I back off. They rarely fight about who is in charge of any given workout. This is another way of listening to my body and staying within myself. I have gained much from being accountable to them.

It is only in the last year that my little ones have let me know the depth of their fears. They continue to expose another layer of my psyche to me as their trust in my constancy and my commitment to our spiritual practice deepens. It is such a relief to be able to begin to put down my fear of being afraid and simply accept how scared I was and could be in the future.

Accountability *to* my little ones is only one part of my internal dialogue. I must also be accountable *for* them. I need to set healthy limits when they act out. I cannot use my little ones as an excuse to slack off, ignore my responsibilities, lash out at someone because I am tired or in a foul mood, move into self-righteous judgment, or look for attention in the wrong places. I cannot justify hurting others because I have been hurt. Now that I know what triggers them, I am accountable *for* their distorted emotions and various roles in the triangle (see appendices). It's on me. When I make a mistake or am triggered, it's on me to clean things up. This is what makes me a trustworthy man.

Being accountable for my little ones isn't about perfection. Rather, it's about honesty and humility. The more I have compassion for myself, the easier it is to own and protect others from my craziness. It's about checking in, choosing the higher path, and making amends when I've made a wrong choice or when my behavior has been discordant with my values. Then it's about checking in again, acknowledging the pain behind my misbehavior, and asking my little one what he thinks we should do to correct things. The solutions my little ones come up with are uncanny once they have had a chance to express their pain without condemnation. Once we have a plan, they hold me accountable for its implementation. The buck stops with me.

I am a work in progress. With each passing stage in life, new issues arise that I haven't faced before. I get triggered when I'm out of my comfort zone. This means my little ones and I must see how the past is now impacting these new life situations. Anne and I know, without a shadow of doubt, that we will be revisiting old wounds, learning more about ourselves, and experiencing fresh moments of humility and forgiveness as we negotiate retirement. We will share our feelings, protect and nurture each other's little ones, and hold each other accountable.

Ah, life.

Boundaries

When I am accountable **to** myself, I am able to establish boundaries that protect me from unwanted interactions. Taking the time to listen to my inner voices, I hear when they are frightened, annoyed, or overwhelmed. I will naturally want to make it safe for them. In saying no to unwanted requests, I am saying yes to myself. As I learn to set firm and gentle limits, I realize that I do not have to run or hide from relationships because I have a say in the pace and degree of intimacy that I have with another person. My ability to stand firm, and to speak my truth in contentious moments emboldens me to stay in relationships because I am capable of protecting myself.

Being capable of setting firm, but gentle, limits means that I must have a healthy relationship with my anger. If I am afraid that I could kill someone if I lost control, I will be less able to speak my truth for fear it will pour out of me like the rounds of a sub-machine gun. When I recognize when I am triggered, and give myself the space to acknowledge old anger, I will trust myself not to dump past resentments onto current interactions.

On the other hand, when I am accountable **for** myself, I am less likely to become invasive of others. When I take the time to listen to my own grief, I am more likely to be present for the pain of others, without needing to interrupt their time of need by blurting out my tale of woe. I do not want my grief to spill out while I am supporting the son of a hospice patient whose mother is dying. I am able to hold the pain of others because I regularly give myself a turn to share my grief.

Similarly, I am able to set boundaries for my needy little one by giving him time on a regular basis. In receiving from me the attention that he craved, he is more likely to give others their turn to be in the spotlight. He does not have to monopolize conversations or blow his own horn. Learning to give others a turn, I stop driving others away. I am less lonely and therefore less needy. His lifelong worldview, that he is not loveable, begins to shift. No one but me (healthy adult) can fill the bottomless hole of childhood neediness for this shift to occur.

Being entitled to have my own space does not give me the right to terrify others. In giving myself a safe place to externalize pent-up anger, I then have the right and responsibility to set limits on the part of myself who wants to hurt others the way he was hurt. Domination, or isolation, is not the same as having healthy boundaries.

Chapter 14

FORGIVENESS AND RECONCILIATION

Genuine forgiveness does not deny anger but faces it head-on.
—Alice Miller

*The weak can never forgive. Forgiveness is the attribute of the strong.
An eye for eye only ends up making the whole world blind.*
—Gandhi

We are taught to forgive. Our left brains, the adult voice of logic and reason, have read the scriptures, believe forgiveness is the right thing to do, and make the decision. But sometimes when we come into contact with the person we have decided to forgive, old feelings get stirred, a painful memory is rekindled, and forgiveness flies out the window. We lash out in frustration or respond with self-righteous indignation. Our best intentions dissolve into acrimony. When we regain our composure, we chastise ourselves, either for failing to do the righteous thing or for being stupid enough to even consider forgiving such a jerk. Clearly despite best intentions, a part of us isn't ready to forgive. For me, this usually means adult Larry has made a unilateral decision without consulting my inner voices.

As I mentioned in earlier chapters, I had unfinished business with my dad, an amazingly brilliant yet narcissistic man. When my parents lived in Delaware or Santa Barbara, visits were relatively brief and infrequent. I was happy to spend time listening to Dad recount old stories and ask him about his daily life. I enjoyed hearing him speak about how he helped some younger people with his or her businesses. He would beam as he told us how happy and grateful the owners had been for his skillful help. Despite his narcissism, Dad made a significant difference in the lives of several entrepreneurs. The assistance he provided to relative strangers while in his late seventies was mutually beneficial.

I have discovered in my hospice work that old age invites narcissism. Our world narrows as we focus on uncooperative bowels, leaking bladders, diminished sensory organs, loss of mobility and energy, and chronic pain. Predictably, my dad's narcissism escalated as he aged, resulting in it becoming a bigger trigger for me.

Knowing they would soon need our help, Mom and Dad moved from California to Tucson in the 1990s. In 2004, when Dad reached ninety, we had to take his car away. We compensated for this loss of independence and their isolation by bringing dinner two to three times a week. With Dad's frailty, I became an extension of his mind rather than someone who was going out of my way to help him. When I stopped by on my way home from the hospital—even before I could say, "Hi, how are you?"—Dad's greeting would be something like "I need a new toothbrush and dental floss, and the toilet is dripping again." For the last four years of his life, I was his right arm, handyman, and part-time shopper.

Dad wasn't introspective. It never occurred to him to inquire about my internal life. I cannot remember him asking a probing question such as, "Hi, how are you? You look a bit pre-occupied today. Why did you stop your lucrative medical practice to work with that Kübler-Ross woman?"

Of course, the hospice physician understood the dynamics of my father's frustration with progressive dependency and his need to feel in control, but my little ones were constantly being triggered as the frequency of our interactions increased. It was one thing to see Dad three times a year, but three times a week pushed the limits of their old resentments and sad regret.

After 9/11, my reactivity with Dad escalated. A black-and-white thinker, Dad went on and on about "bombing them back into the tenth century." I was already beside myself with the Bush administration's response to the terrorist attacks and his invasion of Iraq. I might as well have eaten dinner with Secretary Rumsfeld or Vice President Cheney three times a week. All I could do was keep my head in my food and shove it down quickly so I could have an excuse to leave the table and start the dishes. Occasionally, I even blew my stack at a ninety-year-old man who showed all the signs of early senility.

As a young boy, I spent hours listening to Dad and his friends discuss business and politics. Dad's ability to wade through complex issues and find a simple answer always amazed me. But by the time I was in high school, I began to realize my assumptions about the nature of man were very different from those of my father. I kept my opinions to myself. There was no winning an argument with Dad.

My younger brother, Artie, who was as equally brilliant as Dad, took the opposite approach and went into open battle. Dad loved Artie and couldn't understand how he could throw away his life. Artie didn't complete the last semester of college. He drove Dad crazy when he refused to take jobs he considered tedious and uninteresting.

Artie was bulimic. He spent his days preparing, consuming, and regurgitating his food. Well ahead of his time, he became an expert in sprouting seeds and eating organic, raw foods. Living with my parents in their home in Delaware, he occupied every kitchen counter for most of the day. He constantly tried to convince Dad to eat a healthier diet. Dad volleyed with advice about making money and being a productive member of society. Love oscillated with disdain, as did cogent advice with personal attacks. Mom was between these two men whom she loved.

It was painful watching three members of my precious family trapped in misery. I tried to persuade (even force) Mom and Dad to give Art a car and enough money to leave so only one of the three would be trapped in bulimia and daily fighting.

After Artie finally left home, it took time for Mom and Dad to reestablish their relationship. Once they decided to leave the Delaware winters for sunny Santa Barbara, things were better. Artie would drive up from Venice to see them, but the visits were brief, usually ending when either Art or Dad couldn't maintain the truce. Dad could never understand why his profligate son wouldn't listen to his good advice. In 1989, Artie died of a drug overdose while experimenting with ways to have a spiritual near-death experience.

After Art died, Mom received many letters from friends who described what a kind, loving, and insightful person he had been. He had the gift of sight. He could disarm strangers and friends by seeing through their masks and encouraging them to be their best self. Ironically, Artie enjoyed helping others in the same way our father did.

Even though I was leading workshops, doing my mat work, and developing relationships with my younger selves, I would forget to use the tools I was teaching others with my declining father. I think it's always hardest to find clarity with those closest to us. I began to invite my little ones to tell me how they felt when they were triggered. All I could do was listen because I didn't know how to fix it for them. Sometimes just being heard helped them better tolerate the behaviors that set them off, but it wouldn't last. So I began asking them whether they wanted to come into the house with me as I pulled into my parents' driveway. Sometimes they declined to be part of the visit, and my adult made this visit without them.

Just having this conscious conversation would reduce my inner turmoil. Clearly, I didn't chop off an arm or leg, or leave part of an organ in the driveway, any more than I could leave a real little boy outside. Their refusal to be part of my visit was a symbolic, imaginative, psychic event. It served to shore up my adult self, reducing the mind chatter and frustration that often occurred if I didn't check in with myself ahead of time. I found that I could meet Dad on his terms, engage in whatever conversation he chose, and leave with my to-do list. Sometimes I could feel the old resentments stir, as if my little ones were saying, *If you don't leave soon, we're going to reappear.* Mostly, I felt better for being the son I wanted to be. Dad enjoyed my visits more because I could give him the attention he wanted. It was a win-win.

As Dad deteriorated with congestive heart failure and cognitive decline, I could feel my ambivalence about his impending death. At ninety-four, he had no quality of life. It was time for him to go, but Dad was a fighter. He never once talked about his dying, just about what he could do to get stronger. In the meantime, I was ready to be free of my burden of care.

Four years earlier, at his ninetieth birthday party, I prepared what I felt would be his eulogy. I wanted him to hear that I saw him and honored his intentions and achievements to be a good dad and provider. I spoke about Dad's exceptional intellect despite his limited education, his brilliance as a synthesizer of complex ideas, his uncanny skill as a salesman and merchandizer, and his generosity. I made some humorous remarks about his idiosyncrasies, which everyone recognized as classic Ben Lincoln. I thanked Dad for all he gave me, including my formal, and especially my informal, kitchen table education. I told him I loved him and toasted his ninety years: I was an adult son toasting his adult father. Only once during the eulogy did childhood tears interrupt what I had to say, but I quickly swallowed them. I said my good-bye in front of a crowd of family and well-wishers. Looking back, I think I knew a private good-bye would be much more difficult.

As Dad neared his death, my brother Steve came to town to say good-bye. It was touching to see the pureness of his grief. For Steve, Dad was as good a father as any boy could want. They were a good fit. I was happy for Steve and sad for me because my little ones were so conflicted.

On the day I believed would be Dad's last day of consciousness and my last day to say good-bye, I debated whether I should ask my little ones whether they wanted to come. Even without my asking, I could feel the shake of my head. As I walked into Dad's room, I felt them disappear into the shadows, and I went numb. I recognized this as the old numbness I felt in much of my college, medical school, residency, and early years in private practice.

When Steve told our unconscious father that he was the best dad in the world and then kissed Dad on the forehead, I saw a glimmer of response from deep within the shell that was our father. Even in his unresponsive state, I believed Dad took in the gift my brother gave him.

Later, I returned to Dad's side to thank him for his many gifts. I told him I loved him, even as I felt the vacated place inside me where my little ones reside. I kissed Dad on the forehead, but there was no response. Despite my experiences in hospice and my ability to connect deeply with my own children, I was unable to communicate with my dad, right brain to right brain, heart to heart.

It was an adult who thanked his father and told him he loved him. It was also an adult who felt the grief for all the missed opportunities to connect the way I needed and wanted. I had to choose between my inner child and my dear dad, and I chose my little ones. They weren't ready to experience the grief for the emotional mismatch with my Dad. In his last days, I gained a deeper appreciation for the richness of my relationship with Matt and Rachael.

I still feel sad that I wasn't able to have "the conversation," when Dad heard my need to be seen for who I was and not whom he projected me to be. I felt this wasn't part of Dad's emotional repertoire, especially in his frail state. It wasn't Dad's fault. Nor did I expect Dad to somehow change who he was. If we were to have "the conversation," it would have been up to me to initiate it while he still had all his faculties.

Many of our workshop participants have confirmed that children hold on to the hope well into adulthood that they will someday get what they want from their parents. Many times they make attempts to ask for what they need, only to be retraumatized by parents who feel insulted or minimize the request. Sometimes what might start off as an adult conversation deteriorates into an injured little one either accusing or begging his or her parent. What was hoped to be "the conversation" retraumatizes the inner child by once again identifying him or her as the problem. Therefore, we recommend that vulnerable little ones shouldn't be the ones to have such a conversation. Instead, a strong inner adult, who has learned to love and protect his or her inner children should be the one to speak for them. Ironically, once we have created the voice of this healthy inner parent, our little ones have less need to obtain what they wanted from their biological parents and are more able to accept them for who they are.

With Dad I didn't force my little ones to say their good-bye. Instead, I honored their process, choosing their emotional decision over my hope for some further resolution of their pain. I allowed them to experience their lingering resentment and sadness, and then later to face any regret for not telling one of the most important people in their lives how much they loved him. My little ones retreated, went numb, and I simply didn't push them.

As to forgiving my dad, it has taken time. Occasionally, nonstop talkers trigger me, but I notice my reaction has lessened over the years. Without much prompting, I recognize quickly that it's my Dad stuff again. What has made the biggest difference is my awareness that I'm not so different from my father. My little ones also crave approval and recognition, and occasionally want to climb on their own soapbox. (Yes, my long-winded book.) As I continue to accept my own internal narcissism, my little ones laughingly forgive my dear dad.

My little ones prod me to write that they hope Dad and I will have at least one more reunion. They want to tell Dad's little ones that they are sorry he was also neglected and hurt. They want to tell Dad's needy little boy that they couldn't give him the praise and recognition he so desperately wanted because they were ashamed of their own neediness. I want to tell Dad how proud I am that he achieved all he did with such little guidance and education, and how my tenacity, drive, and competence come largely from him.

I look forward to greeting my father on the other side and laughing with him about the dance we shared. I want to tell Dad that I think it's hilarious that he had so much to do with making me such a touchy-feely man, when what he most wanted was for me to become a titan of commerce. If there is to be this "great meeting in the sky," I expect that Artie will accompany Dad. We will wrap our arms around each other, kiss each other on the cheeks, and laugh until tears of joy flood our faces.

My little ones didn't tell me to write that our dad would finally acknowledge who they are. It must no longer be necessary to them—another sign of forgiveness.

Forgiveness is an organic process, not simply a decision a guilty or even a pious adult makes. When it comes from a place deep inside, where both the vulnerable and perpetrator reside, forgiveness can be a gift of grace. I believe forgiveness begins with the self, from the committed ongoing relationship, which is an examined life.

Forgiveness is a two-way street, between the adult and internal, younger voices. My little ones have gradually forgiven me for treating them just as my parents did, banishing them years ago to survive. I am learning to love and accept them for who they are and not what I wanted them to be. With each level of forgiveness, I become less judgmental and self-righteous. (Oops, as I write these words, one of my little one is muttering, "If judgment and self-righteousness are the measure, you've got a ways to go!") No cures, just a lifelong process.

I find it helpful to remember Elisabeth's fifteen-second rule. It remains my best diagnostic clue that my little ones still have a beef with someone. When I'm accountable, I check in and hear their resentments and pain. My little ones don't want me to lecture them about forgiveness. They will come to it in their own time. If I rush them, I hear something like, *Go ahead, tell the jerk that you have forgiven him, but he'll see that you're just as much a phony as we think he is.* Before I can forgive and reconcile with others, reconciliation must first occur within me.

"Forgive and forget," the saying goes, but forgetting isn't the same as forgiving. Our bodies remember, even if our minds don't. Forgetting requires that I run from anything that triggers the past. We have ample proof in the many centuries-old ethnic conflicts that little ones don't forget. I can temporarily put my pain out of my mind, but I pay a price by going numb. To avoid my feelings, my denial requires that I either minimize or try to fix the misery of others.

If I just don't think about it, events pile up until there are too many things I'm not thinking about. I try to stay positive until I reach overload. Then I will likely explode or disappear into simmering resentment. Avoiding meaningful conversations, I become as unavailable to others as I am to myself. Running from the voices that will not, do not, forget, I once again treat my little ones as they were treated. Once again, they lose trust in me.

It's easy to feel compassion for the victims of violence and betrayal. To have compassion for the perpetrator, I must first recognize and have compassion for the Hitler inside me. When I experienced on the mat the murderous rage I felt for the boys who smothered Teddy, I recognized a little one who fantasized vengeance and could do harm to others. Each time I feel a surge of righteousness when a movie hero takes revenge on the bad guys, I know I'm also capable of righteous murder. In experiencing compassion for my little enforcer, I have developed greater understanding and compassion for the perpetrator in others.

My inner vigilante would like to believe he can destroy the bad guys and rid the world of demons once and for all, but Hitler lurks in each of us. I believe this knowledge is the true source of forgiveness. It doesn't necessarily mean I will become fond of the person I have forgiven, but it does mean I have compassion for their injured little ones and for the story behind their rigidity, disconnection and aggression.

Compassion also requires that I set limits on harmful behavior. Although I cannot help having vengeful feelings, I must take a time-out, recognize their source, and choose not to act. And if I do react, I take responsibility for my behavior and make amends. Similarly, I must speak out against injustice and needless violence of others with the same humility and gentle firmness. As I set limits on my little ones, protecting them from hurting themselves as well as others, I must do the same for the little ones of my enemies. Even going to war must be an act of compassion, not to crush the evil one but to protect him from harming others the way I would myself.

I can show respect for differences in personal reality while still protecting myself. Each time we speak with compassion and respect to the little ones within our enemies, we create a moment of mutual humanity and understanding that may enable a small step toward reconciliation.

The Bible says, "Love thy neighbor as thyself," not more or less than thyself. For years, I considered myself a failure because I couldn't love my neighbor adequately. All the while, the problem was in the "as thyself" portion of the commandment. I now have a glimpse of how profound and transformative loving my neighbor can be as I continue to build this relationship within myself.

Many of us experience the tension of competing needs, desires, taboos, expectations, and longings: work and play, family and outside interests, solitude and public life, honesty and approval seeking, avarice, altruism, fidelity and the lure of the chase, starvation and gluttony, sexual expression and repression, sobriety and addiction, trust and suspicion, faith and cynicism. When we are unaware of the source of these competing voices, we move back and forth from one urge to the other. Competing little ones, each temporarily pushing the other out of the way, take control of our impulses.

We hear about a politician who publicly decries homosexuality, only to be exposed for traveling with a young male companion and wonder how on earth this hypocrisy could occur. We become unhappy when the workday goes on and on, eating into precious family time, only to be preoccupied and anxious when we return home to our loved ones. We awaken to a new day determined to eat healthy food or stay sober; and then, as if an alien invades us, we resume binging or drinking again. Who is running this show?

We can be bystanders in our own lives, unable to regulate our tug-of-war because there is no effective mediator between our competing little ones. In our shame, we continue to justify behaviors and addictions we cannot reconcile with our values and vision of ourselves. Without compassion for an injured little one who learned unhealthy coping behaviors to compensate for his pain, we lack the internal, steady voice of a healthy parent needed to protect him or her from himself or herself and others. We look and dress like grown-ups but react and behave like orphaned children faking it in the big, bad world.

My little ones either disappear or run the show when I don't give them my attention, either dimming my internal light or dragging me around in all their fear and frustration, leaving a trail of psychic debris in their wake. They don't want me to be frightened or condemning of their intense feelings, and they wish me to be able to set healthy limits for them. Internal reconciliation isn't about changing our little ones, because it's too late for that. What happened in our younger life has already happened. Besides, they don't need changing. They need a healthy parent to love, protect, and regulate them.

I don't believe we can have reconciliation in the larger world if we don't have the skills to accomplish it in ourselves. How can we expect Arabs and Jews to create a container for reconciliation when they are unwilling to hear and respect others' reality, especially their fears and vulnerabilities? What will it take for Americans to be willing to walk in each other's shoes? Not until we as a nation accept and confront our own fears, shame, projected rage, and mutual disdain, will we finally stop speaking about "those other people" as if they aren't part of America? I believe only then will we really know we are all in this together and comprehend that how we treat both the least and most fortunate of us defines who we are as a society.

I don't believe inner work is simply a luxury for the self-absorbed. Rather, it's the essential work that will lead to mutual understanding and cooperation, even among those who disagree. Major American congressional legislation is being created with complete exclusion of the minority party, only to be repealed or gutted when the other party wins a majority. We should demand more from our representatives.

In the Middle East, I believe it will be necessary and useful to separate listening from expectations of action and redress. Empathy, trust, and mutual respect must begin with the willingness to walk in the shoes of the other person. Reconciliation begins with psychic disarmament, the risk to be vulnerable, and the humility to let go of mutual disdain. (I always hoped Elisabeth could do one big geopolitical "verkshop.")

As Elisabeth used to say as she shooed everyone out the door at the end of each workshop, "Now go contaminate the world with your love."

Chapter 15
LETTING THE LOVE IN

> *People are like stained-glass windows. They sparkle and shine when the sun is out, but when the darkness sets in, their true beauty is revealed only if there is a light from within.*
> —Elisabeth Kübler-Ross

In my twenty-five years as a hospice physician, it has been a privilege to accompany my patients on their final earth journey. Occasionally, I have been honored to serve colleagues and friends. About two years ago, a former coworker and friend requested that I see her to discuss hospice.

Natalie's Dying Lesson

Natalie was an exceptional nurse I met on a medical-surgical unit more than twenty years ago. She was compulsive, competent, and caring, going out of her way for her patients and the attending docs. I loved working with Natalie, because I knew she gave me excellent medical and psychosocial updates on our patients. In addition to her role as nurse, she had a wonderful relationship with her spouse and was a great mom to her two children.

Despite Natalie's competence, she was always a bit nervous. Perhaps in protection mode, she constantly acted as if someone were about to criticize or yell at her. I never felt Natalie fully appreciated what an asset she was to the hospital or the gift she was to her patients. She was always quick to praise me, but when I returned the compliment, she turned it around.

Natalie left hospital nursing to do home care, and we lost track of each other for about ten years. When I heard through the grapevine that she was diagnosed with stage-four colon cancer, I called to wish her well. We kept in touch off and on during the next three years of her treatments, which included high-dose systemic chemotherapy, a surgical resection of lung lesions, and direct intra-arterial chemotherapy to the liver.

Natalie never wavered on her desire to survive. Only in her midfifties, she wanted to see her new grandbaby grow up. By the time it became clear chemotherapy had run its course, Natalie's energy reserve was nearly depleted. She was losing weight, suffering from bouts of nausea and vomiting, and retaining massive amounts of fluid due to her failing liver. Her husband continued to focus on the next experimental treatment. When Natalie was finally hospitalized because of her unremitting symptoms, I stopped by to see her.

After a quick hug, she burst into tears and said she just couldn't do it anymore. Natalie said she was scared of dying and especially of having horrible pain. We talked about what hospice could offer and how it might help with the worst of her symptoms. I'm not sure she believed me, but she asked me to convince her husband.

I made the call and began the process of preparing him for a mental shift from aggressive treatment to comfort care. He wasn't ready. On the following morning, Natalie looked miserable. Her medications were only moderately effective.

I kissed her on the cheek and said, "It's time for your beautiful soul to leave this useless body of yours." When she looked up, I added, "And you do have a beautiful, kind, and gentle soul."

Even in her last days, Natalie had to turn things around. "Not nearly as beautiful as yours. You've helped so many people."

I shook my head. "Don't change the subject. You've been changing the subject your whole life."

Natalie looked up, nodded, and said, "You're right." And with tears, she added, "They took my self-esteem from me." With no energy to revisit old wounds, that was all she spoke about her childhood. I moved on.

I suggested that she had one last task to do while she remained conscious and still had the energy. It was to say good-bye to her husband and children one at a time, making sure they each knew how important they were to her. I warned her that she would cry and might find it hard to speak the words, but she should push through the grief and do it. Her good-bye would also help to shift the family from aggressive to palliative care.

Then I challenged her to let in the loving words (not only as a wife and mother but also as the little girl who was never seen or praised for who she was) that her children and husband would tell her in return. Natalie closed her eyes and became very still, the most peaceful I had ever seen her. It was as if her little one would finally allow herself to believe the words she longed to hear. When Natalie opened her eyes, she surprised me by saying, "I'm going to start with you."

As she began to tell me what I meant to her as a doctor and friend, I could feel myself wanting her to hurry up so I could tell her who she was to me. I was now doing just what I had chastised Natalie about: I was trying to change the subject. Of course, I had very good reasons why Natalie should stop talking about me. She was dying. She was more important. I could hear the stuff she was saying about me some other time. Besides, Natalie was just being her predictably kind self. My mind was so busy that I barely listened. Despite more than twenty-five years of mat work, workshops, and inner dialogue, I still couldn't sit quietly while a colleague and friend told me, for the last time, what I meant to her.

Why was it so hard to let the love in?

The most obvious reason was that I still didn't believe I was worthy. As Natalie continued, I was aware of lingering shame that prevented me from taking in the wonderful gift she was offering. My little one wanted it so much, but I looked away, condemning myself for yearning to hear the words all children want to hear.

I put that needy little boy under wraps years ago, using false humility to deflect the very words of praise he worked so hard to hear. I didn't allow him to enjoy the gratitude or admiration of others simply because he wanted it so much. The more I punished him, the greater his need, and the more he manipulated to hear it. The last thing I wanted to be accused of was being a braggart. I was still taking revenge on a meek little guy who just wanted some appreciation for being alive. I gave him very little room to move, even as he heard me tell Natalie she should let the love in.

I flashed back to my graduation from Amherst College and Columbia Medical School. I had left college after three years, having been accepted at Columbia. I had requested that Amherst accept my first year of med school as college credit so I would obtain my college diploma. After bringing my request to the entire faculty, Amherst said I could graduate with my class if I completed a final exam in evolution, the remaining prerequisite course of my biology major.

After finals at Columbia, I drove to the college, reviewed the class notes of a friend, and passed the evolution final. Mom and Dad, I later learned, had waited to hear from me, hoping to drive from Delaware to Massachusetts for the ceremony. I delayed calling until the night before, downplaying the event. I got my diploma but without any fanfare. There was no reason for them to attend. I didn't want anyone to make a fuss over me. Four years later, I would find a way to miss graduation at Columbia as well. After all, there was my internship to worry about. My self-deprecation was the flip side of my inherited narcissism.

When Natalie finished saying her good-bye, it was finally my turn. She had taken my challenge to heart. She let herself soak up all I had to say to her. She kept her eyes on me, ignoring the tears of gratitude streaming down her cheeks. She giggled at some of my memories of her on the hospital ward, when we were both young kids in our profession.

In her final days as an adult, Natalie plugged her childhood leak. She proceeded to say good-bye to her loved ones and to take in what she meant to them. Her children commented that they had never seen their mom so alive as in those last days.

Natalie was unaware of her final gift to me. In her last days, she showed me what surrendering to love would look like—and that it was time to take some of my own medicine. Would I, too, have to be dying to surrender to the love all around me?

During my daily check-ins, I began to inquire of my younger voices what they each longed to hear. Their answers were initially vague and perhaps cautious. Maybe they couldn't let themselves feel the grief for what they never had, deal with the shame for wanting it, and overcome their persistent unworthiness. Maybe they didn't yet trust their lifelong harshest critic. At any rate, I couldn't get them to answer my question. Instead, my mind kept drifting away to a current pressing need or worry. I was getting nowhere. When I reverted to lecturing them that wanting love, recognition, approval, and even a standing ovation are universal human desires, I could tell they were humoring me. I talked the talk ... Maybe Natalie would buy those platitudes—but they weren't so gullible. They knew me a lot better than Natalie did. I had to try a different tack.

I remembered Elisabeth's fifteen-second rule, that if you react longer (symbolically) than fifteen seconds, the event or topic is triggering old issues. Mostly, Elisabeth was talking about anger or perhaps sadness and fear. Maybe the fifteen-second rule also applied to love, joy, triumph, and gratitude. I wanted to know whether these powerfully positive feelings were triggering my little ones. I changed my question, asking whether they would let me know when they saw an example of a loving or triumphant moment that touched them deeply. It could be in real life or even in a book or movie. It didn't matter. They seemed more willing to communicate with me in this indirect way. My request turned out to come at the perfect time because I was about to witness what every infant would hope to experience.

Anne had nursed Rachael well past her first birthday. We added food very carefully to her diet because her older brother, Matt, had had serious, life-threatening reactions to eggs and dairy. We also had avoided feeding the kids sweets and junk food during their first few years. For Rachael's second birthday party, Anne decided to give her a taste of ice cream. I was sitting directly across the table from Rachael while we lit the candles and serenaded her with "Happy birthday." With the first mouthful of ice cream, her eyes opened wide, and her face tilted toward the heavens, as if to say, *Ah, so this is why I incarnated!*

Although Rachael remained a relatively picky eater, she always had room for sweets. Later, when she declared she was full after eating just a few bites of dinner, she would solemnly explain, "I have a separate stomach for dessert."

I tell you this story because, when she held her son, Henry, in those first hours, our daughter once again looked to the heavens, this time with awe and gratitude. Henry is more than three now, but I still remember the first time I registered the meaning of Rachael's greeting to him. I volunteered to watch Henry while Rachael and Anne ducked out to run a few errands. They weren't gone long. However, upon their return, I witnessed a look of pure delight that Rachael beamed down at her son, as if she hadn't seen him for weeks. Her greeting held no false-mother self, no contrivance, not a hint of a rehearsed best guess at how a loving mother should greet her child and no look of scrutiny that Henry had to meet some unspoken expectation.

Somewhere deep inside me, a primordial infant whispered, "That's it. That's what I wanted." Later, during my nightly check-in with myself, I tried to recall a memory of such a feeling or look from my mom, but it wasn't there until I was much older. I had a sense that maybe Grandmom had offered me such a greeting, but even she hid her feelings behind a wall of prior loss, fatigue, and resignation to a hard life that tempered her joy.

As a grown man, I have no doubt my mother loved her three boys ferociously. I also can understand that living in her in-laws' home, dealing with a jealous sister-in-law, and worrying when her hustler husband would make enough money for her to feel secure weren't the most conducive conditions to enjoy her second son. My orphaned mom was a worrier. She had every right to be, but the greeting of a worrier has a different look than what Henry saw that day.

Our grandchildren are fortunate to have such devoted parents. I am also grateful to my daughter for inadvertently teaching me what I needed to give myself. When the image of my internal infant comes to me during my twice-daily devotion, I now offer him the same welcome Rachael continues to give Henry.

Although I believe I had shown similar delight when I greeted my grandchildren, I hadn't internalized it for myself until I heard my internal infant say, "That's it. That's what I want." It is ironic that we give so easily to others what we unconsciously deny ourselves.

With gentle questioning, my little ones elaborate on why they are touched by tender or triumphant moments. They also let me know specifically what words they want to hear from me. My timid five-year-old wants to believe his allergies, clumsiness, and meekness have been a gift because they gave him empathy and compassion for others who struggle. He also wants to hear that I see beyond his deficits and love him for the kind, gentle, earnest, and joyful soul he is.

My determined six-year-old needs to believe he can compete with the best of them, that he is a star in his own right, and that excelling doesn't mean it will be at someone else's expense. Although he still struggles with wanting to stand out, he tells me he secretly dreams of taking his own victory lap. He and I are working to sort through the confusing paradox of false humility and underground arrogance. Neither gets me what I want.

I cannot fix my six-year-old's confusion. I can let him know I understand why he struggles, reassuring him that it all makes sense considering his life history. I can also sneak in regular standing ovations when he shows up in my daily life, pushing through an exceptionally grueling workout, making a great presentation, or saying just the right thing to a dying patient.

My adolescent wants to believe he is smart, competent, thoughtful, and insightful. He wants answers to big questions about the meaning of life. He wants to be worthy—and being an adolescent, he wants to be attractive to Anne but without anyone knowing how important this is to him. He and I are beginning to laugh at what a serious guy he turned out to be and how absolutely inept he is at large social gatherings. We also laugh that he wasn't as tall, fast, articulate, or handsome as he wanted to be. And now he looks at me in the mirror and tells me I'm old and looking more and more like my father.

We keep each other honest. Between our bouts of humorous banter, I persist in telling him he is most worthy of life. Gradually, it is sinking in, and the more it does, the more he wants others to feel worthy as well. However, there are words he still resists. When Anne actually tells him he is handsome, he shrugs it off because, after all, she's married to me. (We'll probably go to the grave with this one.).

We talk about desensitization therapy for specific fears and phobias. For the past couple of years, I have been desensitizing my little ones to letting love in. Each day, when I spot their presence in a touching interaction, in a mini competition, in a useful insight, I make sure to tell them, before I fall asleep, how impressed I am by their talent and gifts. I make sure each knows I see his or her particular mark in my everyday life and how grateful I am for the richness and complexity he or she brings to me. In learning to be a better parent to myself, I'm better able to recognize and thank others for their gifts. Just as important, through my personal desensitization therapy, I am beginning to give myself permission to hear, believe, and enjoy many generous and loving comments that come my way. I'm even able to say, "Thank you" without changing the subject.

My daily five- to ten-minute practice of introspection and direct communication with my younger selves has helped me to be less self-absorbed during my day. I find I am less likely to be dragged around by a younger voice while he seeks approval and love in the wrong places. My little ones are satisfied with my self-affirmation, just as they are more open to laugh at our *mishagos* (craziness).

During one phase of this book, one of my inner voices refused to write for nearly a year. We had many internal conversations before he felt heard and respected. He needed time to play and give the whole thing a rest. Although other voices wanted to muscle through, ultimately we waited. It was a wise decision. Once we all got on board, there was a marked change in my writer's voice. Like it or not, I had to wait for consensus.

As I have said before, I don't mention my little ones in everyday conversations. My introspective process, up to now, has been private. Instead, I try to meet others on their terms and discover what drives them to be who they are. As Elisabeth used to say, "I'm not okay, you're not okay, and that's okay."

Chapter 16
REDEMPTION

Kindness is a mark of faith, and whoever is not kind has no faith.
—Muhammed

Jim's Redemption

Jim, a forty-year-old very successful businessman, came to a workshop with an ultimatum from his wife. Jim suffered outbursts of anger with their kids, especially his oldest, nine-year-old Andrew. Jim wasn't happy to be at the workshop. He acted boxed in and trapped. When the mat work started, he became fidgety and gradually slid his chair toward the back of the room.

Elisabeth always said, "There are no coincidences" and that the right people would show up at the workshop to assist us. One time a mother came to grieve the death of her son, the victim of a random shooting. At the same workshop, another mother came to process the life imprisonment of her son, who mistakenly killed another young child during gang-related vengeance. In witnessing the other's pain, each could appreciate the destructive nature of violence for the families of both victims and perpetrators. Jim would soon discover that another participant would be the catalyst for his work.

Bill came to our workshop for depression. He was fifty years old, a college baseball coach. His wife of twenty-five years had attended earlier in the year, and because of the changes Bill saw in her, he applied in hopes of clearing away the layer of fog that pervaded his otherwise very good life.

Frequently, various themes run through a workshop. In this case, it happened to be angry and sometimes violent fathers. After one such story, Bill came to the mat. He soberly described how his father had been a cold, demanding bully who beat his kids just to toughen them up. Bill was too frightened to confront his father about his cruelty. In fact, despite his physical size and strength, he timidly avoided confrontations, wanting to disappear whenever voices were raised in disagreement.

As Bill talked, I placed the hose in front of him. After a while, he picked it up but couldn't bring himself to lift it over his head and bring it down on a phone book. Instead he sat, shaking with rage.

In the meantime, although Jim had moved far away from the action, he was now transfixed by the pent-up rage emanating from Bill. Finally, with near robotic movement, Bill raised the hose and brought it down on the book. Again, he repeated the mechanical movement of the hose onto the phone book; but each time he lowered the hose on the book, he did it with a little more force.

Three, four, and five times, the hose thudded softly on the book. Then, matching the tempo of the hose, Bill began to speak very deliberately to his father, describing the almost-ritualized beatings he and his younger brothers had endured from his hands and fists. With each remembered story, the hose began to move more freely until the force of Bill's swings split the binding and shredded the pages of the phone book. Now Bill was screaming at his father, asking him what kind of a man does that to his kids, as a rage equal to his father's finally poured out of this meek man.

Still in his chair, Jim covered his face with his arms and shook with silent sobs.

When he finished pounding the books, Bill shook his head in amazement that he had carried around so much anger for so many years. Smiling with relief, he thanked the group for witnessing and honoring his work and returned to his seat.

Before anyone else could claim the mat, Jim took possession of the sacred space.

Although he looked ready to explode while he witnessed Bill's anger, Jim shut down the moment he sat on the mat. It was as if his little boy just disappeared. This happens fairly often when people come to the mat for the first time, either because the little ones become scared or the adult, who is proficient at shutting down any feelings, resumes control. It is often best to sit patiently, so I waited for Jim to speak.

Acknowledging that his feelings were gone, he told the story of a sadistic father who regularly exploded in rage and beat his mom and especially his older brother. Jim recounted several horrific scenes but told them dispassionately as if he were a newspaper reporter rather than the child who'd experienced them.

When I asked Jim what it was like for him, he said he supposed it was hard and scary, but he'd "kind of blocked it out." I then asked grown-up Jim whether he would be willing to step aside and allow the sobbing little boy, who I saw covering his face during Bill's work, to be here. I thought little Jimmy wanted to teach big Jim what really went on.

Big Jim consented, lay down on the mat, closed his eyes, and allowed ancient feelings to surface. Tears streaming down his cheeks, he shook with terror, scarcely daring to make a sound, so terrified that his father would turn his hostility from his mother or brother onto him. Finally, he whimpered, "Don't hurt them. Don't hurt me," repeating the words over and over as they morphed from a scared plea to a roaring demand.

Suddenly, Jim bolted upright, grabbed the hose, and lit into his father, telling him what he'd been too little and terrified to say years ago. "If you ever touch my mother or brother again, I'll kill you!" He was drenched in sweat when he finally put down the hose, surprised by the mass of torn yellow pages representing years of unspoken words and stored-up anger.

As if finished with his father, Jim threw down the hose, pushed the phone book aside, and was about to walk off the mat when I placed a pillow in front of him. "This is Jimmy." Jim looked at me with angry eyes, as if he were still talking to his father. "I am *not* going to talk to a pillow." He had no idea how to nurture his terrified little boy. I waited. After a while, he reached over and patted the pillow, and with a mixture of one-part gentle dad to four parts of man to man, he lectured, "You don't need to be afraid anymore."

Ah, the agenda. Jim had spent his adult life telling himself he wasn't going to be afraid. He'd become a man's man, tough in life, tough at home. If his son, Andrew, did anything out of Jim's comfort zone, he lashed out at his son with criticism, threats, and occasionally force. Of course, Jim had no notion that his son's behavior triggered his own fear. As far as he was concerned, Andrew was misbehaving and needed correction.

I challenged Jim to have a conversation with the scared little boy he'd just experienced, as opposed to the little boy he wanted him to be. I then requested that Jim ask Jimmy how he felt about being told not to be afraid anymore. Jim responded without any hesitation. "He feels fine about it." (It was another quick response from an adult who answers for his children.)

Jack Kornfield, a wonderful Buddhist teacher, tells a story that Anne loves and shares at our workshops. It is about a mom, dad, and little boy sitting in a diner. The waitress asks the mom what she'll have, and she responds, "Chicken salad. Dressing on the side, please." When the waitress turns to the dad, he orders steak, a baked potato, and coleslaw. Finally, the waitress smiles at the little boy, and he says with great authority, "I'll have a hotdog and french fries, please."

His mom overrides the order. "He'll have the meat loaf with mashed potatoes and carrots."

Then, without missing a beat, the waitress turns back to the little boy. "Would you like ketchup with those fries?"

After the waitress leaves with their order, the little boy turns to his mom and whispers, "She thinks I'm *real*."

I asked Jim what he'd learned from Jimmy a moment ago. Jim looked at me and said, "I was so terrified I could barely breathe, let alone speak."

I responded, "So, you just told him to pull himself together and stop being scared. Do you think that is possible, based on what you just heard from him? Please ask him again, out loud, how he feels about your telling him that he doesn't have to be afraid anymore."

Clearly self-conscious about asking a question aloud to a pillow, Jim nevertheless complied. I suggested that he close his eyes and be very still so he could listen for little Jimmy's response. About ten seconds passed, and he nodded. Jim looked at me with some surprise. "He says he's almost always scared."

Jim thought he was being helpful and kind, telling the little boy not to be afraid anymore. We want our internal world to be fixed, free from all our old pain so we can be happy and lighthearted. It is a wonderful wish, but we cannot change the feelings stored in our right brain on command.

To a child, telling him or her not to feel what he or she feels is the same as saying, "I will love you if you are different than you are."

I then asked, "Inside of you is a terrified little boy. Does he have to be tough to deserve your love?"

Jim sat perfectly still for about fifteen seconds, then reached over and lifted the pillow to his lap, silently rocking little Jimmy. As tears rolled down his face, Jim whispered to the little boy that he saw how scared he was and that he would be there to protect him when he was scared again.

After a while, Jim looked at me and nodded. His face was soft, without any tough-guy bravado. I made one last request, to see whether little Jimmy had anything to say to him. This time Jim had no difficulty in asking Jimmy whether he wanted to say something to him. He closed his eyes without my asking and waited patiently for a response.

"Jimmy said it was nice that I hugged him and rocked him and that he feels safer than he has felt for a very long time. Then he asked me to promise him I would stop scaring Andrew."

Later that weekend, Jim did another piece of mat work around his relationship with Andrew. He practiced telling his son he was sorry for the way he'd treated him and that Jim's anger had nothing to do with him. On the mat, Jim told Andrew he had learned from his own father to attack when he got scared—and that he had just recently learned he was scared a lot more often than he realized.

Jim started to put the pieces together. On his own, he asked to speak to little Jimmy once again, requesting his inner child's aid. "Please remind me when I am scaring Andrew the way Dad scared you. I want to change." Jim promised that he would take a timeout and talk with little Jimmy before he jumped all over his oldest son.

I was fortunate enough to follow up with Jim several months later. He told me he had apologized to his son and shared his story in a language Andrew could understand. Touched by the forgiveness Andrew had showed him, Jim saw a whole new side to his son. Understanding that his father had tried to make his sons different from how they were, Jim now committed to breaking the generational cycle of rage and violence.

In their new relationship, Andrew was now brave enough to tell Jim when he was hurt. Jim loved this new kind of toughness and courage he was seeing in his son. They had begun to trust each other.

Reclaiming Banished Voices

Near the end of the movie *Gandhi*, someone asked the mahatma why he would visit Pakistan, India's enemy, after the tumultuous and violent partition following India's independence from Great Britain.

Gandhi replied, "To prove to the Hindus here and the Moslems there that the only devils in the world are the ones running around in our own hearts. And that is where all the battles ought to be fought."

"What kind of warrior have you been?" Gandhi was asked.

"Not a very good one," the mahatma replied with a smile. "That is why I have so much tolerance for all the other scoundrels in the world."

No matter how hard Jim tried to compensate for his father's rage and his own fear, he wouldn't find redemption until he reclaimed and forgave himself. He won this life battle when he disarmed within himself, accepting the consequences of his life story without trying to change it. Ironically, with self-forgiveness came a whole new level of accountability. Able to forgive himself when he flew off the handle, he also welcomed Andrew's loving challenge to be the best dad he could be. Andrew also took up the challenge to be a better son.

I sometimes get discouraged when I fall back into old patterns or when I listen to the news and hear about nonsensical violence and fear-based politics.

Then I remember my battle first needs to be fought in my heart. I return to my little ones to honor their fears, frustration, sadness, and self-righteous desire to lash out. They invariably calm down, and together we take up the challenge to be a better man. Redemption sometimes is a daily event. With it comes more tolerance and humility—as well as accountability—for all the little scoundrels who live in each of us.

Chapter 17

CULTIVATING STILLNESS

> There is no need to go to India or anywhere else to find peace. You will find that deep place of silence right in your room, your garden or even your bathtub.
> —Elisabeth Kübler-Ross

The Answer Is under a Forsythia Bush

Roger came to a workshop because of a prior history of alcohol and drug abuse as well as difficulty in his marriage. He had attended AA and remained sober for years. He was separated from his wife and daughter, living with one family member or another.

During his introduction, Roger was extremely animated, dramatically describing how broken, scared, and overwhelmed he was. As the workshop unfolded, he took copious notes of all the teaching, often asking for clarifications afterward for any concept he might have misunderstood. He was desperate for answers.

Roger was in and out of his seat during the sessions, including the mat work, but he didn't come to the mat himself. His anxiety often required an interaction with one of the staff. I began to wonder whether, as a little boy, Roger had to appear that agitated to get attention. Such neglect.

Just as the mat work was concluding, Roger fled the room. I followed to be sure he was safe and to see whether I could help. Although we moved to one of the breakout rooms, where the staff could work individually with participants, Roger wouldn't sit on the mat. Rather, he paced around the room, frantically talking about being broken as a child. At one point he mentioned hiding under a forsythia bush when he was four. He said no one ever came for him; nor did he or she seem concerned that he was missing. The more he talked about his early years, the more frantic Roger became.

I asked Roger to lie down on the mat. Surprisingly, he complied, continuing to talk nonstop about how scared and broken he was. Becoming a bit agitated myself, I blurted out over him, "Sh, Roger—no more words." He stopped talking for about ten seconds but started all over again.

"Shhh, no more words. The answer to your question is under the forsythia bush."

"Shhh, shhh, shhh," I kept repeating in a soft sing-song voice to the grown man lying on the mat. "No more words, Roger. The answer to your questions isn't in your notebook but under a forsythia bush." I placed a pillow on Roger's chest. "Go find that little boy."

"Nobody ever came for me. I was so scared and lonely, so broken and—"

"Sh, he doesn't need to hear any of that. He just wants to be held, to feel safe and loved."

Roger became still for the first time during the workshop. A few tears squeezed out of his closed eyes, and his breathing relaxed.

"Yes, it's okay for him to breathe." He allowed himself to take more relaxing, deep breaths. I sat quietly next to the mat while big Roger held his little boy for about fifteen minutes. No more words were spoken.

I knew one of the staff was about to teach a section on shame, a topic Roger had specifically asked whether we were going to discuss. Knowing how important this was to him, I finally said the teaching was about to begin, and we could end our session so he could join the group to listen.

I waited. After about thirty seconds, Roger opened his eyes, turned to me, and in a soft, very grounded adult voice said, "He (the little boy) wants me to be with him right now. You go on. We're fine right here."

I never leave people alone while they are on the mat, but this time I told Roger I needed to be in the main room for the teaching. I asked him to check in with his little boy to see whether he felt safe with Roger alone. Roger asked his little one aloud so I could hear. After about ten seconds, he looked at me again and nodded. "He just wants me to hold him a while longer. We'll be just fine."

I left them together.

After the teaching, I went back to the breakout room. Roger wasn't there. I found him sitting outside, warming himself in the sun. He smiled at me and thanked me for being with him earlier. For the rest of the workshop, Roger remained calm. He listened to the teaching but no longer frantically wrote down every word. The desperation to find answers outside himself had subsided.

As we were saying good-bye at the end of the workshop, I asked him whether I could tell others about the forsythia bush. Roger took a moment, as if to check in with his little boy who had spent so much time under the forsythia's protection, and then proudly told me he would love it if I could help someone else by telling his story.

I saw Roger a year after his workshop. He had integrated his mat work into the twelve- step model that had kept him sober for over a decade. He told me he now understood the source of his anxiety and elaborated on the violence and neglect he experienced in his childhood. "Now, when I get scared, I nod my head to my little guy and let him know he isn't alone." Roger shares his wisdom with the men he sponsors.

Sometimes stillness is simply the acknowledgment and acceptance of our anxieties and grief. In what I call my "spiritual practice," I enter the space of introspection before I climb out of bed to start the day. I ask whether any voice needs my attention. Sometimes nothing happens. They all remain quiet. I wait and ask again. Depending on my mood, the request is serious, pensive. "Good morning. Does anyone need time?" Other times, it is playful. "What's up in there? Ready for the day?" Sometimes it begins with a body sensation.

This morning I felt tension in my solar plexus at the top of my abdomen. I tried to listen, but all I heard was my mind making a list of what I had to do today. I asked, "Who's making the list this morning?" Of course, I already knew. It was the six-year-old who is always proving himself. I placed my hand on my abdomen, letting him know I felt his energy. I didn't tell him this was "stillness time" and that he needed to chill out and get with my spiritual program. I just let him know I was with him.

After a while, my hand moved as he took a deep breath. "Ah, yes, it does feel good to breathe," I said jokingly to him. He took another breath, and I felt him smile.

"That's me, always running scared," he half-joked.

I added my smile to his. "Anything I can help you with?"

"Not now, but I'm about to get into high gear. Today, you aren't retired! I'll give you our to-do list soon." And so it went.

Once the six-year-old and I had checked in, I asked whether any other voice had anything to say. No words, but I felt the sadness of the five-year-old. He didn't require that I fix him. "Yes, I know, the sadness and fear are never far away." He just appreciated that I knew he was there, even in his silence. This morning, my very little one requested a minute just to be held. The others never refuse the infant his request. We all gave him a moment as I gently squeezed a pillow to let him know we were there for him.

Then my adolescent asked that we at least take the afternoon off, free of small talk and life maintenance. Anne was away, looking after grandson Henry while Rachael rehearsed for a performance. My adolescent wanted to chill. I didn't realize until this morning's request how much alone time he needed. I always thought it was the younger one who wanted to be alone. Maybe during tonight's check-in, I will ask the older one about this new piece of information. I could tell he didn't want to pursue this conversation right now. Maybe if he got his quiet afternoon ...

All this took less than five minutes. I left my bed, put on workout clothes, and started my day. Once the workout started, I checked in to see who wanted to set the pace. Today there was a consensus not to let my driven six-year-old take control of the workout. This would be a recovery day. But the six-year-old was already planning tomorrow's workout.

Where is the stillness in all this? Mostly, it is in acknowledgment and acceptance of who I am. I can be still, even with all the chatter that goes on inside my head. It is the "ah so" that follows from listening to the whisperings of my heart.

I continue to discover new information about myself. With each life passage, new issues appear that enhance my understanding of my past and how it affects my present. When a current loss or new stress plunges me back into old habits of hyperactivity, emotional withdrawal, neurotic fear, compulsivity, or overeating, I look at myself once again with new lenses. My little ones teach me more about who they are and request that I don't abandon or condemn them again. They also demand that I show up for them, including setting healthy limits so they don't hurt themselves or the people they love.

As a parent to myself, I still have a way to go. I forget or choose to ignore what I know is best for me. But my little ones just keep encouraging me. They have generous, forgiving hearts. The stillness is in the love and respect we have for each other and the desire and intention to deepen the kinship. They continue to teach me how to be the man I want to be. They give me the courage to contaminate others with my love. Once banished, they are now truly a gift.

Chapter 18

TILL DEATH DO US...

It is not the end of the physical body that should worry us. Rather, our concern must be to live while we're alive—to release our inner selves from the spiritual death that comes with living behind a facade.
—Elisabeth Kübler-Ross, MD

Some friends say they just want to play and be happy, that they don't want to go back into the past, rip the scab off old wounds, and that frankly they are tired of all the drama. I want to say to them, "Play and play and play. Laugh, too"—until or unless you need to cry. Then cry like you play with fierce abandon and let your tears form a big puddle that your little ones will splash in.

I have very serious little ones living inside me. Fear does that to some of us. I have envied those who can dance and laugh and live so fully in the moment. At times, I have been skeptical of other's joy because it was so distant from my reality. My skepticism has diminished with my commitment to the spiritual practice of checking in with my little ones, who continually surprise me with their humor. They constantly entertain me, just like my three grandchildren do. In return, my laughter has emboldened my little ones to come out and play in our new neighborhood, which is filled with interesting and caring people. We have indeed left that mob of neighborhood boys behind.

I remember back in 1984, on the fourth day of my first workshop. Elisabeth talked about what happens when and after we die. At the time I was wide open from my mat work, and her teaching felt like I was greeting an old friend. I continue to present a modified version of what Elisabeth spoke about, not so much to focus on after death as to use the information to live a more fulfilled life. Teaching about what happens when we die rekindles my feeling of peace when I first heard this information in 1984, but it doesn't eliminate a persistent skepticism that resides in my logical brain.

I have both a deep faith and belief that there is a higher power, God, absolute reality, from which we all come, as well as an almost equal skepticism that we are simply a product of nature's evolution. My belief in God, I believe, emanates from the youngest part of me, a source of nonverbal, intuitive knowing. My little one's vision is fresh from the source, unencumbered by logic or thought. I suppose it is what the adult world would call *faith*, filled with awe and gratitude for the miracle of life. I felt this at the birth of my children, Matt and Rachael, and when I have held my three grandchildren for the first time and felt their unique life force.

When I push my youngest self for details of his knowing and faith, I receive only the image of the safety of loving arms cradling him. It isn't intellectual knowing but experiential wisdom of the unity of all things, such as the greeting from an old and trusted friend. Sometimes the little one's knowing isn't enough for me.

Although I believe love is all that matters, my mind often tells me meaning is manmade, at best an evolutionary (albeit glorious) survival mechanism. My skeptical mind dismisses the possibility of a God who communicates with me or cares about me. Yet I choose to live a conscious life, God or no God, because when I close my eyes and check in with the voices that are the sum total of who I am, I feel a collective sigh of peace and the joy that comes from our deepening relationship.

Because I am writing this chapter right now, I spontaneously asked the youngest, intuitive part of me during our check-in last night whether there is a God. He rolled his eyes and shook his head at me. As if he were talking directly to God, I heard the little one mumble, "You see how immature he is." Still my skeptic wanted proof.

I looked for support from the older voices during my check-in. My driven six-year-old basically said he was too busy to worry about such matters. The scared five-year-old, whom I buried all those years ago, replied that he really hopes God exists. The adolescent said he went along with the infant. *He knows more than all of us.*

On a good day (when I am centered in who I am, have checked in with myself, and have given space to my frustration, fears, and grief as well as my talents and gifts), I see God's handiwork in all things. Over the last thirty years of Growth and Transition, I have decided to end the program at least ten different times. Within hours of my final decision, I invariably bump into a former participant (sometimes I don't even remember who he or she is), who tells me his or her workshop weekend changed the course of his or her life. The regularity and timing of such an encounter has seemed beyond coincidence. Each time I have had to let go of my need to control where my energies will be spent and listen to where the universe is leading me. Each time I have been grateful for the gentle nudge.

I'm always amazed and tickled when one of my dying patients hangs on for days longer than human physiology would predict so the children can get past old, familial patterns of jealousy and bickering, and come together to celebrate with gratitude what their mother or father was able to give them. I once again see the handiwork of a loving force, much larger than any individual.

I pray. Mostly I thank God for giving me a life of abundance. I rarely ask for specific personal requests. I figure God will sort out what I need. Maybe it seems selfish to ask God for His time and attention. Maybe I still feel unworthy. When I am skeptical, I wonder whether He listens to the cacophony of requests from the faithful. I also wonder why He never speaks to me. I've never heard His voice. I used to think He was too busy to talk to his flock. Lately, I've been thinking He talks to me all the time, but I'm unable to hear Him over the never-ceasing drone of my mind.

When I am disconnected from myself, when I fail to take notice of my little ones, when I am triggered, reactive, and judging the unwelcome parts of myself, my skepticism and cynicism about the presence of a loving God increase. I find that when I feel most isolated, I want to deny God or project my anger and judgment of others onto Him. I recognize the fundamentalist who lurks inside me. I want God to do the right thing and dish out justice the way I see it, and I want Him to love me more than He loves others because I deserve special treatment. I make God in my own image. Fortunately, I believe God doesn't take my arrogance personally.

The God of my faith is all love, both in compassion and accountability. He doesn't punish simply because He is jealous of my false gods, because I disobey Him, or because I assert my own power and control. The Creator of this unimaginably grand universe isn't so petty as to need my unquestioned devotion; nor do my anger and skepticism threaten Him. He doesn't love me better or worse than His more prodigal or saintly children. Unlike many parents, God doesn't take any of my human failings personally.

It is all very humbling either way: to be a mere, yet treasured, mortal speck in God's wondrous creation; or to be an evolutionary coincidence. Humility continues to be a good thing for me. I continue to spew out self-righteous judgment despite all my best efforts. I continue to withdraw in isolation when I am stressed, withholding from those I love and cheating them out of the opportunity to gift me with their love and redemption. I continue to respond from the need to be right. Yes, humility is a good thing for me.

Much like shaving, my reclamation is an ongoing, daily activity. Arrogance and pride return each morning like the stubble on my chin. I'm not and will never be cured. I remain a moving target, still being triggered by daily interactions and each new, challenging phase of life. I already know I am guaranteed to meet my old friend fear as I awaken to daily life without my professional career, private medical office, and paycheck.

If I remain conscious, I will continue to put the pieces of my puzzle together, continue to learn more about my little ones, and engage them with compassion and accountability. I hope I will remain conscious and learning until my dying breath.

Dying Breath

About three years ago, Evelyn arrived in our hospice in-patient unit in respiratory distress. She required fifteen liters of oxygen flowing through her nasal cannula to maintain an adequate oxygen level in her blood. She had been admitted to another hospital, while very short of breath, and treated successfully for pneumonia. Unfortunately, her heart then failed, and her lungs filled with fluid. She and her family requested hospice care.

Evelyn was a small woman with short-cropped hair and a wiry body, who looked as if it had been in perpetual motion most of its ninety-three years. Except for fluttering her eyes to my voice and exam, Evelyn made no other response. Her chest moved in and out with twenty-four medium breaths a minute faster than the normal twelve to fourteen. She hadn't consumed food or fluids in eight days. She would go through the end-of-life process of dehydration now that her intravenous fluids had been stopped. Ironically, as she dehydrated, the fluid in her lungs would also diminish, improving her respiratory distress and prolonging her days in hospice. I explained this process to several members of her family. Since Evelyn was already unresponsive, I also offered the option of turning off her oxygen, which would likely result in a more rapid death.

Pulmonologists have told me that low-blood oxygen isn't painful. In high altitude climbers, hypoxia doesn't cause pain. Generally, when families opt to discontinue this life-prolonging intervention, we administer morphine and a sedative, lorazepam, to relieve potential air hunger and anxiety.

Very few people die "on time" in hospice. It is split pretty evenly between too fast or too slow. The problem solvers, the type A personalities, sign their name on the hospice forms and then give us the look that says, *Let's get this show on the road*. They become bored and impatient with waiting for death. Others cling to earth by their fingernails, resisting with every ounce of remaining life force. Sometimes it is a fear of the unknown or of eternal judgment. Sometimes they just don't want to miss anything on this side of the veil. Or they cannot conceive how their spouse or children can make it without them.

Families of the dying often have similar timing concerns. Those who see only the suffering their mother is experiencing want it to end. Those who have been the primary caregiver for months and years are often very ready for their own sake as well as that of their loved one. On the other hand, some continue to hope that, with a little more time, Mom's body will recover. They choose to love their mother by keeping her alive at all costs. Sometimes guilt propels them. Sometimes they cannot pile one more loss on a life of losses, so they protect themselves from their mountain of grief by postponing the inevitable straw that will break the camel's back.

Conflicts appear when members of a family have different needs during these last days or weeks of life.

Fortunately, Evelyn's family members were in agreement. After waiting for the last child to arrive, they came to consensus that Mom wouldn't want this phase of her life prolonged. After taking some individual time to say their private good-byes, Evelyn's family requested that we turn off her oxygen.

I ordered a bit of morphine and lorazepam before removing the mask covering Evelyn's nose and mouth. Normally, I would leave the room and continue my daily rounds, checking on other patients and families. I might poke my head in briefly to see whether Evelyn was comfortable or to answer additional questions from the family. Sometimes I would come in after the death to say a private good-bye. On this morning, I surprised myself when I heard an inner voice declare that I was going to stay right there with Evelyn. I moved next to the bed and placed my hand in hers.

Evelyn was unresponsive but a bit restless. After I turned off the oxygen, her heart soon raced at 140 beats per minute. Her respirations increased to forty rapid, gulping breaths a minute, as if she were running her last race. One daughter was squeezing her hand, telling Evelyn, "Mom, it's okay to let go." The others sat on the sofa and chairs around the bed, talking quietly.

I looked to see whether anyone was regretting the decision to turn off the oxygen or was upset with me because of how hard Evelyn was struggling to breathe. In fact, Evelyn's muscles were very relaxed, and her body otherwise demonstrated no evidence of distress. The family seemed quite content with what was happening. I tried to answer their questions matter-of-factly while I casually pushed the button for our nurse. When she arrived, I repeated doses of morphine and lorazepam. I was the one who was becoming anxious.

I suddenly needed more air. I began hyperventilating quietly along with Evelyn. I looked at each family member to see whether they were also short of breath, but they were calm and patiently waiting for Evelyn to die, even laughing about old times. Several more minutes passed, with Evelyn heaving her chest at forty times a minute. Even though she was unconscious, I half-expected her to sit bolt upright and claw her way to the surface of the primordial pond suffocating her.

I pushed the button for our nurse again, or was it a terrified little boy who was now prescribing? I was attending my worst nightmare. But at that moment I had no awareness that a five-year-old was breaking through my professional persona.

I had served as the medical director at Tucson Medical Center Hospice since its inception, at that time more than twenty years ago. I had signed hundreds, if not thousands, of death certificates and witnessed almost every possible type of death in all age groups. What was happening to me?

I considered excusing myself. Doctors always have legitimate reasons for moving on. I didn't move. I tried calming my breath but couldn't concentrate enough to relieve a rising panic. I calmly gave another medication order to our nurse as a drop of sweat trickled down my back. I couldn't believe Evelyn's body, at ninety-plus years, hung on, breathing this rapidly for more than thirty minutes.

I gasped for breath as I watched the boys pile on top of Teddy. They wouldn't get off. They just kept jumping back on the pile. He couldn't get any air. I wanted to scream, "Get off, get off, let me breathe—" But I didn't utter a sound.

There you are again. Won't we ever be finished with this?

My little one felt my impatience with his fear of suffocation. I wanted to tell him to get a grip, that even Evelyn's children were calm. I thought about all the times in the last sixty years when he had put me through moments of panic: in the dentist's chair, mouth open, with the irrigation spray preventing a breath; in the ICU, suddenly imagining myself flat on my back, hands in restraints, with an endotracheal tube down my throat while I desperately fought to override the ventilation machine programmed to force air into my lungs at only twelve times a minute. Or it came while I was waiting for a massage, lying facedown with my forehead resting on the head attachment, my mouth surrounded by foam and cloth, about to have someone compress my chest while I fought the urge and embarrassment of suddenly leaping off the table. Even on occasion, there was the sudden, unexpected urge to lunge out of bed when Anne moved close to rest her head gently on my chest.

In response to my impatience with him, the little guy answered me with another memory. During my first year of college, I was training for the start of wrestling season by working out in the gym and sprinting up hills. It was a cold New England afternoon on the day when I decided to do twenty sprints up Memorial Hill, a very steep prominence overlooking the athletic fields.

After about the third sprint, I couldn't catch my breath due to wheezing. I had suffered mild asthma in the past, mostly triggered by exercise. In those days, nobody knew much about asthma, and treatment was limited. My asthma manifested mostly as unexplained shortness of breath despite vigorous conditioning. However, I never had a full-blown attack like this one, brought on by the cold Massachusetts air. As the sun set over the Berkshires, I could barely make it to the infirmary. When I arrived, I was breathing just like Evelyn.

I don't want to die like Evelyn, my little guy whispered to me. His plea brought me back. Using my right hand to hold Evelyn's, I moved my left hand to my side, as I symbolically took his small hand in mine. "That makes two of us. This time, you aren't alone," I silently reassured him.

Our breathing slowed, and my focus returned to Evelyn and her family. I wondered whether she had been a sprinter. It dawned on me that one of the reasons I had exercised so hard all my life was to convince myself that I could regain my breath no matter what happened to me.

Evelyn's breathing finally began to slow. I released her hand, stepping back to let her family surround her. Letting out a final sigh, she crossed the finish line. After saying my good-byes, I walked outside, still gripping the little hand of my five-year-old. I tried to console him.

Little one, we've been doing aerobic training and running scared for the last sixty years, just in case we'll have to breathe the way Evelyn did. Not everybody dies this way. Hopefully, when it's our time, we'll just be able to close our eyes and rest. I promise that I'll warn all our caregivers of your fear. But if we can't breathe and you are still afraid, remember that you won't be alone this time. I may be a shriveled old man by then, but there will still live inside us a strong, young wrestler, who will throw us both on his back and make a final charge up Memorial Hill.

Sprinting to heaven.

We all die alone. No one on this side of the veil can accompany us on our last journey. I won't be in control, either of its cause or its timing. I cannot say whether I will die with the name of God on my lips, as Gandhi did, or whether I will be lunging out of bed in panic as I feel my soul leaving my body.

Hopefully, I will be with all my little ones on our final journey, not abandoning any one of them to fear, bitterness, or grief in our final hour. As I cradle them for the last time, I hope we will finally merge just in time for the powerfully gentle arms of God to welcome us. My infant will smile in recognition as Mom rests him on her bare chest, able to be pure mother, no longer a frightened little girl. My five-year-old will inhale a completely satisfying last breath and release his final sigh as Dad reassuringly rubs his feet for the last time. My driven six-year-old will giggle with delight that he no longer has to do anything to feel worthy. My adolescent will dissolve his wall of shame and self-protection and open his arms to all that is love. And I will feel enormous gratitude for the abundance that was my mortal life.

During graceful and grace-filled final moments, I will have the opportunity to tell all my loved ones one last time how precious they are to me. And I will be able to thank them for seeing and loving all of me.

Appendix 1

NATURAL AND DISTORTED EMOTIONS

> Fear keeps us focused on the past or worried about the future. If we can acknowledge our fear, we can realize that right now we are okay. Right now, today, we are still alive, and our bodies are working marvelously. Our eyes can still see the beautiful sky. Our ears can still hear the voices of our loved ones.
> —Thich Nhat Hanh

Elisabeth taught that we have five natural emotions that help us live fully present lives. There are, of course, many different words to describe emotions. I will use Elisabeth's nomenclature. Each has a purpose, a natural expression, and many distortions.

They are, in no particular order, the following:

- Grief
- Anger
- Fear
- Natural jealousy
- Love

Grief

The purpose of healthy grief is to process separation and loss. In this context, I'm not referring to the grieving process, which utilizes all the emotions. Rather, I mean the sadness that comes from loss.

Losses can be big and varied, such as the death of a child, an attack on our country, the stealing of a childhood because of abuse and neglect, divorce, retirement, the loss of a job, or the loss of identity because of debilitating illness. Losses can be less devastating in the scheme of things, such as an injury that prevents us from exercise, a bad investment, or storm damage to a home. Losses can even be trivial, such as misplacing an earring or locking our keys in the car.

Knowing which losses will affect us the hardest can be surprising and unpredictable because a particular experience may symbolize very different things to each of us. A financial loss may trigger doubts about our competence. A cheating spouse may reveal our essential ability to judge and trust people. A physical injury may challenge our identity as strong and healthy. A lost earring may question our ability to be in control of our lives.

But the biggest grief is for the things we never had and always wanted: a safe and nurturing childhood, a love we never received, a future with a child who died prematurely, the loss of a homeland for future generations. Perhaps the greatest loss of all is the abandonment of lifelong dreams and passions or the inability to delight in the magic and serendipity of an unburdened, open heart. At the very bottom of a bucket of shed tears, I have often heard the same five-word supplication: "I want my joy back."

Grief is expressed with wailing and tears, the sharing of a ritual, and the telling of our story. Anne and I heard one of the most dramatic sounds of grief when we were in southern Iran. After a death, the women of the family made a circle on the street corner outside the hospital, held hands, rocked side to side, and wailed. We could hear them several blocks away. The wailing went on for a very long time, notifying the community that this clan had suffered a painful loss. It was such a contrast from Western stoicism.

The repetitive telling of our story helps us to own all our feelings about a loss and then make sense of the loss in the context of our lives. When our son, Matt, was a toddler, one of his favorite pastimes was sitting with his grandmother on a hill outside our home and identifying the vehicles that whizzed by. "Truck! Convertible! Motorcycle! Station wagon!"

One day when we were visiting friends who lived in the woods along a river in the Pacific Northwest, we took a family walk along a dirt road and came across a car that was rusted out and upside down.

"Car—upside down. Car—upside down!" Two-year-old Matt couldn't make sense of this anomaly. It was so upsetting that he took us back three or four times a day to see this car. He was grieving a world that was somehow less predictable. I believe he needed to know he was still okay, even though this car wasn't.

Our culture sends many negative or minimizing messages about tears and grief. *Big boys and girls don't cry. Pull yourself together. I'll give you something to cry about. Time will heal all wounds. Be grateful for what you have. She's with God now. We'll get a new puppy tomorrow. Let me get you a Valium.*

If it isn't safe to express grief, our losses accumulate, stacking up on top of each other, only to be triggered by the next loss. This pile of losses requires increasing energy to carry. We keep ourselves numb with work or addictions, platitudes, or drugs. When a fresh loss faces us, we are unable to deal with it because it might open Pandora's box of sadness, and we will never stop crying. We pull ourselves together, give and receive pep talks, and go on with life because "that is what Mary would have wanted."

Some argue that pulling ourselves together and getting on with life are what we all need to do. Certainly, moving forward with life is a good thing. When we grieve, we acknowledge the loss has changed us. We redefine ourselves. Sometimes our losses propel us to look at our past behaviors. Sometimes they expand our empathy. Sometimes they force us to reconsider what is truly important and what is trivial. Sometimes they humble us with our powerlessness to change things and to appreciate how comical we are in believing we are in control. Sometimes they plunge us into the pit of despair while we decide whether to go on or to give up. Losses melt rigid steel into molten metal, ready to be reforged—that is, if we stop to see and feel what we have lost.

In my rush to make morning rounds during my residency, I locked my keys in the car with the motor running. I gave myself hell, screaming at myself in the large VA hospital parking lot. Leaving my overflowing briefcase and stethoscope on the hood, I ran to find a security guard, who had a tool to unlock my car. I sensed that he took a perverse pleasure that an Ivy League hot-shot doctor needed his assistance. I humbly thanked him.

I wanted to race into the hospital. Instead, I channeled Peter Sellers's portrayal of Inspector Clouseau. I straightened my tie and strolled into the hospital as if I had all the time in the world. I was grateful that I even realized what I had done before the end of the day, when I would have not only frantically looked for my keys but also discovered my car had idled its way through a whole tank of gas. Grief expanded my self-image to include the buffoon and gave me permission to be humorously imperfect.

Losses happen. They can paralyze or transform us. Grieving allows us to find a resting place for our losses and find forgiveness for our imperfections and mistakes. Grief allows us to choose life with new self-awareness and priorities. Losses bring us to our knees, where we can humbly find our authentic selves.

We distinguish the sadness of grief from the grieving process, which includes all the emotions. It is often necessary to shake our fist at the unfairness of life and come to terms with our fear of future losses and more pain before we can decide to reengage fully in the gift of life.

When I first trained with Elisabeth, I soon realized many other professionals came to the workshop to watch her work her magic. Elisabeth had an uncanny way of plucking the right string to move people to where they needed to go. When people asked how she did it, Elisabeth would invariably answer, "You need to learn symbolic language, which is the language of the spiritual-intuitive quadrant, the language of the soul. It is the part of us that knows everything, even though we do not know how we know. When someone is in crisis, their intellect may not know what they need, but their spiritual quadrant always knows. When your spiritual quadrant listens to their spiritual quadrant, you will know what to say. But first, you must silence your own skeptical intellect, which will warn you to keep your mouth shut so you won't look like a fool or make someone upset."

When we listen with our hearts, magic happens.

Roger's Grieving

During my third workshop as a trainee, Roger introduced himself to the group and told us he had come because he was homeless. We were in a country where homelessness was nearly nonexistent. He explained that a friend had offered to pay for his attendance and that he wouldn't mind a clean bed, a daily shower, and steady meals for a few days. About ten years ago, his only child, Billy, had died after a two-year illness. Roger said he had died as well. He'd lost his job and then his marriage. He lived in his car and then on the streets. He told us he had seen several shrinks and had been medicated and hospitalized, but no one could bring back the dead. Then he sat down.

Much later, Roger described that at first he had obsessed on his son's delayed diagnosis and the oncologist's inadequate care. All the what ifs. He remained bitter because of what had been taken from him; his anger increasingly leaked out at work. He resented other parents who talked about celebrating their child's next birthday. Although these feelings may be a normal part of the grieving process, after five and then ten years, it was beyond the norm. Gradually, the bitterness and remorse that had covered the pain of his tremendous loss faded into depression and resignation.

Roger had lost the ability to grieve, to shake his fist at God for taking his precious son away, and to weep over the only person in his life he could love completely and innocently. He was unable to arrive at the stillness at the bottom of his sobs, the gratitude for the miracle that had been his son, and the humility of knowing that even his ferocious love—and medical science—hadn't been able to keep his son alive. He had never arrived at the decision that he could honor his son best by loving others with the same intensity and innocence. Because his natural emotions had been taken from him years before, he was unequipped to deal with the earlier losses that had piled up, let alone the loss of his precious son.

When Roger arrived at Elisabeth's workshop, he remained frozen in time, separated from humanity and himself. He appeared to be the same person he had been on the day his son died ten years earlier, one of the walking dead.

As others came to the front to share their stories, Roger sat very close to the mat, listening without emotion. We heard poignant stories, bringing everyone to tears, except Roger, who watched with dry eyes. On the afternoon of the second day of intense sharing, I returned from one of the back rooms, where I had facilitated the continued work of another participant. Just as I sat down next to Elisabeth (every chance I could, I sat close to my teacher to soak up whatever I could), she looked at Roger and pointed to the empty mat in front of her—symbolic, nonverbal language for *You may be here on a free ride, but it's your turn to do your work*. With compliant indifference, Roger crawled the few feet onto the mat. He had given up a long time ago.

Elisabeth said, "Through all the pain and anguish of the last few days, you sit there like a stone."

Roger turned to the group. "Please don't think I am disrespectful. I see your pain and see that this is helpful for you, but when Billy died, my heart turned to stone. I have no tears. I feel nothing."

I knew that one day I might be leading workshops, facilitating in front of a group just like this. I wanted to be as skilled as possible, to be of as much help as I could. After Roger spoke, I anxiously thought, *What on earth is Elisabeth going to do now? She can't tie up the mat with a two-hour counseling session. This time it's not going to work.*

Elisabeth sat quietly for nearly a minute while the whole room waited and watched. Roger had our complete attention. He had nothing more to say. The waiting seemed endless. Finally, Elisabeth looked up and asked the group whether they knew the words to a specific song and requested that someone with a good voice start the singing. After the first two phrases of the song, Roger began to sob, continuing to weep through the rest of our singing and for two or three minutes thereafter. When he finally caught his breath, he looked at Elisabeth and said, "That's the song I used to sing to Billy when I tucked him into bed each night."

I don't think Roger was aware of how much he needed some evidence that Billy wasn't completely lost to him. Hearing the song gave Roger permission to open the floodgates and collapse into his grief, shedding the tears lodged behind the dam of childhood loss.

Later, in a back room, Roger proceeded to recount the story of his own lonely and isolated childhood. As Billy grew, Roger loved playing with him and being with him every moment he could after returning home from work. Billy's eyes would light up upon seeing his dad, something Roger had never experienced as a child. In fact, Billy was Roger's only friend.

I asked Roger, the father, to step aside and let his lonely little boy grieve the loss of his only friend. It was one thing for Roger to talk about having a lonely childhood. It was another to feel the despair and emptiness of his inner, desperately lonely little boy, who had lost the miracle of Billy's friendship with the crushing reality of his death. He cried and cried for the utter loneliness of his childhood and then screamed at God for his cruelty of taking his only friend. By the time his little boy was finished, Roger realized his lonely inner child was more devastated by Billy's death than he was.

I gave Roger two pillows to hold: one represented Billy, and the second represented his devastated inner little boy. Roger tearfully thanked Billy for opening up his heart and for being his best and only friend, a precious gift worth having, even if it had been much too brief. He then told Billy he would honor him by looking after this new little boy, who had been playing all along, right beside both of them.

Roger returned to the group to tell them what he had learned and to introduce his devastated inner little boy to them. He told us he didn't realize this abandoned little boy had been wandering the streets for the past ten years. He then made a promise to us that although he had lost Billy to cancer, he would now be making a proper home, with a roof and furniture, so he could father another precious little boy.

We finished the day's mat work at two o'clock in the morning. As soon as we arrived at the staff bunkhouse to get a few hours of sleep, I asked Elisabeth, "Where did that come from?"

The other staff members hadn't been in the room twelve hours earlier when Elisabeth requested the song. Although the staff didn't understand what I was asking, Elisabeth did. She simply smiled, put two fingers to her lips, and then raised them to the heavens in gratitude.

In the emotional quadrant, there is no linear time. Loss triggers loss. Our feeling of sadness over a current grief may linger for years because it is sitting on top of older, buried grief.

Distortions of Grief

When natural emotions aren't expressed, they often surface in distorted ways. One common distortion of grief is an overflow of pent-up tears when we watch a sentimental television commercial (such as the old AT&T "Reach out and touch someone" ads) or a sad movie. If an incident or a movie continues to sadden us for days, we are likely tapping into a personal reservoir of unresolved grief. As Elisabeth said, someone's sad story can touch us, but "when we cry, we cry for ourselves."

Another distorted expression of grief is prolonged remorse or regret. Examples of this distortion include, "I should have taken him to the doctor sooner. I should have made one more trip to see her before she died. I should have told him how much I loved him every day. I should have been stricter." We blame and punish ourselves rather than accept the reality of our loss. This can lead to depression or morph into persistent self-pity or narcissistic "Everything always happens to me" martyrdom.

By the way, as Anne likes to say, "Normal grief is narcissistic." For a while, we feel that no one has gone through what we have. We may temporarily resent others, who are taking life for granted or whining over stupid, trivial issues. However, when we remain stuck in self-righteous pity, this usually means we are holding on to guilt, or our loss is piggybacking older pain.

Some families are unable to let go of a loved one at the end of life because they cannot add one more loss to their unprocessed pile. Futile and prolonged medical care may result because a family member cannot deal with yet another loss. The flip side is a cynical renunciation of life. The feeling is, *After all, what is the point of living if we are all going to die anyway?*

If our tears were ridiculed, we may have learned to displace feelings of sadness into expressions of anger and frustration. I believe more fists are punched through walls because of unexpressed grief than anger.

We can also avoid our grief by over analysis. Our media will sometimes support this distortion by endless reviews and commentary. Analysis can lead to misplaced blame, needless litigation or retaliation, or endless remorse. Rather than feeling our helplessness, wailing out our pain, and exploring any older losses, we resort to blaming others. Some medical malpractice lawsuits are a distortion of grief.

Vengeance can be another avenue of unexpressed grief. Holding on to our pain, we take justice in our own hands in endless tit-for-tat revenge. Perhaps we feel better temporarily. Ultimately, our burdens increase as we create more pain. No one finds a resting place. Without healthy grief, we are unable to look back with gratitude at the gifts we have received in living a vulnerable life.

Anger

One purpose of anger is to change things that are disturbing to us with appropriate assertiveness. Healthy anger is also for self-protection, both physically and emotionally. We need to be able to say, "Stop saying that because it hurts my feelings" or "Stop threatening me."

Intimacy requires the capacity to set limits. Otherwise we risk being smothered, controlled, or treated like a doormat. We lose respect for ourselves when we cannot say no. And our yes becomes meaningless and untrustworthy.

Anger is also for self-definition. When our daughter, Rachael, was about two years old, she was in constant motion. Putting a dress over her head and into her arms was a bit like roping a calf, but after several misses, I managed one morning to fill the three apertures of her sundress with the correct body parts.

I congratulated myself a bit too hastily. Rachael had other ideas. She pulled the dress over her head, dragged off the leotards, and rummaged through her dresser to find a pair of jeans with multicolored patches on the legs, a bright yellow shirt, and two mismatched socks. Had she been verbal enough, she would have raised her chin and declared, "I'm not a sundress girl today. I'm a jeans girl!"

Toddlers say no a lot, because they are defining who they are, separate from their parents. This behavior is more than just plain stubbornness. It is a creative journey in separating and discovering their uniqueness. We often must endure our children's second opportunity to redefine themselves during adolescence.

When our son, Matt, was a junior in high school, he announced at the peak of his rebellion that he wasn't going to study anymore. Anne and

I expressed our fear that he might be jeopardizing his college choices by risking his critical junior-year grades. As you might expect, our helpful comments backfired, so we bit our tongues.

The semester rolled on, and Matt performed a minimum of schoolwork. We did our best to accept his decision, telling each other that even if he didn't go to college, Matt was still the bright and loving boy he had always been. That sounded good when it came out, but it was still hard to watch our plan for our son's academic career being thrown out the window. Finally, about two weeks before the semester ended, we surrendered.

It may have been sheer coincidence, but no sooner had we truly let go of our academic hopes when Matt knocked on our bedroom door and flopped on our bed. "I've been experimenting this semester to see if I was getting A's for you or for me. I've got two weeks left this grading period, and you haven't laid a guilt trip on me. I've decided to end my experiment because I now know that I want to achieve for myself."

Matt quite amazingly pulled the airplane out of its nosedive. I think he really appreciated his success in school after he ended his experiment. It also emboldened him to take nontraditional paths in college, with surprising detours later, before finding his passion. He has continued to take risks to find interesting and challenging work.

The natural expressions of anger are a "No, thank you" for adults and a tantrum or a chin-jutting "No!" for the little ones. Elisabeth used to say that natural anger lasts a symbolic fifteen seconds, appropriate to the stimulus. If our response to a situation is dramatically longer and more intense than we would expect for the event, it usually means old, unfinished business is triggering us.

If we are unable to express healthy anger, we become mired in its many distortions.

Once we can recognize that we are reacting longer than fifteen seconds, we can use this information to diagnose and resolve earlier unresolved pain. This fifteen-second rule has helped me on many occasions to take responsibility for surprisingly strong feelings generated by an unwitting soul. Clarissa Pinkola-Estes, a wonderful Jungian analyst and storyteller, calls those who trigger such strong reactions in us "God in drag." They offer us the opportunity to identify and clean up old messes. I am constantly "blessed" by God's many disguises.

Distortions of Anger

Resentment gnaws at us from the inside out. The degree to which we hold on to old hurts is a measure of our childhood injuries. We simply cannot let things go. We get into a dispute with a loved one, and we bring up something that happened twelve years ago. Then we wonder why our partner throws up his or her hands and walks away.

For some of us, anger was taboo. "We don't behave that way in this house." Healthy anger is replaced with the silent treatment and brooding or cynical passive-aggressive remarks. Unexpressed resentments and fantasies of retaliation create ticking time bombs that never go off or explode unexpectedly, creating chaos and more resentment.

For some of us, rage and violence replaced natural anger. In some homes, one parent has the corner on the anger market, using threats, intimidation, or beatings to control everyone else. The other family members tiptoe around the house, appeasing the angry parent because raising a voice in protest risks further harm. Children stuff their anger, becoming weak and timid. Unsafe to show any assertiveness, they feel hopeless and turn their anger inward. Often one child rebels and carries on the tradition of rage and intimidation. The others remain powerless, falling into despair and depression, or become pleasers and appeasers. In our workshops, many participants define anger as rage because they have never experienced healthy assertiveness in their homes.

We may look in the mirror and swear we will never be like them, but our repressed anger builds into adulthood. Intuitively, we know it's best to keep our mouths shut, because a monster lurks just beneath the surface. Our boss or friend makes a minor request or criticism, triggering our built-up resentments. We swallow our words and sneak away, but the resentment builds until we cannot take it any longer. We explode with dire consequences, often on our unexpecting loved ones. We become what we hate.

Or we humiliate ourselves by bursting into tears, unable even to speak. Our tears aren't of sadness but of impotent rage, making us feel weak and unstable. Then we might humiliate ourselves by accepting support and consolation from those we are angry with.

Our inability to change things and take ownership of our feelings and beliefs may leave us feeling impotent and hopeless. We turn our anger inward, hating ourselves for being powerless doormats. Our self-disdain becomes the ultimate distortion of anger.

It is exhausting to keep a lid on years of pent-up resentments. During a routine day, we may be triggered multiple times. Needing to appear competent, appropriate, and in control, we divert our energy from the tasks at hand to controlling unexpected emotional and physical reactions. When our anger leaks out unexpectedly—or we get those looks that say, *What the hell is wrong with you?*—we feel even worse. For self-protection, we make our anger about everyone else. If others would only …, then we wouldn't need to be angry. By the end of the day, we return home, exhausted, and wonder why we have a headache. Not from the stresses at work but from our unresolved past, we burn out and mistakenly decide to look for a less stressful job. Unfortunately, our past follows us.

As Elisabeth used to say, negativity breeds negativity. The list of crimes against humanity seems unending because we pass on distorted feelings and behaviors from one generation to the next. When we lose the ability to express our anger safely, we are doomed to recreate and perpetuate a world view of mistrust and tit-for-tat revenge.

Fear

The purposes of fear are survival, caution, and discrimination. We have two innate fears: falling and making sudden loud noises. All other fears are learned. Many are necessary for survival: look both ways before crossing the street, stay out of the swimming pool during a lightning storm, and don't provoke a rattlesnake.

Healthy fear is expressed by screaming, freezing, or running, known as the fight-or-flight response. If we are allowed to express our fears during childhood, we learn to ask for reality checks, reassurance, and encouragement; and we make healthy decisions about which risks we are willing to take and which fears we will try to overcome. With each new risk we take, we develop better judgment and become more facile in taking risks. We also aren't ashamed to say, "This is still too scary for me."

After my knee wore out and I could no longer run, I began to cycle. Occasionally I rode with men who were better and more experienced.

Several years ago, I accepted an invitation to go on a week-long cycling trip. I liked the challenge of the climbs but couldn't stand the feeling of the nearly out-of-control downhill careening at forty to fifty miles per hour on two very thin rubber tires.

In my youth, when pride was more important than safety, I'd have sucked it up and just done it anyway. But I have since learned to listen to the voices inside, especially when they are adamant about their limits and abilities. After a day of several rapid descents, I awakened the next day to a voice that declared he wanted to take the day off from cycling. I knew enough to ask myself why. The response from the younger part of me was, *It's just too scary to be holding onto two handlebars at forty-plus miles an hour.* He didn't want me to talk him out of his feelings about this, and he didn't care if my friends thought I was a sissy. I validated his feelings and asked whether he would cycle if I gave him full control of the brakes. I felt him smile. He agreed to try it.

The morning began with a long, flat ride through farmland and then gentle, rolling hills that evolved in a steep climb. On the way down, I remembered to turn the brakes over to my younger self and soon lost contact with the group. Once I was back on flat land, I kept up a good pace but still didn't see them.

After about ten minutes, I came around a turn, and there they were, taking a drink and waiting for me. "Did your chain come off?" one of my buddies asked. I was given an easy out, but there would be other downhill rides to explain. More importantly, the only reason to lie was whether I was ashamed of my being scared. So, without making excuses, I confessed that it made me crazy to go so fast downhill and that they should go ahead; I'd eventually catch up.

The men are great guys, good friends. They all murmured, "No problem."

About ten seconds later, one of the guys in the group offered, "Hey, I'll stay back with Larry so he won't have to ride alone."

Then another said, "Me, too."

We split into two groups, and everyone had a great day.

Distortions of Fear

If we are ridiculed for expressing our fears or constantly talked out of them, we are left to sort them out on our own. As children, we don't have the intellect and experience to do this, so our fears magnify. We can become phobic, preoccupied with our personal safety and unable to enjoy life. Our energy is diverted to avoiding what might hurt us. The list of phobias is endless: fear of heights, fear of spiders, fear of success, fear of failure, or fear of public speaking. We can become so paralyzed that we can't leave home.

If not from specific fears, we can suffer from generalized anxiety or obsessions. We can use up our energy in repetitive silent worry or overt compulsive behaviors. My partner and wife, Anne, always tells her story when she is teaching about fear and anxiety. Before her exams while working on a master's degree in counseling, Anne would go on a cleaning frenzy. Instead of a final touch-up review of material, Anne made our house sparkle. Anxiety trumped preparation. For the record, she always did very well on the exams—and our home continues to be clean but not with quite the same focused determination. I won't elaborate on what she would say about yours truly.

Unacknowledged and unexpressed fear can lead to panic and flashbacks. Stored and incompletely processed hidden memories can flood us with the raw, emotional data of past experiences. Our hearts pound, we break into a cold sweat, and we hyperventilate until our hands and lips go numb. We feel as if we are dying. We will do anything not to feel fear. Our biggest fear becomes fear itself. We avoid all stressful situations so we don't feel as if we are dying over and over again.

If we live in a chaotic and dangerous home, we can learn to split off from our experience or dissociate. We leave our bodies, cutting ourselves off from the hurt, returning to consciousness sometimes long after the danger and pain have passed. As adults, when we are in situations that are even slightly scary, we find ourselves shutting down again. We cannot stay focused in meetings, and we miss important portions of conversations. Unable to concentrate in the classroom, children become labeled as stupid or troublemakers. This very ingenious survival mechanism unfortunately burdens our daily interactions and affects performance and relationships.

We cannot undo what happened, but the past can find a resting place if we are fortunate enough to find a safe place to do the grief work we were unable to do. Most importantly, we get to reclaim our lost younger selves and stop punishing ourselves for being too scared to function. Because of what we have endured and survived, we can be grateful for the wisdom we have earned and have the serenity to look at life's new challenges as opportunities for growth.

Of course, there is also the flip side. We can become so disconnected from our fear that we are never afraid. Several years ago, we consulted for a hospital to work with its staff about the emotional aspects of change. We decided to spend one session on fear in the workplace. When we asked them to talk about how their fears manifest at work, the staff, to a person, said they didn't have any fears. One session expanded into three. The staff began to see that fear was so taboo for professionals that the feelings became displaced by obsessive work, frustration, resentment, judgment of other colleagues or the administration, and finally burnout. Gradually, they began to recognize specific behaviors that clued them into the fact that they were afraid.

In retrospect, I understand that many of my mother's angry outbursts were her distorted responses to fear. Dad's gambling scared the little orphan within her, who never had the safety to utter how terrified she was to be separated from her brothers and sent to live with strangers. Mom was a sweet, tough woman, a survivor who allowed no room for fear in her psyche. Rather than tell her husband how scared she was with his flush-or-broke financial status, Mom attacked with rage and contempt. Fortunately, Dad put his gambling aside and went on to become a successful entrepreneur.

One of the most common reflexes to avoid feeling fear is to jump to anger. I had been teaching the natural and distorted emotions for more than two years before I could see how clearly I jumped to anger when I was afraid.

A Father's Misplaced Anger

Our younger child, Rachael, has greatly stretched our family literally and figuratively. She is a magnificent dancer. In motion from the moment she was born, Rachael has been kinesthetic in a family where intellectual or feeling functions have been dominant. She has blazed her own trail, doing cartwheels off the diving board when she was three and prompting her four-year-old brother, Matt, to utter incredulously, "She doesn't know the meaning of the word *fear*."

Although I should have been prepared for what was to come, the speed and intensity of Rachael's adolescent rebellion blindsided me. By eleven, Rachael was maturing physically, experimenting with newfound power and certainly under the spell of surging hormones. Often defiant and angry, she spent much of her time with friends. She was grounded regularly, which only put a temporary hold on her acting out. Things came to a head just before her twelfth birthday when she moved out to live with a friend's family, whom we barely knew. (What we didn't know until many years later was that Rachael was discovering that the grass wasn't always greener on the other side.) Anne and I were flying by the seat of our pants. At any rate, after about a week, we arranged for a truce.

It was during our meeting, as Rachael aired her grievances and demands, that I suddenly realized how my participation was making matters worse. When it was my turn to speak, I confessed that I had been very angry with her. It was as if I had kissed my little girl good night and by the next morning an alien had taken over her bedroom. My sweet daughter had been kidnapped, and I was furious with this strange being who had taken her place. With tears in my eyes, I told the intruder I missed my little girl and that I was very afraid she was going to do something stupid or dangerous that would hurt her permanently. I then apologized for being so angry and confessed that I was mostly scared.

I suppose I was hoping that my sincerity and vulnerability would somehow bring my little girl back. Instead, and much to her wise credit, the intruder looked right at me and, without blinking, said, "Well, your little girl is dead and never coming back, so you better get to know me now."

Every once in a while, our children give us an opportunity to look deep into their beings to see who they are and what they are made of. These moments can be threatening for parents and can result in conflict, attempts at control, and laying guilt for daring to break the family rules. Or they can be head turning and humbling, filling us with newfound respect for a child who dares to fly when her family has only taught her to walk.

I dried my tears, and, seeing part of my child for the first time, I said with all sincerity, "Yes, I do believe that I should get to know the young woman [emphasis on 'young'] sitting in front of me." I have never been disappointed with my decision.

Over the next few years, Rachael continued to be grounded with regularity. Sometimes toward the end of her rebellion, Anne and I thought she did things just so she would get caught and have an excuse to chill out for a few days from her otherwise superheated life. I made sure I didn't confuse my fear with anger, and I told her how scared I was when she asked to take a road trip or go to a concert.

As her rebellion ended, Rachael responded with a tender hug and said, "Dad, I hope you're learning to manage your fear." The more I managed my fear, the more I realized I could trust the young woman who supplanted my little girl. By the time Rachael was in her final year of high school, we lifted all restrictions, simply asking that she let us know where she was and to call us at any hour if she needed a safe ride. Rachael surprised us many evenings by arriving home well before her prior curfew. She chose to have a good night's sleep rather than burn the candle at both ends. Today Rachael and I happily admit that "my little girl" is alive and well, and I now marvel at the nurturing, wise woman and terrific mother Rachael has become.

Sometimes we are so ashamed of our fear that we constantly try to defeat it with daredevil stunts. We become Evel Knievel, proving to ourselves that we are brave and taking enormous risks we don't even enjoy. We are most dangerous to ourselves and others when we are afraid and don't know it or when we confuse bravado with bravery.

When I first began working with Elisabeth, many Vietnam vets came to our workshops, burdened by posttraumatic stress. They described that they medicated themselves with drugs and alcohol to maintain their bravado, and many confessed to using excessive force and committing atrocities in the heat of battle because they had been so terrified. Fear then led to shame.

One man sobbed his confession of shooting an approaching five-year-old child because he couldn't be sure whether she was armed with a bomb or grenade. He saw the face of that girl and the anguish of her mother night after night. Finally, after telling us his story and confessing his murder, he looked up, expecting to see horror and condemnation. Instead, he saw compassion in our eyes. He began the process of self-forgiveness. He could find a resting place for a little Vietnamese child and for the young soldier who took her life.

Recently, we were privileged to care for Jim, another Vietnam vet, in our hospice. A big bear of a man, he had been a biker and retained many burly male friends, all there to care for him in his last days. They sipped beers, laughed, and swapped stories. Our nurse was present when the topic of Vietnam came up on one of his last nights. The mood changed. He talked about how he alternatively acted tough to cover up his fear, or simply stayed numb. Finally, he looked at our nurse and made his confession. With tears in his eyes and in the eyes of all his buddies, he said, "I killed a lot of people over there, and it remains a stain on my soul."

We put guns in the hands of terrified young boys, and then are horrified by the atrocities they commit. Our entire species is responsible for creating a world full of unacknowledged fear and then arming children and young men with pumped-up bravado and weapons of violence. It isn't just the children who are afraid and don't know it. Many times we have replaced diplomacy with anger and violence, sending young men to war as a manifestation of the unconscious fear of our leaders.

I can imagine that if I hadn't lived in a culture of fear, another scenario might have occurred after the incident with Teddy. I can picture his father knocking on the doors of the neighborhood and requesting that the families come together. He might have described that his boy begged for the others not to crush him, that he couldn't breathe from their cumulative weight, and that the kids all ran away because they knew what they had done was wrong. I can also see him request that no child be punished but instead that each child apologize and promise that that no other child would suffer in this way again.

Neither Teddy nor I should have had reason to carry this shame into adulthood.

Healthy Jealousy

By the term *jealousy*, we mean the innate desire to mimic new behaviors and develop new skills. Recently, neurobiologists have discovered the "mirror neuron" near the premotor cortex in the brain. In response to another's action, these mirror cells fire and set in motion a similar action from the observer. Within weeks after birth, newborns mimic adults when they wiggle their tongues. Scout pushed out her tongue between two closed lips like a turtle poking its head out of the shell. We played tongue games for several minutes together. I was very impressed.

The purpose of natural jealousy is to propel growth and develop competence. Rachael watched her brother, Matt, reading a book on the sofa. She waddled over to the bookcase, chose a story, climbed up on the sofa, and thoughtfully turned the pages. It didn't matter that the book was upside down.

The ingredients for natural jealousy are the healthy motivation engendered by positive role models, encouragement and generosity of spirit. "I want to be great just like my mom!"

When we have healthy role models, we want them to be the best, and we want to be just like them. Inherent in healthy jealousy is a wonderful generosity that cheers on everyone to become the best he or she can be.

At Thanksgiving many years ago, Anne and I invited her family to join us for our feast. We stuffed ourselves with delicious food. After dinner, the adults decided to take a digestive walk before they faced dessert. I volunteered to stay behind with the children and began to tackle the dishes. My four-year-old niece watched me scrape the plates and place them in the sink. With great seriousness, she offered her assistance. I pulled a chair over to the sink, turned on warm water, and handed her the bottle of dish soap. She didn't spare the Dawn. We had mounds of bubbles. I hovered so dishes were safely handled and (mostly) clean. We were both very wet, with bubbles to the armpits.

I received my payoff when her mom and dad came back from their walk. She was luminous with pride for helping Uncle Larry do the dishes. I still remember her face. I also remember the *Better you than me* look her dad gave me. Encouragement is food for the soul.

Encouragement and praise aren't the same thing. Encouragement acknowledges and cheers on someone's dreams and the desire to conquer new challenges. It leaves room for self-evaluation and the necessary experimentation to learn where our passions and talents lie. Praise is applause for what has been accomplished. Whereas encouragement doesn't require a specific outcome, praise is a response to an outcome. Praise can be wonderful. We all wish for a standing ovation. But praise can also be tricky.

False praise can be confusing if it doesn't jibe with the recipient's inner knowing. It hinders children from learning healthy self-appraisal. Later, they misinterpret healthy feedback as harsh criticism, and they resent not receiving constant praise from teachers and supervisors. Instead of being driven by inner passion and motivation, they may be taught to rely on external rewards. Of course, we all enjoy praise, but it should be the icing on the cake rather than the cake itself.

Excessive praise may be interpreted as parental expectations. Children may bury their own passion in life to pursue what makes their parents happy. On the other hand, lack of any acknowledgment may make us feel invisible and unappreciated.

Too much scrutiny can suppress creativity and develop into fear of failure. I was recently talking to a coaching friend of mine, who told me about his young wrestler, who excels in practice but freezes during a match. The boy loves the sport but hates the competition because it is so loaded with expectations of performance. This young wrestler not only faces his weight-matched opponent on the mat but must also deal with overbearing expectations of others. The best of intentions can break a promising spirit.

Discouragement can be just as harmful as too much attention. At our workshops, we hear repeated stories of how people have "settled" for a career because they were told they weren't smart enough to be a doctor, thin enough to be a dancer, or talented enough to be a writer.

Parents who haven't grieved their own unfulfilled dreams may be envious of the dreams of their children. Other parents, trying to protect their children from their own failures, discourage their children even from trying. "I just don't want you to be disappointed, that's all."

If we grow up with comparisons and criticism, some of us give up and prove our critics right about us. We seek role models who welcome us into the fold of the disenfranchised and expect little of us except loyalty. We see gangs filled with children who have given up. They wear the colors and give their obedience to belong somewhere. Desperate children without hope are at risk of being brainwashed and manipulated by role models who are less altruistic than healthy parents and teachers.

Resisting criticism, some children overcompensate to prove they are good enough. They set goal after goal to achieve, but their successes are hollow and short lived because they cannot banish the voices of their childhood critics. They push themselves to be the best. Their role models and colleagues have become their unknowing competitors. Lacking healthy encouragement, they are preoccupied with their own need to show them. Being better than someone else or winning becomes their only goal.

They envy those who are more successful and see everyone as competitors. Some will even cheat to win. They see the world as filled with winners and losers. Since they were criticized, they become critical of others. Winning at all costs replaces the natural desire for growth and exploration. Living their lives in endless comparisons, they have no empathy for those who try and fail or who have never had a chance in the first place.

Many of us are tormented by our internalized judge, who constantly whispers an unending tape of criticism. We can never be good enough for our internalized judge, so we endlessly seek scraps of praise from others. Sadly, praise can only temporarily override the endless chatter of the internal judge, who, among other things, constantly asks, "What have you done lately?" There is never celebration, only another yardstick, which isn't of our choosing.

Bob's Powerful Judge

Bob came to our workshop because he was burned out at work, had no energy for life, and felt depressed. He had done everything he was supposed to do. He'd played sports in high school, gotten good grades, graduated from a prestigious university, started his own business, made a lot of money, married a good woman, and fathered two children, whom he adored but spent little time with. His work was his life. Even though he didn't need more wealth, he remained driven to grow his business and multiply his net worth. He rewarded himself with fancy toys and provided everything his family wanted, but his enjoyment was transient. He always needed to know what his friends and business competitors were driving and where they were going on vacation.

Intellectually, he knew he was successful, but inside he still felt like a failure—maybe not exactly a failure but definitely not good enough. When he looked in the mirror, all he saw was what was wrong with him; he was too fat and bald, and his nose was crooked. He was worn out running from his internal judge, the voice that constantly critiqued who he was and what he did. He could explain all this in front of the group, but he seemed powerless to change it. When I asked him to defend himself from the judge, he said he couldn't because basically it was all true.

Our judge retains power over us because of its stealth. No one else can see or hear it but us. Its whisper in our ears is both subliminal and deafening. One way to take its power away is to insist that the judge speak aloud.

So I spoke directly to Bob's judge and demanded that whatever he had to say to him must be said aloud, for everyone to hear. As it turned out, Bob's energy lay in his own self-hate. His judge tore into him with anger and disgust. It proceeded to put Bob out on the phone books, calling him a loser, describing how ugly he was, and telling him the only reason his wife stayed with him was because of his money. He was lucky rather than talented. The judge went on and on. Bob's self-hate was strong and powerful.

Finally, when the judge was finished, I asked Bob whose voice that was. "My father. He didn't even have to say anything. I could tell by the way he looked at me that I was a disappointment."

Then, without my saying another word, Bob confronted his father. The voice heard was that of an eight-year-old. He told his father to leave him alone, to shut up and let him be, that he was a good kid who was smart and talented, and who cared about people. After his rage, the tears followed, tears for all he had missed, for all the years of frantic activity, hoping to hear from his father words that were never spoken.

Very calmly, Bob looked around the room and introduced his eight-year-old. Bob described in great detail how gifted and caring this boy was, how proud of him he was, and what kind of man he would grow up to be.

That morning, in front of twenty-five witnesses, Bob gave his little one a new internal father. Of course, the voice of the judge would return, but Bob was able to recognize it, utter a "Thank you for sharing," and use the voice of his new internal father to equalize the chatter. Months later, Bob reported how his relationship with his two sons had improved. He now had an eight-year-old consultant who advised him about what little boys need and crave.

After releasing his pent-up feelings, Bob could integrate the raw, unconscious, emotional data of his early experience and replace his rigid, retraumatizing beliefs and behaviors with newfound compassion and gentleness.

Healthy competition recognizes the gift our competitor gives us by motivating us to become all we can. In sumo wrestling, each contestant bows in acknowledgment to the other both before and after the match. Without an opponent, there could be no match at all. Healthy competition encourages and values both the winner and the loser. Unhealthy competition becomes solely about the winner, whether he wins by cheating or because his opponent messes up. "Talking trash" has replaced the bow of respect in many of our sporting and political arenas.

If we aren't raised with loving encouragement and generosity of spirit, we become envious, greedy, and self-centered. Like Ebenezer Scrooge, we hoard what we have and demean those who have less. Life becomes a zero-sum game.

Love

By love, we mean joy, playfulness, intimacy, passion, empathy, forgiveness, and connection. Love begins with self and our Creator, and it spreads outward. These words sound like platitude until we see self-love in action.

Natural love is unconditional. *I love you for who you are, not for who I want or need you to be.* Healthy parents delight in the birth of a new soul on the planet and resonate with the words of Kahlil Gibran.

> Your children are not your children.
> They are sons and daughters of Life's longing for itself.
> They come through you but not from you.
> And though they are with you yet they belong not to you.
>
> You may give them your love but not your thoughts,
> For they have their own thoughts.
> You may house their bodies but not their souls,
> For their souls dwell in the house of tomorrow, which you cannot visit, not even in your dreams.
> You may strive to be like them, but seek not to make them like you.
> For life goes not backward nor tarries with yesterday.
> You are the bows from which your children as living arrows are sent forth.
> The archer sees the make upon the path of the infinite, and He bends you with His might that His arrows may go swift and far.
> Let your bending in the archer's hand be for gladness.
> For even as He loves the arrow that flies, so He also loves the bow that is stable.

With loving curiosity, healthy parents seek to discover the awakening nature of the children they birthed. Parents gift their children by seeing, encouraging, and rejoicing in who they really are. At the same time, they don't spoil their children. Parents teach their children to take responsibility for their words and actions, delay gratification, and share in the work and benefits of family life. They allow their children to make mistakes and learn from them.

Apologizing when they overreact, parents demonstrate respect and humility. Matching their behavior with their words, parents model discipline and healthy boundaries in their relationships. They set limits with their children. Expressing their own needs for balance with family activities and time alone, they teach their children to make similar requests.

Distortions of Love

Many of us have grown up with conditional messages, the "I love you ifs": *if* you are pretty, *if* you are smarter than Jimmy, *if* you are good, *if* you take care of me, *if* you are quiet, *if* you are happy—but not too happy.

The list of "ifs" is endless. Conditional love is a commodity that can be bought and paid for. Elisabeth used to say that when we perform to be rewarded, we become prostitutes. We learn that all gifts have a price. We stop trusting others' motives because we know our own are suspect as well. We become manipulators, and after a while, we begin to believe our motives are genuine. Without trust, life becomes a game of what we can get.

When we are loved conditionally, we learn that who we are is never enough, that we are valuable only for what we do. We become seducers, because we doubt our inherent self-worth. Yet from a distorted sense of entitlement, we resort to demands rather than requests of loved ones. Believing we are unworthy of love, we are needy, clingy, and possessive because we know it's only a matter of time before our family and friends find someone more attractive or interesting. Some of us can't deal with this anxiety, so we reject preemptively. "I'll leave you before you leave me."

Constantly giving ourselves away in relationships, we can be truly ourselves only when we are alone. We are either compliant or resentful. Authenticity and intimacy are mutually exclusive. Some of us just give up and take the geographic cure. *I'm going to an island in the South Pacific, and the hell with everybody!* As Paul Simon says,

> I am a rock.
> I am an island.
> And a rock feels no pain,
> And an island never cries.

But when our loved ones see who we really are, warts and all, and still love us, they melt away our nagging sense of aloneness. That isn't to say that there will never again be disagreements, differences of opinion, or even flares of anger and frustration. But the bridge of love and trust isn't broken.

I recently told a friend about a family ritual we have developed since our two children graduated from high school. After Anne and I began working with Elisabeth, we developed a close friendship with another couple, who also worked with her. Sharon and Shannon became a part of our family Thanksgiving for twenty-five years, beginning when Matt and Rachael were young teenagers. Initially, the four adults would take time alone to have a talking circle, sharing what we were doing but, more importantly, what was going on inside us. Speaking without comment or interruption, a very sacred rule of our check-ins, we each took a turn to say what was on our minds and in our hearts. We found that having time to be still would often bring out feelings and thoughts we weren't consciously aware of. We all learned the value of cultivating deep introspection. Our check-in time always brought us closer.

After graduating from high school, Matt and Rachael began to ask exactly what we did when we went off by ourselves. We explained in great detail how our check-in worked and why we took this time for ourselves. We invited Matt and Rachael to join us. Without hesitation, they both said yes.

All six of us were surprised by the depth of sharing during our first year together. Our children heard us talk about current sadness and joy, and refer to childhood injuries that still bubbled up in the present. They witnessed our childhood vulnerability as well as our tears, anger, humor, and resilience.

In turn, they spoke courageously and with great dignity about their struggles and triumphs, their fears and frustrations, without blaming, shaming, or protecting their mom and dad from their truth. They also showed great compassion for our blunders.

Most importantly, we have been able to tell each other, in these times of great openness, how much we love and appreciate each other, even with all our *mishagos* (a Yiddish word for craziness).

Over the years, Matt and Rachael have invited their partners to join our circle. Our family is spread out over both coasts, and we cherish the few times a year when we're all together. We have learned that taking the time to "check in" when we first come together brings us closer and makes us aware of how we can best meet each other's needs.

"Wow," my friend said. "Your kids are really mature. Didn't they ever use what you shared against you?" Of course, that question told me a lot about my friend's early life. But it made me appreciate how the love we have in our family supersedes any disagreements or irritations. It wouldn't even cross my mind that any of us would attack the young and vulnerable voices that reside in each of us.

We try to fight fair when we fight. When we spot a scared little one in the fray, the other disarms. The child is held and supported with reverence until an adult reappears. When I have reacted from those old hurt and defended parts of myself, I am treated with tenderness until I return to my center. Once again solid within myself, I am then able to own old behaviors I no longer want and to make amends. The nod of love and acceptance that follows deepens our connection.

Unconditional love means we can speak honestly with each other and respect differences of opinion. It gives us the self-confidence to engage in respectful inquiry into why someone else feels and believes differently than we do, rather than jumping to immediate judgment or unrelenting advocacy of our opinions.

Carl, the Tough Marine

Many years ago, Carl came to our workshop because he had begun to feel out of control. When he was a boy, his father had ridiculed and humiliated him each time he cried. He had been taught that life was hard and that only the strong survive. Carl learned his lesson well, stuffing his grief so deep that he was no longer aware of it. He didn't cry for over thirty years.

Unfortunately, the cost of this repression was that he lived his life on autopilot. He didn't feel sadness or joy. He didn't feel at all. When his parents died, his eyes remained dry. Carl and his wife had no meaningful conversations and were basically business partners in their marriage. They lived separate lives until one of their children became ill. Carl began to feel things he didn't want to feel. He couldn't sleep for worry. He pushed his fear away the only way he knew: be tough, be positive. He comforted his son the same way he did himself, with pep talks and false cheer. His son humored him until one day, nauseated from chemotherapy and scared that he wasn't going to survive, he told his father, "Shut the fuck up and leave me alone." A friend gave Carl a brochure for Elisabeth's workshop.

Listening with rapt attention to one participant after another, Carl couldn't believe others had also buried their anguish deep inside. He saw the transformative power of quiet attention rather than pep talks or advice.

Finally, he came to the mat and explained to the group that he had been taught to bury his feelings. Joining the marines to fight for his country, he'd watched men die while he continued to carry out his duty. Grief was a luxury for the weak and certainly not beneficial for a marine. But now his son was fighting for his life, and Carl was terrified. Trying to stop the unexpected sobs that burst from his chest, he made fists and began pounding on the mat.

Elisabeth, who was a tiny woman, got up from her chair and took this big, strong marine in her arms. He sobbed like a little boy for maybe five minutes. We all sensed he shed tears for events that had happened long ago. It didn't matter that we didn't hear the words he whispered to Elisabeth. When Carl finally looked up, he saw tears in many eyes, kindness instead of judgment, and respect for the risk he had taken by coming to the mat.

Carl had reclaimed a small and tender boy who had been browbeaten into being tough and unfeeling. A loyal and good man, he had lost the ability to be vulnerable and empathetic. He now understood that being vulnerable wasn't a weakness. Right now, in fact, he felt stronger and calmer than he had felt for years. Carl couldn't wait for the workshop to end so he could go home and apologize to his son for not being there for him.

It was only after Carl found love and tenderness for himself that he could be present, vulnerable, and strong for his son. In loving himself in this new way, he could return home and give his son what they both had never had.

Carl's son recovered, and his boy's illness became the catalyst for a new intimacy with his wife and the other child. Carl later wrote that not only was he more effective at work, but his relationships there gave him newfound pleasure.

Natural Emotion	Purpose	Natural Expression	Distortions
Anger	For Change Self-Definition Self-Protection	Assertiveness Temper Tantrum ("No!")	Rage Intimidation Resentment Retaliation/Revenge Violence Passive-Aggressive Sarcasm/Cynicism Silent Treatment Withdrawal Powerlessness Despair Self-Hate Defiance
Fear	Self-Protection Survival Caution Discrimination	Fight/Flight Scream Freeze	Anxiety Phobias Obsessive Thoughts/ Behaviors Panic Numbness Daredevil Acts Misplaced Anger
Jealousy	Impels Growth (Emulation)	Mimicry Role Models Encouragement	Discouragement Compare/Criticize Internalized "Judge" Ugly Envy Quitting Overachieving Unhealthy Competition False Praise

Grief/Sadness	Express Loss Redefine Self	Crying Tell Our Story	Always on Verge of Tears Remorse (If Only) Regrets Martyrdom Blame (Self, Others) Self-Pity Glorification Intellectualize Numbness
Love	Connection with Self, Others, Creator Joy, Play	Touch Attunement Empathy Sexuality Unconditional Set Limits	Conditional: I Love You if … Prostitute (Buy Love) Clingy Possessive Seduction Manipulation Do It Alone: No Needs Rejecting Demanding/Entitlement

The deeper we can explore who we are, the more comfortable we become in learning and seeing who others are, including their pain, fear, and rage. As we develop self-forgiveness and empathy for the banished voices inside (including those aspects of ourselves that are capable of hurting others), we can offer that same gift to others.

Appendix 2

NO CHOICES: THE VICTIM TRIANGLE

> The oak fought the wind and was broken, the willow bent when it must and survived.
> —Robert Jordan, *The Fires of Heaven*

With childhood abuse and neglect, we suffer twice, first from the injury and second from the shame of our vulnerability, weakness, and neediness. Most of us survive the abuse, but the shame can mark us for life.

Most parents do the best they can. The desire for our kids to have happy lives often motivates parental invasiveness. I would bet that Kyle's father truly believed he was preparing his kids for a hard, uncaring world, where only the fittest survive and thrive. Most parents have the best of intentions, often trying to protect their children from their own unresolved, painful childhood memories. In wanting to protect their kids from disappointment, failure, homeliness, and rejection, parents can inadvertently send the message that their kids must be perfect to be loved.

Some children give up on their true passions to please their parents, while others rebel. If kids are allowed to safely protest, midcourse corrections in the relationship between parent and child happen naturally. But if parents are either insecure or perfectionistic and haven't dealt with their own childhood pain, their children's deficiency becomes a threatening reflection. Kids pay the price. Unable to rise to unstated standards makes them feel like failures in the eyes of their parents. Kids lose either way, on the one hand feeling shame for prostituting themselves for parental love and on the other for feeling inadequate.

In the 1960s, a branch of psychology called "transactional analysis" described the roles people played in shame-based, dysfunctional relationships. In 1964, Eric Berne wrote *Games People Play*, which was followed by Stephen Karpman's *Drama Triangle*. Karpman described three classic roles (victim, persecutor, and rescuer) that enabled people to be in relationships and at the same time avoid feeling pain. Sharon Tobin and Shannon Steck, two very gifted therapists who worked with adults suffering childhood trauma, began teaching this model in Elisabeth's workshops. Anne and I have continued to use and modify this model to stress the importance of doing our grief work to improve our relationship with ourselves and others.

Equally descriptive names for the "Drama Triangle" would be the "Triangle of Reactivity," the "Shame Triangle," or the "Victim Triangle," because it is our sense of unworthiness that propels us into these unhealthy roles. The major fuels of the triangle are fear, guilt, and our need to avoid emotional pain.

We manifest all the distorted emotions listed in appendix 1 when we live in the triangle. To change our relationships, we must first identify and own the behaviors we manifest in each of the three roles. Sometimes we move so rapidly from one role to another that it can be difficult to identify each dysfunctional pattern. No role is inherently better or worse than another. However, beauty is in the eye of the beholder. For any individual, one role may be seen as healthy, another abhorrent. These preferences speak to the specific childhood adaptations to their injury. Getting out of the triangle often requires revisiting these past events.

The Victim (Shame) Triangle*

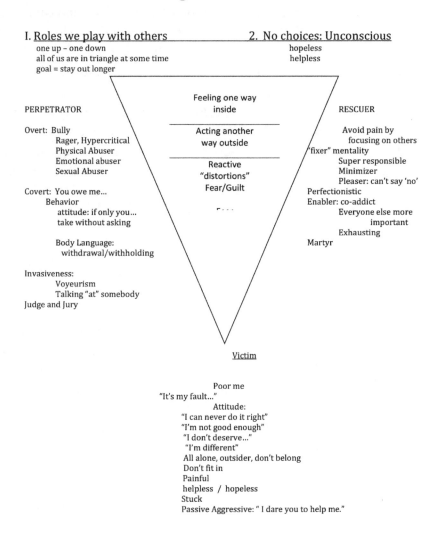

The Victim

We *all* enter the triangle as a victim: helpless, not good enough, and at fault. If children are reinjured or exiled when they dare to protest hurtful behaviors of their caregivers, they have only two options: to remain helpless and extremely vulnerable or to blame themselves for all that is wrong in their world. Since we humans cannot stand to be powerless or feel out of control, we unconsciously take responsibility for the chaos and emptiness in our lives. As small children, we construct a world in which we are both bad (unlovable) and simultaneously all powerful, because of the unhappiness *we* have created. No longer safe to shake our fist in protest, we resign ourselves to a lonely life.

As victims, we aren't deserving of love and support. Feeling unworthy, we don't ask for help. We remain stuck in despair. No matter what we do, the deck is stacked against us. Isolating from others or complaining for the sake of complaining, we drive people further away and confirm our world view that we aren't lovable. We never feel that we belong or fit in, even among a small group of friends. We are stuck but unable to see how our childhood decision has paralyzed us.

The triangle is defined by one-up, one-down relationships. Clearly, "victim" is a one-down position. Yet each location on the triangle has its own power. Even as victims, we may silently carry the banner and arrogance of uniqueness. No one has suffered as we have; no one can understand what we have been through. Our pain, if nothing else, makes us special. Each position in the triangle is infused with its own particular brand of grandiosity and righteousness. For the victim, our grandiosity is in what we have endured; our righteousness is in our martyrdom.

Victims appear helpless, with no choices or means to change. We carry the mark of Cain; we are bad, unworthy, hopeless, and without redemption. Yet we have more power than we realize or care to admit, because we generate guilt in rescuers and contempt in perpetrators.

I use the pronoun *we* because most of us have the voice of each of these roles within us. We touch the victim place, even if briefly, with our pessimism and cynicism. I have found that when I am having a particularly strong reaction or judgment to one of the roles of the triangle, I need only to look inside to see what I despise about myself, what part of myself I have banished to avoid feeling my vulnerability. When I find myself condemning someone who is, as Elisabeth used to say, marinating in self-pity and at the same time congratulating myself for being strong enough to climb out of my pit of despair, I only need to wonder how much more abuse, neglect, or humiliation I would have had to experience to make me give up. Then I return to a place of compassion and gratitude.

As victims, we harbor simmering resentment. Had we received the love and attention we needed, we wouldn't be in this place of despair. We attract rescuers, but with passive-aggressive and self-righteous bitterness, we punish those who offer help by rejecting their advice. We flip-flop from not deserving help and compassion to silently daring, almost demanding, that others try.

In this way, victims stay in relationships. As victims, we don't want to own our power because it implies that we are capable of change. Rather, we need others to confirm our world view; rescuers imply that victims are incapable of surviving without them, while perpetrators condemn our powerlessness. Rescuers and perpetrators mirror the disrespect the victim has for himself or herself.

In a perverse way, the victim's self-esteem comes from suffering. As victims, our whining and complaining occupy a large part of our time and energy. We remain trapped in our past, unable to grieve and move on, because we don't believe there is any hope. We wear our feelings as a badge of suffering, rather than use them as an opportunity for growth. It is a very lonely and painful role, mirroring the abuse and neglect of earlier times.

It's important to remember that the triangle is one of our most useful survival tools, because it allows us to stay in relationships, even abusive ones, without which we literally couldn't survive childhood. When we are in the victim role, we push away the agony, powerlessness, and emptiness of an unsafe or unseen childhood. Attracting rescuers to save us and perpetrators to judge us, at least on the surface, prevents us from being completely alone; and the dance of power between these roles distracts us from dealing with our pain.

In all three positions in the triangle, we become stuck in habitual thinking and behavior. It takes tremendous courage, will, and often help to break such ingrained patterns. For many of us, the role of the victim, though powerful in its own way, is intolerable. Feeling unworthy and much too vulnerable, hopeless, and powerless, we move to another spot in the triangle.

The Rescuer

This role looks healthy at first glance. Doing for others is rewarded in our Judeo-Christian culture. I became my mother's little helper and protector. I wanted to help the meek and infirm as well as to be tough and scrappy like my father. Praise and reward reinforced the role. My unconscious motivation was to banish my shame by being a hero. The role of the rescuer is therefore not, in essence, altruistic. The rescuer must have people in need to redeem himself or herself. I had to be one up in order not to feel one down.

Like most people, I had, and have, a strong desire to be of service; but my unconscious drive to focus on the needs of others, at the exclusion of my own, was unhealthy. There are times when the desires of the rescuer are so submerged; they don't know what they need or want. When asked about a simple choice of restaurant or movie, the classic rescuer response is, "I'm open. You decide."

The rescuer or caretaker must find others who need fixing. If there are none around, he or she will fix what isn't broken. Much like the cartoon of two boy scouts escorting a healthy, robust woman across the street, the rescuer can be invasive. My dad was a rescuer and a good one at that; but I just wanted him to listen to what *I* felt, not lecture me about what he thought I needed. At times, I still get angry when I'm given unrequested advice or assistance; and yet I still find myself on occasion talking rather than listening.

The rescuer gives unrequested advice, pep talks, and sermons. He or she asks questions just long enough to be able to pontificate and proselytize. The rescuer, therefore, covertly uses the frailty of others to make himself or herself feel important and to avoid his or her own sense of unworthiness. The rescuer focuses his or her energy relentlessly on others so he or she doesn't have the time to experience the emptiness of his or her own life. The rescuer is often very uncomfortable being in his or her own company.

The rescuers are super responsible. Companies do well to hire them. They will take full responsibility, even for things completely out of their control. Out of fear and shame, rescuers will enable addictive behavior, appease brutish bosses and relatives, and sacrifice any personal life. Everyone else is more important. They'll work overtime without extra pay. They cannot say no. They are perfectionists, and they are indispensable. The rescuers' brand of grandiosity is in their indispensability. "Without me, everything would fall apart." Their righteousness is in their selflessness.

Rescuers often work harder than the person they are helping. When a friend asks for help painting his or her living room, rescuers go to the hardware store and buy the paint. While their friend takes a long lunch, they keep working to finish the job. Then they do the cleanup. Usually, it's only in retrospect that resentment creeps in. When their effort isn't worth the unconscious payoff, they find themselves asking, "What's wrong with this picture? Why doesn't anybody do this for me?"

I have had the privilege of being the physician for some very good friends. It can be a delicate balance at times. My friends are the first people to tell me not to work so hard … until they have a medical problem.

One afternoon, I was visiting a very good friend and long-time patient at his office. He is an extremely loving and generous man. During our conversation, he was bemoaning that people called him only when they wanted something. I looked at him and said, "I know just what you mean." I raised my eyebrows.

"Oh, I do that to you, don't I?" We laughed hysterically for a few moments and then moved on to other topics. About three days later, my good buddy called me in the middle of a busy day. I always try to answer his calls, but on that day, I did it while shaking my head and thinking, *I don't have time for another problem right now.*

"Hi, Larry."

"Hi, Jim, what do you need?" I was all business.

"I need to see how my good friend is doing today and ask him if there is anything that I can do for him." We laughed again.

Rescuers can count on the fingers of one hand how many people ever call just to see how they are doing. They project self-sufficiency and strength. If someone offers help, it is kindly refused. Even when the rescuer asks for help, it is done with apology. Sometimes when help is given, rescuers put up a wall, feeling invaded by the person offering assistance. Their vulnerability triggers fear and anger, which often is projected at the one trying to help. Rescuers like to be in control.

If someone brings a gift, it is immediately reciprocated. The rescuer doesn't feel deserving of an unconditional gift. Suspicious of an ulterior motive, rescuers refuse gifts, even those offered with an open heart. Rescuers hate to feel indebted because it confirms past vulnerability.

Jim still calls me regularly to ask how I am. I still smile with delight, remembering the laughter we shared in his office years ago. Each time he calls, I take a deep breath of gratitude and open my heart to this gift of unconditional caring. Rescuers don't want others to check on them. They are always just fine. Unable to accept the gift of concern, they often turn the table on the caller.

Rescuers ultimately exhaust themselves. I used to think Ford Motor Company put a mood-altering chemical on the seat of my car. I would leave work as Super Doc, but by the time I pulled into my driveway, I was beaten down and weary, and I just wanted to be alone. I wasn't good at faking it with my astute wife and jumping-all-over-me kids. The people I most wanted to be with were getting the least from me. What kind of father and partner was I? Poor me. Exhaustion erodes the most fortified caregiver. I move back to victim again.

Sometimes some unsuspecting soul asks me to do one more thing. He or she has no idea my day has been a disaster, with what seemed like a hundred phone calls, fifteen emergencies, and too many consults, for which I have pretended to be grateful. I attack or treat him or her dismissively. The poor person just requested some help. Rescuer moves to perpetrator.

The Perpetrator

I tried to make myself indispensable to many people, to be the ultimate caring and dedicated physician. Then when they had the audacity to need me, I got angry at their dependency and fearfulness. It's like a wonderful therapist I know, who admitted to me that there were days when she wanted to tell all her clients, "Get a life!" With exhaustion, we can slide seamlessly from rescuer to perpetrator. Irritable and judgmental, we throw caring and concern for others right out the window.

Although I dressed in a shirt and tie, and had a stethoscope around my neck, there were days when a frustrated five-year-old was practicing medicine. Even though I was a pro at faking that I had all the time in the world for them, my patients would invariably comment on how tired I looked. If they only knew how much energy it took to contain a seething five-year-old, they would understand why I was tired. At the time, I didn't know why I was tired either.

Mainly my family experienced the seething time bomb, saw the clenched fists, heard the controlled rage, the dismissive responses to questions, or the silent withdrawal. I never dared show this part of me in public. I was a nice guy. I wasn't like *them*. My resentments and judgments hovered just below the surface: *Everyone else gets to relax, play, and have nights and weekends off.* All the distortions of the natural emotions have full range in the triangle.

I should say that many days went reasonably well. The practice of medicine, like an illness, is unpredictable. Some days my schedule moved along without interruption, and I finished at a reasonable time, enjoying poignant interactions and appreciative patients for my skill as an infectious disease specialist. Other days I could put my stress in cold storage for the night and be a good enough mate and dad.

I remember nights when I collapsed with fatigue, falling asleep midsentence during a story I was reading to Matt and Rachael, only to have them shake me awake so they could hear the ending. Occasionally, I was beyond reach. Survival overshadowed even the love I had for my family, and no amount of cajoling from them would break the spell.

Clearly, healthy adults get tired, angry, and frustrated as well. When we are outside the triangle, the healthy adult doesn't take it out on others. We let people know we've reached a limit, apologize for any inconvenience, and make a request for help and support. My five-year-old acted like an angry martyr, not because he was bad but because he lacked a healthy adult to acknowledge his frustration, set limits on his behavior, and seek support and understanding. My adult was pleasant, even charming, during times of low stress; but during times of chaos, I often lacked the knowledge and tools to be present for an overwhelmed little boy.

I suppose I assumed that if I sacrificed enough, one day I would be pardoned. Shame, however, is a cruel and enduring taskmaster. It asks only one question of the rescuer: what have you done lately?

Perpetrators give up trying to make reparations for their shame. Instead, they act from a perverse entitlement. They take without asking, monopolizing conversations, touching someone without his or her permission, and reneging on agreements.

Perpetrators blame others others for their lot in life. They take no responsibility for their choices or feelings. It's the system, the boss, weather, kids, or spouse. "If only you changed, I would be fine. The only reason I yell or complain is you! You don't listen. You spoil the kids. You never help." You, you, you; never I.

Perpetrators bury shame under a mountain of entitlement, which can erode core values. We butt in line, humiliate a waitress, make fun of a colleague because getting a laugh is more important than someone's feelings, steal a towel from a hotel room, sneak into a movie or onto a train without paying, or blast music so loud no one else can think. *If someone is going to do without or suffer, it's not going to be me.* Perpetrators find innocent people to hurt so they don't have to feel their own pain. Often they hurt the people closest to them.

When we move from victim to perpetrator, our self-righteousness justifies almost any behavior. War, terrorism, theft, revenge, murder, drug and alcohol abuse, and sexual exploitation are rationalized by what the world did to us. We can even weaponize religion and spirituality. Elevating ourselves to judge and jury, the perpetrator in each of us is capable of excluding, condemning, or manipulating others. We can even declare which of us is going to heaven, which to hell. The perpetrators' brand of grandiosity is in their willingness to use their power to get what they want. The end justifies the means. Their righteousness is in the certain knowledge that, no matter what anyone says, everybody has a price.

I believe many perpetrators are unaware of their unconscious hatred. In fact, they see themselves as victims or rescuers. Adolf Hitler projected his childhood abuse onto the Jews, who were taking over Europe. He was "saving Germany" from these outsiders. Hitler, the victim and rescuer. In each of us lives the victimized and saintly perpetrator.

Perpetrators aren't only the classic physical, emotional, or sexual abusers. They don't need to be violent sociopaths. Most of us demonstrate the subtle behaviors of the perpetrator in body language—rolling the eyes, withdrawing in silence, taking passive-aggressive jabs, or making a disapproving and condemning look. A look of disgust can be as brutal as a fist.

Believing they don't deserve a standing ovation, perpetrators resort to bragging and self-inflation. They aren't at all bashful about pontificating, making pronouncements to family members or even total strangers about the best flavor of ice cream, the appropriate dress code, or the one true path to nirvana. As high priests, their truth is the truth. They use others by taking up all the space in a conversation, giving unsolicited opinions, or telling self-inflated stories. No one is smarter or more interesting to a perpetrator than himself or herself.

Perpetrators are cynical about altruistic motives, since they have known only deceit and manipulation. Underneath all the banter lie enormous fear and mistrust. For the perpetrators, it is survival of the fittest. They aren't their brothers' keeper.

We perpetrate by controlling relationships. We may isolate our partner from friends and relatives; demand inappropriate loyalty and devotion; and even invade our partner's private letters and journals. During a disagreement, perpetrators might attack emotionally or physically or not speak to someone for a week. Or we might engage in risky, self-abusive activity while telling our partner it will be her fault if we injure ourselves. We are unable and unwilling to take responsibility for our thoughts, feelings, and behavior.

Although we tend to have our fallback spot in the triangle, we move with great fluidity from one role to another. Shame is monochromatic, black or white. Gray requires perspective, a willingness to look for the good in everyone and acknowledge with all humility our own shadow. When I was beyond reach, I was unwilling to be wrong. Pride infuses the triangle. I didn't apologize.

We can perpetrate on ourselves. My internal judge would condemn me with the question "What kind of a father and partner are you?" My response "Poor me, never good enough" took me back to the victim. When there is no one else to play with, we move from one role to the other all by ourselves.

Whereas healthy self-evaluation brings me back to my core values, self-condemnation plunges me into victimhood. The internal judge whispers in my ear the constant message that I'm not good enough. It is one of the subtlest and most pervasive forms of violence.

Abuse and neglect may breed a unique form of narcissism. In the triangle, life is always about *me*: the heroic martyr-rescuer; the downtrodden, self-flagellating victim; or the entitled perpetrator. An example would be a man who yells at his partner in front of his kids, scares them to death, then later plunges into such dramatic remorse that his wife and kids have to encircle him with forgiveness and take the blame themselves. Or how about "God made it rain just to ruin my day at the beach"? Life is always about me.

When I get tired of bathing in self-pity (victim) and self-disgust (perpetrator), I can move to rescuer, enabling myself by binging on food or buying expensive toys. When the MasterCard bill comes due, my judge takes over … around and around I go.

For many children around the world, their choice is reduced to either victim or perpetrator: kill or be killed. They haven't experienced the rescuer. Child soldiers bounce from one to the other until they either are crushed under the weight of abuse and violence or find the power to dish it out themselves. Some succumb, giving up in despair. They use alcohol and drugs to anesthetize their pain and shame, and they stifle the rage that puts them at risk of becoming what they hate.

Others survive by fanning the flames of their hatred. Kidnapped boys become child soldiers, surviving by creating fear in others to protect themselves from their own terrors. They bury their fear with acts of brutality, torture, and rape. No one is more dangerous than armed men or women who are unaware of how scared they are, including world leaders with armies at their disposal.

I was fortunate to have examples of caring and generosity at home. The rescuer became a viable option for me. I had the opportunity and received praise for helping. I gravitated to the more socially acceptable spot as my fallback position, but having a preference didn't prevent me from visiting the other points on the triangle. I was just as trapped in dysfunction as someone who had a different fallback choice.

Of course, none of us is perfect. We all make mistakes, but when we recognize we are in the triangle, we stop, take a time-out, check in with ourselves, and break the spell. We take responsibility for our behavior and make amends.

I wish I could tell the reader I no longer find myself spinning around the triangle. Alas, I remain very human. Knowing about these dysfunctional roles and having loving help to remind me, I can break the spell more quickly. I become less defensive, which is another hallmark of the triangle. I speak my truth, allowing others to do the same. I disarm.

Rachael Wants to Go to the Mall

When our kids were teenagers and flexing new muscles, Anne and I split shifts during the summer so one of us was mostly home all day. On this particular day, I started about four o'clock in the morning to finish by two or three in the afternoon. Keeping one eye on the clock, I rushed around, seeing patients and doing my best to present a caring, professional face. On my drive to work, I had promised myself that once I got home, I would just hang out and relax. Having recently identified a young boy inside who always had to be productive, I was working on giving him time just *to be* rather than always scanning for things to do. He was really looking forward to an afternoon of R&R.

Rachael had other plans for us. As soon as I walked in the house, Rachael and her friend greeted me with, "Dad, we have to go to the mall right now!"

Without taking even a breath, let alone checking in with the little guy, I said, "Okay."

I immediately felt the heat rising inside my chest. I quickly added, "But we have to go right away." My little one was in no mood to sacrifice the rest of the afternoon. Already I was moving to martyr.

As the girls ran off, I began the process of appeasing myself. I told myself I would still have close to an hour to relax. The little guy wasn't buying it. I had made too many false promises to him. Of course, I had done the same thing to Matt and Rachael, and they didn't like my broken promises any more than my little one did.

I kept busy to avoid what I was feeling. I opened the mail and scanned the morning paper, which hadn't even been delivered when I left for work. Five, ten, fifteen minutes burned away, with still no sign of the girls, who so urgently had to be at the mall.

I stormed down the hall to see about the holdup. Side by side in front of the bathroom mirror, in a sea of cosmetics, the girls were in serious discussion about the best shade of lipstick. Primping could go on for at least another hour. Victim moved to perpetrator.

"I thought you said that you had to go to the mall right now? You always do this. You *always* wait until the last minute. You could have told me last night that you wanted to go to the mall." (Blah, blah, blah.) "The bus leaves in five minutes," I heard myself say, not even vaguely aware that the voice that spoke those words was much too young to be driving.

Ten hours ago, I had promised my five-year-old self that we could do whatever he wanted after I had sprinted through my day. The little one had no desire to awaken in the middle of the night so I could start my hospital rounds at four o'clock in the morning, but he had kept his grousing to a minimum because of my promise to him. Even when an angry family member in the hospital accosted me, my little guy had kept his mouth shut and calmly accepted the wrath of my patient's daughter, as much as he wanted to tell her, *You ought to be grateful that your mother's receiving such good care. She wasn't the only one on planet earth who didn't get enough sleep last night—and if you don't like the care she's getting, why don't you take her across town? That'd be one less person I'd have to see today.* Instead I calmly apologized while politely reminding the nurse that my patient wasn't to be awakened during the night.

Now it was three o'clock in the afternoon, and my little guy was waiting for lipstick, eyeliner, and hair spray. I paced back to the kitchen, noting the time on my watch so I could cancel all travel if the girls took longer than five minutes. While the clock ticked, I stuffed my face with a half-dozen cookies I didn't even taste (rescuer/addict). With thirty seconds to go, I walked out to the driveway so I could be standing next to the car and pointing at my watch when the girls came out. The five-minute ultimatum passed.

By then, the five-year-old turned his sights on his true villain. *You don't keep your promise to me, and you make idle threats to your daughter. You're a jerk and a wimp to boot.*

I returned fire with another voice, maybe someone about twelve years old. *Wimp? You're calling me a wimp? I'll give them two more minutes, and if they don't come out, you'll see how tough I am. They'll be hoofing it to the mall!* I'm now living through a civil war between two inner voices I'm supposed to have under control.

I'm a professional. I handle life-and-death situations without so much as a bead of sweat, but when my sweet daughter unwittingly asked me for a ride to the mall, all hell broke loose? Now I turned the judge on myself.

What kind of father are you? You should be happy to take your lovely daughter and her friend to the mall. Instead you look like a jerk. I managed to exhaust myself running around the triangle as Rachael and her friend strolled out to the car. One look at me, and her friend headed for the back seat. Rachael climbed in front.

"You're in a bad mood," she commented as I backed down the driveway.

"No, I'm not."

After about a mile, Rachael said, "You've been in a bad mood a lot lately. I just asked if you could take us to the mall. You could have said no."

I had two voices inside me that were both ready to maim and kill, and my teenage daughter showed no fear. As if I were a hired chauffeur, Rachael returned to her animated conversation with her friend.

Rachael didn't bite. We could easily have gone around and around the triangle together, calling each other names, beating each other up verbally, and carrying the resentment and accusations well into that evening or the next days. Instead, she spoke her truth without judgment or anger. She didn't enter the triangle with me. She left me to deal with myself, refusing to give up her happy afternoon.

After the girls got out of the car, I sat for a while, examining what I was feeling. I hadn't realized how worried I was about our adolescent daughter, how tired I had become compressing my medical practice so I could be home with her, how conversations with Anne sounded more like business meetings as we passed the baton on our way in or out the door, and how I hadn't taken time to recharge despite the pleading from my inner voices.

I was leading workshops and teaching others to take care of themselves but not following my own advice. I apologized to myself for making promises I didn't keep.

Later that afternoon, when Rachael and her friend climbed back into the car, I was able to tell Rachael I had considered what she said and that she was right. I apologized for saying yes when I really wanted to say no and then taking it out on the two of them. Rachael just smiled and reached over to squeeze my arm.

I watched myself act out behaviors that were clear diagnostic signals that I was in the triangle. It could have been much worse. I could have gone on the attack immediately after Rachael made her urgent request. "Why didn't you call me two hours ago? You never consider anyone else but yourself. With you, it's just gimme, gimme, gimme."

Or I could have played all-knowing rescuer. "If you go to the mall now, you'll be too tired for your swim meet tonight. You need to rest this afternoon." As perpetrator or rescuer, I could have made it all about Rachael, escalating the tension and pushing Rachael to defend herself. Instead I said yes when I meant no. Poor me, the dutiful martyr. I had no choices.

Instead of reflexively agreeing to something my little guy had no input in, I could have told Rachael I needed a moment to collect my thoughts and had a rational conversation with myself. In all likelihood, my little guy would have weighed the options and chosen to spend part of the afternoon talking with Rachael and her friend on the way to the mall. He has always adored Rachael, even during her most flagrant rebelliousness, and would never miss an opportunity to be with her. It would have been his gift to her and himself.

Instead I said yes without checking in with myself, treating him the way he'd been treated while growing up. He was angry with me, not Rachael, but I almost made it about her. I gave myself no choice, the classic predicament of the triangle. Rachael and her friend experienced my resentment without having any idea what it was about. Fortunately, they were healthy enough not to let it ruin their day. But I cheated myself out of gifting my daughter with an enjoyable ride to the mall, and I denied Rachael a "cool dad." The act of taking my daughter to the mall didn't define whether I was in the triangle. Rather, it was my lack of choice that set up my whirlwind tour of dysfunction.

Understanding the triangle helps us all to make amends and realign ourselves with our values. But we will always have blind spots. The shadow never disappears. My children are approaching or have just passed their fortieth birthdays. They have richly textured lives, full careers, and wonderful families. They are bright, passionate, kind, thoughtful people; and I am very proud to be their dad. And now and again I see in them the teeth-clenching time bomb, the judgmental critic, or the need to control, which they experienced in me during the first decade of their lives. I wince as if I am being forced to watch a reality TV show starring me in my thirties.

I look over at Anne. Most days we give each other a loving nod. I want to put my arms around Matt and Rachael's little ones, kiss them on their foreheads, and tell them how much they are loved and adored. I want to apologize for my shadow times, which have contaminated their lives, and wipe the slate clean, never to have to look in the mirror again. But it will be up to my grown children to put down the excess baggage I passed on to them.

Ahh, blind spots. Be gentle with yourself.

Appendix 3

GETTING OUT OF THE TRIANGLE

> Until you make the unconscious conscious, it will direct your life and you will call it fate.
> —C. G. Jung

Spotting Troublesome Thoughts and Behaviors

To get out of the triangle, I have to recognize I'm in it. Here is my partial list of diagnostic clues, which you can expand and personalize:

Saying the Opposite of What I'm Feeling

The classic example is saying, "Sure, I'll drop what I'm doing to help you" when inside we are screaming, "No way!" We betray ourselves with a reflex *yes,* never taking time to check in with ourselves.

The inverse is subtler. We reflexively say, "No thanks, I've got it" when someone offers us help, even though inside we may be begging for support. Similarly, when we are given a compliment, we divert the gift with, "Yes, we have a great team." Although we may prostitute ourselves our whole lives for a standing ovation, we can't even let in a simple "Good job." Our shame prevents us from acknowledging the basic human need of being seen and appreciated.

Being Careful in My Interactions with Others

When I find myself rehearsing what I will say to someone, I know I'm afraid. I don't trust that my spontaneous remarks will keep me safe from another's anger, judgment, or guilt trip—or that I won't hurt someone with my anger or self-righteousness. Responding from experience, I don't risk speaking my truth, because I believe (not necessarily the truth) someone always gets hurt if I get what I want.

Being careful doesn't determine whether I'm in the triangle. Rather, it is the unconscious behavior and the lack of choice and personal responsibility that define a dysfunctional behavior. At times, I may make a conscious decision to measure my words and take the safest course, but I will take the responsibility without blaming the other person.

Giving Unrequested Advice

I might want to fix someone because his or her pain hits too close to home. Or perhaps I don't have the patience and stamina to sit with the person in his or her need. Due to guilt or fear, I cannot say I'm unable to offer the person what he or she needs. Instead, I give the message that the person needs fixing because he or she isn't capable of his or her own repair. When I'm in the triangle, I breed mistrust and disrespect.

Gossiping or Judging Others without Compassion

Yes, I can very easily become self-righteous in all three roles of the triangle. It is a one-up, one-down system. Since I cannot be vulnerable, I'll be one up by putting others one down.

Being Perfectionistic

When I cannot make mistakes, a small, little voice that is afraid he will be hurt or ridiculed again is dragging me around. He tries to silence the voice of my inner perpetrator, the judge, by doing everything right. He is only lovable if he is perfect.

Beating Myself Up (Believing My Judge)

I continue to treat myself the way I was treated. My judge demands that I be someone I'm not, and I continue to wear outworn masks, trading safety for authenticity.

Speaking for Others or Allowing Others to Speak for Me

Fear and guilt require that I rescue or be rescued.

Passive-Aggressive Withholding of My True Feelings, Even from Those Who Are Safe

When I was in pain as a child, my safe place was to go inside and shut down. I am still afraid my anger could hurt someone and that I would become what I hate. But I cheat myself out of the love and support available to me. I also cheat those who love me by declining their gift.

Being Overly Defensive

When I attack someone who offers feedback or disagrees with me, I know he or she is simply confirming what my judge has been telling me all along: I am not good enough.

Not Being the Same Person in All Settings, at Home or Work, Public or Private

One measure of health is that we are the same person in all settings. Do I have a secret Internet life or beat my kids on Saturday night and then parade them into church on Sunday as the benevolent patriarch? Am I obsequious to my superiors and demeaning to my subordinates? Do I show respect to others in their presence and then belittle them in their absence? Do I kowtow to older kids and then smother a timid five-year-old? When we can be our true selves, we are who we are in all situations, consistent and trustworthy.

Feeling Shame

Shame tells me I am unworthy of love, which is how I entered the triangle in the first place.

This list represents some diagnostic feelings and behaviors that tell me I'm avoiding what's going on inside me. Once I recognize a dysfunctional behavior, I can go through some steps, which help me break the old patterns.

Doing Things Differently

Make Friends with Your Judge

First, I try to be gentle with myself. My internal judge attended the same workshop and learned about the triangle the same day I did. He doesn't hesitate to beat me up for being in it, even though he often has a starring role.

Over the years, I have tried lots of techniques to banish my judge. I pretend he doesn't exist; cover my ears and making funny, humming noises when I hear his voice; attempt to drown him … until I run out of air myself; repeat affirmations louder than he can criticize; tell him to *shut the f … up*; and even plead with him to give me a break—all with only marginal success. One day when he was especially prolific, I dragged myself and the judge into the bathroom, locked the door, stared at him directly in the mirror, and told him to give me his best shot. I forced him to tear into me aloud, where I could get a good look at him.

The judge repeated all the deafening condemnation he'd been whispering in my head for years. As he ran out of things to tear me down about, I baited him. "Is that the best you can do? Don't you have anything new and fresh to say, something I haven't already heard two or three thousand times?" I stared right into his eyes until the judge ran out of gas. The quiet was surprising. I dusted off my shirt and thanked him for sharing.

On occasion, when I do something especially stupid, I invite the judge to lock and load again, always looking directly in the mirror and forcing him to criticize me aloud. The barrage comes to an end more quickly these days because the judge knows the rest of the routine. I laugh, dust myself off, and thank him for sharing.

After many years of practice, even my judge rolls his eyes when I drag him into the bathroom. He knows it will all end in knowing and forgiving laughter. We are becoming friends. My laughter at the end of the condemning monologue isn't simply dismissing the judge. It also contains a layer of acceptance that what the judge says is partially true: I am a stupid, proud, ugly, overeating, narcissistic, pompous, yada yada idiot ... *at times.*

My laughter acknowledges my fears, recurring bad habits, and need for perfection; and says, "Yes, I am human. Even I can make mistakes, be a jerk, and manipulate for attention."

My laughter also thanks the judge for keeping me honest as well as reminding me that I can be better. My laughter disarms my critic but also my pride. Once I forgive myself, I'm able to own my unhealthy behavior and make amends. I give myself room to improve.

Take Risks to Speak Your Truth

In the beginning, I took small risks in stepping out of the triangle by speaking my truth and owning my preferences. I could tell Anne her very favorite chocolate bread pudding didn't do it for me. Surprise, surprise, she didn't melt into a puddle of tears; she didn't accuse me of putting her down; and best of all, Anne continues to make it for favorite guests and thoroughly enjoys serving and eating it.

We warn participants who may have expressed their anger for the first time in many years and have found a new and powerful voice not to let it all hang out when they return to their normal lives. Sometimes we overshoot "our truth" with a bit more emphasis than is helpful. Having decided that I will "speak my truth" no matter what the cost and then get fired from a good job because I mistake my boss for my father, I see just another way to revictimize myself. Better to start with bread pudding than tell my boss he is, was, and will always be a jerk.

Take a Time-Out

I've had to learn to recognize when I'm bringing old issues into the present, to hold my tongue until I can attend to my feelings, and not to react with old behaviors. Emotional clarity leads to better choices. Instead of making an automatic response I might regret, I've learned to say, "Let me think about it." This approach gives me time to weigh the pros and cons, and discover whether I have competing needs around the request. Sometimes I hear very different needs when I check in with myself. If I take the time to reconcile my internal differences before I respond, I come to a conscious choice. I avoid resenting the person who is asking for help. When I take full responsibility for my yes, I can enjoy the gift I offer because it's my choice rather than a have to.

Life is full of competing needs. Taking the time to listen and show respect to all my internal voices makes for a much more settled decision, even when no internal consensus is reached. This internal consultative process has spilled over into my work, greatly improving my ability to listen openly to the different needs of my colleagues.

Struggling couples can get bogged down in resentment because of unmet expectations, believing their partners should magically know what the other needs and give it to him or her without the person's asking. This leads to each trying to extract concessions from his or her partner while keeping a running score of who gives what to whom. Winning a battle is hardly the same as a freely given gift of love and caring. Saying yes when we really would like to say no feels like a defeat for the giver. The relationship becomes a competition rather than one of gifting and nurturing the other.

When we take time to listen to our inner voices, we might discover that our desire to gift our partner is greater than our desire to conserve our own time and energy. We can learn to say yes with an open heart rather than with resentment. Gradually, the partnership builds trust. Acts of caring and generosity build on themselves. "No, thank you" is no longer proof that the other doesn't love and care. Being able to say no makes the yes that much sweeter. In the story of Rachael going to the mall, my playing the martyr gave neither of us pleasure. It was up to me to sort through my competing needs, make the best decision at the time, and enjoy the gift I was offering.

Remember the Fifteen-Second Rule

I try to remember Elisabeth's motto. When I react longer than fifteen seconds, I'm being triggered by unfinished business. Recognizing my old patterns of behavior helps me to take a time-out.

- As a victim, I might feel bad about myself and cynical about other people's motives.
- As a rescuer, I may be working harder than the person I am trying to help, becoming compulsive and perfectionistic.
- As a perpetrator, I may find myself withholding or being particularly self-righteous and judgmental.

When I'm able to stop myself and rewind life's tape, I can follow the thread of my feelings. Recognizing I am under the spell of reactivity will help me to come back to adult awareness, even if I don't have time to process all my feelings. Later, I can sit with myself or get help from Anne about my exaggerated response to the trigger. Each time I do this, I develop a richer internal relationship, which helps to heal old wounds and brings gratitude for the "teacher", who upset me so much. I always seem to have a ready supply of teachers.

Sometimes I am so completely under the spell that I stay in the triangle for days. Once I awaken to my part in the dysfunction, I may need to let out steam on the mat or release it symbolically, picturing myself using the hose on a telephone book. Then I can own my part in the dance and make amends. Whether the counter party chooses to own his or her part in the process is completely up to him or her. At least I have stepped out of the triangle by looking inside and taking responsibility for my feelings and behaviors.

Friends, family, and coworkers may try to keep us in the triangle. They bait us with their problems, criticism, and "shoulds," keeping us in a dysfunctional relationship because they don't want to lose us. This behavior is usually not premeditated, although sometimes we wonder. They will try to get any reaction out of us, even anger, because it means we are still engaged with them. I try not to put the bait in my mouth; and if I've opened too wide, I try not to chomp down on the hook.

I have a friend who couldn't stop himself from trying to fix me. If he asked how I was doing and I responded honestly about the good and tough things in my life, he would immediately try to talk me out of feeling upset, giving me a pep talk about staying positive. I tried to tell him what I needed was for him to just listen and give me support until I was ready to ask for something more. Unfortunately, it didn't work. I became angry and pulled away. Then when he asked how I was, I simply gave him back his own words: "Everything's great." The relationship became more superficial. I bit the hook, and his incessant caretaking made me feel victimized. I lost compassion and became judgmental and self-righteous toward someone I love.

When I bite the hook, it usually means I am reacting longer than the symbolic fifteen seconds. When I stop to check in with myself, I discover I am, once again, frustrated with my parents' minimizing my feelings and offering unrequested advice. Once my anger is released, I can acknowledge how much Mom and Dad loved me and didn't want me to suffer. Of course, I also recognize and appreciate my friend's kind heart. Now, when I receive his unrequested but often very useful advice, I can thank him for trying to make me feel better. With compassion, there is always an opportunity for change.

A coworker is a bully, and he doesn't ask for my opinion about how he chooses to live his life. I bite down hard. I want to wring his neck or ask him why such a bright, talented man can be so clueless and insensitive. While other colleagues ignore the blowups or just laugh, I avoid being around him. He is taking the pleasure out of my workday.

Once again I find myself reacting longer than fifteen seconds. My distorted emotions are the hallmark of the triangle, including paralyzing fear, resentment, vengeful fantasies, and powerlessness. When I am able to call an internal meeting and ask who inside is experiencing which feelings, I discover a scared little one who was intimidated by a bully and an enraged one who wants to kill the guy. In the safety of our own internal home, I allow these voices to be heard. After the fear and anger are acknowledged, I ask myself what sets my coworker off. My internal expert on fear gives me the answer. When things aren't going his way, his fear manifests as anger, intimidation, and domination. I tell my little ones they aren't responsible for changing this man, but I will try to connect with him the next time he acts out.

When my colleague goes on the attack for what I consider to be insignificant, I choose a quiet time to tell him I appreciate the high standards he holds for himself and others but that I believe it's counterproductive to attack others when he gets scared and frustrated that his standards won't be achieved. I spit out the hook. I request that he consider an alternative approach to reach his goals and offer to discuss this with him if he would like.

Each time I take another step in reconciling my past and decoupling a current relationship from old baggage, I'm better able to look underneath irritating behavior and find a renewed compassion for myself and the "teacher" who was the source of my reactivity.

Say No When I Mean No, with Kindness

I remind myself that saying no to someone is actually saying yes to myself. If my image of setting a boundary is shoving someone out of my space, I am loading my submachine gun with each potentially difficult interaction. Each time I begin my sentence with, "You did this, said this, behaved this way," the relationship becomes all about the other person. My only part is to tell the person what he or she is doing wrong.

When I recognize I'm actually protecting or nurturing a younger part of myself, I am able to begin my conversation with "I need to let you know that the best way to communicate with me is … If you can remember, I'd like to request that you …" I have no control over whether the other party hears my words or needs, but my little ones always listen when I speak for them. My yes to them has greatly deepened their trust in me.

I need to make it clear again that I don't speak about my little ones in day-to-day adult conversation. I don't want to appear foolish, and my little ones don't wish to be ridiculed. I am using my imagination to create an image of myself at different ages, because I can more readily give love and compassion to someone younger, not what I call my adult self. These imaginary conversations have deepened my ability to be self-aware, to listen to the whisperings of my own heart, to reduce self-criticism and judgment of others, and to be able to engage with understanding and compassion in daily interactions.

Ask for What I Need

Asking for what I need sounds easy, but I must first believe I am worthy of such a request. Often our little ones, so full of shame and self-loathing, are too scared to ask. In any case, a five-year-old child shouldn't have to make such a request. Nor should a young child be the one to reach out to an adult. It's up to a parent to notice distress and reach out to the child. Similarly, my adult self needs to find the time to sit quietly, access my younger voices, hear their concerns and needs, and speak for them. It's up to me to demonstrate, even to myself, that I am worthy.

"Deserving" is another issue, separate from "worthy." When love is unconditional, "deserve" isn't really part of the equation. I love my family; no ifs about it. They are worthy because they exist, children of God. Love isn't God's commodity—it is his blessing.

When we are in the triangle, we live in a manipulative world, trying our best to avoid and survive our pain. Our choices are unconscious, based on self-protection. We have lost our sense of innate worth, so "deserve" takes on greater importance. The rescuer makes restitution and then feels deserving for his or her martyrdom; the perpetrator takes what he or she wants out of a perverse sense of entitlement ("the world owes me"); and the victim remains undeserving, marinating in self-pity or angry despair. "Deserve" keeps us in the triangle.

Out of the triangle, we make conscious choices, overseen by a functioning adult. For example, I may choose to work long hours because I need the job. My employer hasn't enslaved me; nor has he lied to me about the time commitment. Once I take responsibility for my decision to stay at my job, I can set down any bitterness toward my employer. I may ask him respectfully, honestly, and without expectations for better work conditions. In turn, my employer will benefit or suffer the consequences of his choices, losing good employees if he isn't responsive to their concerns. There is no "deserve" in our relationship; rather there is mutual respect, even in disagreement.

For little ones whose physical, emotional, or sexual space has been violated, having someone enter their space to offer a gift can be terrifying. To make a request, I need healthy anger to say, "No, thank you" when someone offers more than my vulnerable little ones are ready to receive. We cannot feel safe saying yes until we are strong enough to say no, to set limits. Otherwise we risk retraumatizing ourselves.

Asking for what I need presumes I know what I need. When I take the time to ask myself what I need to feel safe, loved, and respected, I may get different internal responses. I have a very independent one who puts safety above nurturing. He chooses not to risk rejection or feel beholden to someone because he doesn't trust in the existence of unconditional giving. Also, he has no expectation that he will receive emotional support or even that someone will inquire in how he is doing. Over time he has become more trusting of me, since I listen to him and acknowledge his reality. Sometimes I see he has the capacity to recognize and be pleasantly surprised by an unconditional act of kindness or generosity. But it always comes as a surprise to him.

A slightly older voice needs regular validation and emotional support. When I don't give him what he needs or don't speak for him, he seeks it out in manipulative ways. He may downplay his abilities so he can get a rescuer to praise him.

Sometimes my needs are quite pedestrian: a shirt to be ironed, a favorite dessert, an errand to be run, or help with the computer. By asking, I offer Anne the opportunity to give me a small gift; and I get to express my gratitude for her love and devotion many times a day.

When I dare risk to ask for unmet childhood love or attention, I know that on some level I am speaking for all the wounded and vulnerable children on the planet. On those rare occasions when we humbly dare to ask for what we never had, we speak for all humanity. Whether I receive what I have requested has become less important. My little one knows I have heard his plea and have spoken for him.

As I learn to say no, I find it easier to ask for what I need because I don't take rejection so personally. I accept the notion that no can be bidirectional. I have also stopped assuming people in my life should be psychic and somehow know what I need from them. In asking for help, I take responsibility.

My requests remind me that I'm vulnerable, that I am human, and that I need support. I don't always have to be the hero. They also let the people in my life know I respect and trust them. Despite understanding all this intellectually, I am still surprised when help and support have been waiting for me all along. Old habits die hard.

I find myself in and out of the triangle all the time, which isn't so different from the many food plans and exercise regimens I have tried. I relapse. Sometimes I want to beat myself up for having no willpower, being lazy, or being so unconscious.

I had a breakthrough week at my first Life, Death, and Transition Workshop. In many ways, I changed. I was lighter after releasing years of pent-up rage I never knew I was carrying. I listened to myself differently, discovering a voice that predated the donning of my mask. I was no longer so afraid of anger and much less ashamed of my grief. It was easier to sit with others in strong feelings. Even my fear was less scary. I became aware of little miracles that blessed each day.

Hilda's Unending Need

Hilda was a seventy-four-year-old who had required multiple joint replacements because of severe, crippling rheumatoid arthritis. I first met her in 1984, about two months after my first workshop with Elisabeth. She was on a gurney, being rushed from her room on the orthopedic unit to the ICU, in septic shock from a raging knee infection just three days after her joint replacement. Fortunately, I chose the correct antibiotic for the unusual organism infecting her knee and bloodstream.

Once she was stabilized, her surgeon washed out the joint. With prolonged antibiotics, not only did Hilda survive, she was able to keep her new knee. Timing is everything.

Hilda mentioned several times that the only thing she remembered was looking up into my eyes and holding my hand as she was being taken to the ICU. Despite my protests, she projected her entire recovery onto me. I was her hero. About two months after she left the hospital and rehab, Hilda asked whether I would be her primary care doctor. I told her I didn't take patients from my referring doctors, but she said she had already called him and that he had given his blessing for her to transfer to me. I called her doc, who reassured me that he was completely fine with the transfer. In fact, he almost seemed eager. I should have seen it coming, but gratitude and flattery …

Within another few months, Hilda was calling the office with questions and minor problems nearly every day, requiring more and more time from my nurse and me. Office visits also dragged on longer. I would ask her how she was doing, listen to a litany of minor complaints, examine her, and begin backing out of the exam room, when she would drop the bomb. "Oh, I meant to tell you that I have been having these crushing chest pains when I walk to the mailbox or try to put on my clothes."

More questions and a stat EKG, and twenty-five minutes later I would be reaching for some drug sample to give her to get her out of the office, knowing full well that the medication wouldn't relieve her myriad of symptoms caused by years of her devastating disease.

As I was leaving the office at the end of a long day, I glanced at my schedule and noticed Hilda was once again penciled in for one of my emergency slots the next day. When I felt myself wince and shake my head, I knew I had to follow the thread of my irritation—or else she was going to torture me for years to come.

After beginning our training with Elisabeth, Anne and I had set up a mattress, hose, and phone books in our guest room for those days when we needed to release our frustration. After arriving home that day, I kissed Anne, hugged my kids, and then closed the door to our guest room and put Hilda out on the mat. My reaction to Hilda was way beyond the fifteen-second threshold.

I grabbed a phone book, picked up the hose, and gave her a piece of my uncensored mind as I released my frustration onto the yellow pages. "You are a manipulative, sorrowful woman. I don't care how crippled you are. I am tired of you calling every day and wasting my time, and I'm tired of you taking forty-five minutes for a fifteen-minute appointment. There's not a damn thing I can do for you. I can't help you!"

Bingo! I couldn't help her. Each time Hilda called or came to the office, she reminded my perfectionistic little one that he wasn't good enough. He was getting more and more upset with her and disappointed in himself. After he and I had a chat, we were eager to see Hilda the next day in my office.

I had to find language to speak my truth without aiming a submachine gun at Hilda. This strategy meant my sentences would begin with "I'm feeling ..." rather than "You are such a ..." In other words, my truth was only about my reactions and reactivity, not about taking Hilda's inventory.

The night before on the mat, I happily took Hilda's inventory and gave her a piece of my mind. I labeled her, judged her, condemned her, and hated her all without hurting her. It felt great. By expressing my built-up distorted emotions, my shadow came safely out of the darkness. My uncensored feelings brought about needed insight.

Before the workshop, I wouldn't have considered that Hilda would be a catalyst for my healing. I would have just labeled and judged her, suffered her presence in my practice, and acted out unconscious passive-aggressive behaviors that would have humiliated her or driven her away. Now that I understood how I was being triggered, I could nurture and reassure my little perfectionist and speak with Hilda without making it about her or purposely hurting her. I prepared a bit before her visit to be sure I would take responsibility and allow her to do the same if she cared to.

It is scary for a rescuer to say no because it always feels like it is at someone else's expense. If I say no to Hilda, I might upset her. She might fly into a rage and attack or exile me. As a doctor, I really didn't want Hilda to go into my waiting room (or put a full-page ad in the local paper), accusing me of being a terrible and insensitive doctor, and then filing a lawsuit. Then all my patients would request transfer of their care to other physicians. I would be completely disgraced, and our family would lose our home. Fear creates amazing catastrophes that leave me once again the victim, helpless, hopeless, a failure. It is way too risky for a rescuer to speak the truth. Fear keeps me silenced, in the triangle.

Or here's another scenario: I might make Hilda cry, in which case she might go home, give up, take an overdose, and nearly die because of me. I am a killer, no different from *them*. I am the perpetrator.

Saying no, the rescuer loses either way. So, I might as well swallow my truth and just put Hilda's needs above my own until fatigue or resentment gets the better of me. I wind up becoming what I dread anyway. I take a deep breath. It takes practice and courage to say, "No, thank you." My little one wouldn't risk such horrible, potential outcomes unless he knew I would be there for him.

When Hilda came in, I asked her about the urgency of this visit. After she gave me a list of several of her routine complaints, I put down my pen and looked up at her. "Hilda, I want to tell you that I realized something about our relationship last night. I have done a disservice to you. I've been getting frustrated with you and even more annoyed with myself. I need to be honest and tell you that, unlike your knee infection, I cannot fix most of your current long-standing symptoms. I realized last night that I have felt like a failure and resented you for it. I have even given you sample medications that I really didn't think would help just to end our appointments, because they have been taking much longer than my schedule has allowed.

"So today I want to apologize to you. I am sure that you've felt my tension. But I also need to say that I am unable to help you with your chronic aches and pains—and, most importantly for me, that I cannot respond to phone calls from you every day, nor give you prolonged office visits."

This time I spoke my truth gently and calmly.

Hilda burst into tears, saying she was so grateful for my care and that she knew I couldn't fix her. She confessed that she called our office because she felt so lonely and desperate since her husband had died. For about five minutes, she mourned the loss of her best friend and life partner and the years of chronic debility caused by a disfiguring, cruel disease. I just listened and acknowledged her pain. Then I took the risk to ask for what I needed.

"Hilda, I hear you, and I am sorry how hard it is for you. But I need to ask you not to call every day. I am willing to speak with you briefly, once a week, on the phone but no more. If you call more frequently, I won't be able to return your calls unless I believe it is a true medical emergency. Also, I am able—and would like— to see you for a fifteen-minute appointment once a month."

Hilda began what would be another lengthy response, but fifteen minutes had already elapsed. I calmly told her I needed to see my next patient, stood, and asked whether I could give a lonely widow a hug. Hilda smiled. We gave each other a hug, and she thanked me once again.

At her next month appointment, I entered the exam room, gave Hilda a big smile, and ceremoniously looked at my watch. Hilda rapidly went through her list of aches and pains, telling me she knew I couldn't fix them but just needed to let me know how uncomfortable she was. Then she proceeded to tell me she had joined a church group, which gave her an outing once a week. She chatted about how she still struggled with loneliness but had reached out to her daughter and enjoyed some really good conversations with her.

I did a brief exam and asked whether she had any questions or needed any medications. She laughed and said, "No samples today." We both giggled. Fifteen minutes had passed.

Hilda had chosen not to waste her time talking about her chronic symptoms. Instead, she told me about her life. I ceremoniously looked at my watch again, and we smiled at each other. I had seen more of the real Hilda that day than I had for the past year. We shared a small miracle because I had learned to listen to myself.

Hilda and I had many laughs over the next several months, mostly at ourselves. (We also clarified the definition of "medical emergency.") She brought me cookies and told me to nibble when I felt like a failure again. I always looked forward to our visits.

Nine months later, Hilda died from a massive stroke.

It is scary to step out of the triangle. All of us have learned to get some of our needs met in our dysfunctional relationships. The triangle is like an old pair of shoes.

When we begin to get out of the triangle, our friends may change. I believe we can risk stepping out of the triangle only when our little ones know we won't desert them and that they aren't alone because we will be available to hear their fears and grief. Stepping out of the triangle requires the presence of a committed adult within our psyche.

It's normal to be afraid of speaking our truth. We should practice being careful of our loved ones' feelings when we take the risk to say what we need. We also must expect that others will feel hurt or angry when we step out of the triangle, because they will feel we have abandoned them. We have disturbed the old equilibrium.

In stepping out of the triangle, rescuers risk being hurt again (victim) or becoming what they most hate (perpetrators) and being the cause of another's pain. In stepping out of the triangle, victims acknowledge that they are now responsible for their future choices and for the well-being of their injured little ones. Victims can no longer blame their abusers for their future. The perpetrators must acknowledge their vulnerability to stop making themselves feel better by passing on their childhood fears and powerlessness to their victims. These are scary, wonderful decisions with sobering and potentially life-enhancing consequences; but they must not be taken lightly.

The Triangle of Health

Bad things happen. If we have the tools to grieve our losses, we find meaning and joy where we can. If we have lost our ability to express our rage, grief, and fear, we become victimized by life's inevitable losses, doomed to repeat dysfunctional patterns of behavior that don't get us what we want. We may marry and eventually divorce a self-centered, narcissistic partner only to choose another partner who is equally unavailable.

Being unconscious in the triangle, we are protected from the pain of our grief, but we no longer have choices or insight. We are programmed to repeat past behaviors until we recognize the old protective patterns, which are now self-defeating.

In the triangle of health, the place of victim becomes a place of resilience, born out of successfully grieving our losses. We own and share our pain, tell our story, howl at the moon, lick our wounds, laugh at our fallibility, and choose life once again.

The place of the rescuers or caretakers becomes the site of the caregivers, who choose to offer care and concern after checking in with themselves. The caregivers place the oxygen mask on their face first before attempting to help their neighbor. They honor their own needs, set healthy limits, and recognize when they are working harder than the person they want to help. They allow their friends and family the autonomy to learn and grow from their mistakes. Yet they know the deep joy of giving when there are no strings attached, and they are blessed and honored when someone trusts them to ask for help.

The site of the perpetrators becomes healthy assertiveness, without blaming or judging. We can ask for what we need and set appropriate limits. We are strong in our beliefs without finding it necessary to shove our truth down someone else's throat.

The triangle of health describes us when we are spontaneous and real. Grandiosity is replaced with humility, righteousness with gratitude. We enjoy a full range of emotions and don't fake who we are. Although we may not be happy all the time, we are content. We display serenity much of the time until we don't. Then we ask for a supportive ear to hear our fears and grief. Reconciled with internal voices, we are capable of compassion when we plumb the depths with others. Finding compassion for both the saint and sinner who live inside, we have the humility to take responsibility for our part in a disagreement. Our pride doesn't prevent us from making an apology. We enjoy our own company as well as working and playing with others. We are flexible, creative, and cooperative in identifying and solving problems. We display a generosity of spirit, an open heart and mind, and a sense of humor that comes from the hard work of reclamation. And we know we are much more alike than we are different.

Resources

Adverse Childhood Experiences Study: Felitt, V, Anda, R, Nordenberg, D, Willaimson, D, Spitz, A, Edwards, V, Koss, M, Marks, J (1998): "Relationship of Childhood Abuse to Many of Leading Causes of Death in Adults." *American Journal of Preventative Medicine*: 14: 245–258.

Ainsworth, M., and Bell, S. (1970): "Attachment, Exploration, and Separation: Illustrated by the Behavior of One-Year-Olds in a Strange Situation." *Child Development* 41: 49–67.

Bos, K, Zeanah, C, Fox, N, drury, S, McLaughlin, K, Nelson, C (2011): "Psychiatric Outcomes in Young Children with a History of Institutionalization." *Harvard Review of Psychiatry* 19: 15–24.

Brown, Brene. *The Gifts of Imperfection*, Hazeldon, Center City, MN, 2010. *Rising Strong*, Randon House, New York, 2015.

Earley, Jay. *Self Therapy*, Pattern System Books, Larkspur, CA, 2009.

Elisabeth Kübler-Ross Foundation: www. EKRfoundation.org.

Gerhardt, Susan. *Why Love Matters*, Brunner-Routledge, New York, 2005.

Gibran, Khalil. *The Prophet*, Alfred Knopf, New York, 1974.

Golomb, Elan. *Trapped in the Mirror: Adult Children of Narcissists in their Struggle for Self*, William Morrow, New York, 1992.

Gottman, John. *Raising an Emotionally Intelligent Child*, Fireside Press, New York, 1997.

Growth and Transition Workshop: www.growthandtransition.com.

Hollis, James. *Under Saturn's Shadow: The Wounding and Healing of Men*, Inner City Books, Toronto, 1994.

Johnson, Robert. *Inner Work*, Harper Collins, New York, 1986.
Living Your Unlived Life, Penguin Group, New York, 2007.

Karpmann, Stephen. *A Game Free Life*, Drama Triangle Publications, San Francisco, 2014.

Kornfield, Jack. *A Path with Heart*, Bantam Books, New York, 1993.
The Roots of Buddhist Psychology (audio)., Sounds True, 1995.

Kübler-Ross, Elisabeth. *On Children and Death*, Touchstone, 1983.
On Death and Dying, Scribner, New York, 1969.
Working It Through, Touchstone, New York, 1982.

Lawrence, Susan. *Creating a Healing Society*, Elite Books, 2006.

Meaney, M, Aitken, D, Van Berkel, C, Bhatnagar, S, Ssaampolsky, R (1988): "Effect of Neonatal Handling on Age-Related Impairments Associated with the Hippocampus." *Science, New Series:* 239, no. 4841: 766–768.

Middleton-Moz, Jane, and Dwinell, Lorie. *After the Tears: Reclaiming the Personal Losses of Childhood*, Health Communications, Deerfield, FL, 1986, 2010
Miller, Alice. *The Drama of the Gifted Child*.

Nhat Hanh, Thich. *Reconciliation*, Parallax Press, Berkeley, CA, 2010.

Sacks, Oliver. *Musicophilia*, Vintage Books, New York, 2007.

Schwartz, Richard C. *Introduction to the Internal Family Systems Model,* Trailheads Publications, 2001.

Siegal, Daniel. *Brainstorm,* Penguin, New York, 2015.
    Mindsight, Bantam Books, New York, 2010.
    Parenting from the Inside Out, Penguin, New York, 2004.

Tatelbaum, Judy. *The Courage to Grieve,* Harper Collins, New york, 1990.

Van der Kolk, Bessel. *The Body Keeps the Score,* Penguin, New york, 2015.

Whitfield, Charles. *Healing the Child Within,* Health Communications, Deerfield, FL, 1989, 2006.

Witt, Keith. *The Attuned Family, iUniverse,* Bloomington, IN, 2007.

Acknowledgments

I cannot possibly acknowledge all the people in my life who have encouraged me to become the person I am and to risk telling my story.

I have had successive editors. My thanks to Nancy Linnon, my initial cheerleader who listened with an open heart and told me to keep writing; to Wynne Brown, whose copy editing turned a primitive manuscript into the first semblance of a book; to Karen McKelvey, hospice nurse and poet, who graciously volunteered to clean and prune my language (your father would be proud); to Adam at Balboa Press, who did final polishing; and to Anne Taylor Lincoln, who encouraged me (a cattle prod just posted on eBay) and made the most important contributions to both content and style.

Special thanks to Teddy, to the numerous people who entrusted their stories and "little ones" to my mat, and to my medical and hospice patients: you are all my teachers.

To Mom and Dad, Steve, and Artie—what a clan. Artie, I know you would be pleased.

To Grandmom. What strong and gentle hands. I know you are waiting for me.

To Elisabeth Kübler-Ross, a great teacher and storyteller; all her staff; and all those who have helped us with the Growth and Transition Workshop: a no more dedicated, talented, and loving group of people.

To those who offered their time to engage with my entire manuscript and offer valuable insights and suggestions: Danny Blake, Eugenie DuPont, Kate Edgar, Liese Groot-Alberts, Hauke Groot, David Henschel, Carol Hogue, Lorraine Kupfer, Marie Miyashiro, Bob Pontarelli, Andy Stone, Steve Stone; and Matt, Rachael, and Lindsay Dart Lincoln.

To those who cheered me on, and offered suggestions about portions of the manuscript: Ron Estes, Elaine Flannagan, Parlan McGaw, and Pannill Taylor.

And to Tucson Medical Center, for sponsoring our Growth and Transition Workshop for thirty-one years.

CPSIA information can be obtained
at www.ICGtesting.com
Printed in the USA
BVHW031127030319
541644BV00001B/52/P